# UNLIKELY ALLIES

*Fort Delaware's Prison Community
in the Civil War*

Dale Fetzer and Bruce Mowday
Foreword by Leland C. Jennings

STACKPOLE
BOOKS

Published by
STACKPOLE BOOKS
5067 Ritter Road
Mechanicsburg, PA 17055

Printed in the United States of America

10 9 8 7 6 5 4 3 2 1

FIRST EDITION

Fetzer, Dale, and Mowday, Bruce.
    Unlikely allies : Fort Delaware's prison community in the Civil War / Dale Fetzer and Bruce Mowday. — 1st ed.
        p.   cm.
    Includes bibliographical references (p.   ) and index.
    ISBN 0-8117-1823-9
    1. Fort Delaware (Del.)   2. United States—History—Civil War, 1861–1865—Prisoners and prisons.   3. Prisoners of war—Delaware—Fort Delaware—History—19th century.   I. Mowday, Bruce.
    II. Title.
    E616.D3F48   1999
    973.7'72—dc21                                                              99-29577
                                                                                  CIP

## *Over the Carnage Rose Prophetic a Voice*

Over the carnage rose prophetic a voice,
Be not dishearten'd, affection shall solve the
    problems of freedom yet,
Those who love each other shall become invincible,
They shall yet make Columbia victorious.

Sons of the Mother of All, you shall yet be victorious,
You shall yet laugh to scorn the attacks of all
    the remainder of the earth.

No danger shall balk Columbia's lovers,
If need be a thousand shall sternly immolate
    themselves for one.

One from Massachusetts shall be a Missourian's comrade,
From Maine and from hot Carolina, and another
    an Oregonese, shall be friends triune,
More precious to each other than all the
    riches of the earth.

To Michigan, Florida perfumes shall tenderly come,
Not the perfumes of flowers, but sweeter, and
    wafted beyond death.

It shall be customary in the houses and
    streets to see manly affection,
The most dauntless and rude shall touch face
    to face lightly,
The dependence of Liberty shall be lovers,
The continuance of Equality shall be comrades.

These shall tie you and band you stronger
    than hoops of iron,
I, ecstatic, O partners! O lands! With the love
    of lovers tie you.

(Were you looking to be held together by lawyers?
Or by an agreement on a paper? Or by arms?
Nay, nor the world, nor any living thing, will so cohere.)

—Walt Whitman

# CONTENTS

# FOREWORD

*by Leland C. Jennings*

The viewing of an artist's masterpiece is always a deeply moving experience. The painting, the sculpture, the poem, or whatever form the work may assume conveys the deepest instincts of the artist in such a powerful way that the beholder cannot help being moved. It is rare that an architectural work designed primarily for destructive purposes would stir such a profoundly emotional response. Yet John Sanders's masterpiece on Pea Patch Island in the Delaware River is a magnificent structure. Sanders did not live to see the completion of his work, but from the grillage timbers of its foundations to the fine, finished brickwork of its casemates, Fort Delaware bears the stamp of a man whose great attention to detail and ability to overcome incredible logistical difficulties raised it out of the compressible mud of Pea Patch Island.

Six years ago, I began to research Fort Delaware. The primary focus was to locate the engineering documents required for preservation and stabilization of the old fort. Sanders's notes, his letters to the engineering department, and his daily orders shaped a story not so much of the construction of a gun battery but, more to the point, the construction of a town. The story of the brick-and-granite structure is inextricably woven with the story of those who built and maintained it. The research project grew to encompass the lives of the workers, the soldiers, and those who were imprisoned during the War between the States.

The story continued and took a number of surprising twist and turns. The postwar years found Fort Delaware in caretaker status but still very much a vibrant town. Families and descendants of the men who had built the fort still occupied the buildings both inside and outside the walls. In 1860 Patrick Gunning, an Irish immigrant, came to the fort as a carpenter. He lived out the rest of his life on Pea Patch Island, married a laundress, and raised five children. Most of the children remained on Pea Patch as well. Mrs. Paterson's inn became a hunting lodge operated by the Gunning family, and once again proved a very profitable business.

The twentieth century took a toll on Sanders's work. Projects intended to modernize the fort necessitated the removal of buildings both inside and outside the walls. The most significant act took place in the first decade, when the Army Corps of Engineers shaped a plan to prevent storm surges from flooding the small island, creating a nearby channel-dredging project that deposited millions of cubic feet of dredge spoils. The muddy sludge filled the island to the top of the seawall, simultaneously changing its topography and entombing its most significant artifacts. The island fortress was manned and ready in World War I and briefly during World War II. In 1943 the official curtain finally came down.

The late 1940s and early 1950s were witness to the looting of Fort Delaware. The war effort was in need of scrap metals, so local "patriots" removed iron stairs, traverse rails, and even 10,000-pound cannons for profit. Teak powder-magazine doors, as well as the oak walls, were removed. Brass and bronze, steel, iron, and hardwoods all fetched handsome prices. Many a home added doors or windows. Others in the area soon sported granite steps or stoops.

Time and weather also took a toll on the hard fabric of Fort Delaware. Chimneys toppled, water and ice split stone and brick, insects devoured the woodwork. Fortunately, Sanders's work inherited the staunch will of its builder. The primary structures conceived and executed by the brilliant engineer are as sound today as they were in 1860. Sliding pocket doors in the general's office still glide effortlessly, proving that in more than 130 years less than one inch of settlement has occurred in this massive structure.

The State of Delaware Division of Parks and Recreation is committed to the restoration of Sanders's masterpiece. Years of research and many months of hard labor have succeeded in setting a stage. It is on this stage that schoolchildren and visitors from around the world will have the opportunity to view firsthand life in the mid-nineteenth century. Here, the story is told of the blacksmiths, the laundresses, the carpenters, and the farmers.

I have always considered the writing of a comprehensive history of Fort Delaware a vital catalyst. The research that began six years ago continues and has expanded to include scholars from the University of Delaware, as well as interns from a number of other institutions. The information gathered to date required the interpretation of scholars whose understanding of the technical, military, and social aspects of nineteenth-century America could form the context of the work as an interesting hybrid of social and military history. I believe that *Unlikely Allies* has achieved that end remarkably well. Mr. Fetzer's and Mr. Mowday's broad knowledge of the Civil War and engaging style have succeeded in giving us a close and personal look at Fort Delaware's creators and its inhabitants.

The research that began six years ago has yielded a great deal of important information, and it leads us in some instances to change our perception of events or to broaden the context for them. As time passes we will view events with different perspective, and different scholars will proffer new and exciting theories concerning events that took place at Fort Delaware. It is possible that this book will be the inspiration for a young scholar. *Unlikely Allies* is accessible history. It has successfully merged disparate data into a story of powerful human interest. As the primary researcher for the project I am extremely pleased to see this story told so well.

# ACKNOWLEDGMENTS

This work owes its existence to a great number of dedicated folks whose work for Fort Delaware spans many decades. When we decided to collaborate on a history of Fort Delaware, we knew that there had been at least fifty years of archival work preceding our present endeavor. Historians, genealogists, archivists, Civil War buffs, and reenactors had gathered information and used it to augment their specific pieces of work—from term papers to living history programs. But no one had tried to combine all the sources to paint an overall picture of Fort Delaware and the events that affected the community on Pea Patch Island during the American Civil War. What we found was surprising, engaging, and truly inspiring.

We made a few decisions from the outset that we hoped would facilitate the writing of this book. Our division of labor proved, for us, to be an excellent collaboration: Bruce collected and organized much of the research, Dale took the organized data and created the narrative, then Bruce added the polish. In effect, we created a two-man team. But in a larger sense, we were a team of thousands. We owe our work, above all, to the courageous men and women who lived on Pea Patch Island during the years our narrative covers. Their strength and perseverance during those difficult times were often the source of inspiration during those long nights when we had trouble finding the right words, or the long days when a primary source was elusive as a Sasquatch. We came to appreciate how little we understood suffering and imprisonment. We hope their experiences will become our lessons.

An important consideration in all of our decisions concerning the material in this book was our deliberate effort to use as many primary sources as possible. Whenever we found contradictions, we used the documents closest to the time and place rather than reports and monographs written from memory, many years after the fact. Keeping in mind the old adage, "all history is testimony and all testimony is suspect," we sought sources that, we hoped, would paint as accurate a picture as possible of life on Pea Patch Island within the time covered by our account. To be sure, there are many articles, books, and reminiscences written by survivors of the prison camp in the years following the war. And naturally those works relied on the memory of the writer. We did not want to make light of those valuable resources, but at the same time, individual memory is often clouded over the course of time. Our intention was to present a picture of the activities at Fort Delaware from the sources on the scene.

The help of so many people is reflected in this book. We thank each group, organization, and individual that sustained, reviewed, and supplemented our work. For Dale, the help of Barbara Robbins—who put up with the endless hours, the trips, and all the labor that took away from family life— was instrumental in seeing this through. Fort Delaware State Park Historian Leland Jennings Jr. opened all his research and provided critical analysis as the work progressed. Lee's remarkable research, especially on the construction of Fort Delaware, was invaluable. Lee, as the park historian, has spent the last six years plumbing the archives, tracking down obscure leads, and compiling the hard data upon which much of this work is based. Special thanks are extended to Kelli W. Dobbs of the University of Delaware's Center for Historic Architecture. Kelli's organization of the construction of Fort Delaware and the thorough time line she created from the engineer's reports put the continuing construction in its proper perspective. It was amazing to discover that work on Pea Patch Island continued throughout the Civil War and beyond. The Fort Delaware Society and their archivist, Martha Bennett, provided all the help and support that was humanly possible. Martha made every piece of paper in the collection available without question. The collection of the Stanislaus Mlotkowski Memorial Brigade was an invaluable resource. Kellee Blake of the National Archives, Eastern Regional Office, could not have been more cooperative, locating little-known engineers' documents that enriched the texture of the narrative. All the folks at the Library of Congress Manuscript Division, most notably John R. Sellers, pointed us in the right direction on a number of occasions. Of course, the resources of the National Archives in Washington, D.C., as well as the Historical Society of Delaware played a conspicuous role in the sources required for this narrative. Mr. and Mrs. Frederick Freund, of Paris, France, in graciously loaning their cottage in Normandy, provided an enclave where Dale wrote much of this narrative.

Bruce thanks all the members of his family, especially his wife, Katherine, all of whom put up with Bruce's fanaticism about Fort Delaware and the Civil War. Bruce's daughters, Megan and Melissa, visited far too many Civil War sites, at least to their wishes, during their childhood. Katherine and her family and friends, especially Betty Derrick, gave Bruce their Southern perspectives on the War of Northern Aggression.

# INTRODUCTION

During the American Civil War, Fort Delaware served as a U.S. prisoner of war facility, housing more than 30,000 Confederate prisoners over the course of three years. Those days of captivity were burned into the memories of those who experienced them—Yankee guard and Rebel prisoner, man and woman, black and white, slave and freeman. It was that time that forever marked a place in our nation's history for America's premiere fortification on Pea Patch Island. It was a time of conflict, urgency, bustling activity, and extreme boredom. With barely seventy-five acres of ground, this tiny island maintained a population of more than 16,000 at its highest concentration. But as the war ended, so ended the usefulness of the sprawling prisoner facility. Fort Delaware's days of fame were gone, and while it was still maintained by the U.S. Army, the high drama of the Civil War was never repeated on its shores. In 1942 the last of the garrison was transferred, and Fort Delaware seemed destined to fade away, a crumbling ruin standing in mute testimony to what was once the most modern fortification in America's history.

When we began the study of Fort Delaware, we thought the work would simply be a narrative history of her war years. It seemed to have all the elements of good melodrama: wretched living conditions, poor rations, uncaring bureaucrats—all against the backdrop of civil war. But the research changed our perceptions. This Civil War prison was different. There were many layers to the story, many twists and turns, but the surprising ingredient in the mix proved to be the natural isolation of the fort.

As it became obvious to the Federal authorities in Washington that the exchange system for prisoners of war was not working, an alternate plan had to be rushed into place. No one in authority had given much thought to the staggering number of prisoners this seemingly endless war generated. The exchange system proved to be a bureaucratic quagmire, with longer and longer waits between parole and exchange. Meanwhile, thousands of men caught in the limbo of red tape had to be housed, clothed, and fed. When the Federal government turned to its existing facilities, Fort Delaware seemed a natural. It was located on an island, brand-new, and thought to be impregnable, with ample space for the erection of outbuildings for prisoners. Escape would be difficult; furthermore, it was evident that the Confederate navy could never muster the strength to assault the fort.

The decision was made that Fort Delaware, the nation's premiere fortification, would play its role in the war as a backwater facility. In time she became one of the largest prisoner of war camps in the United States and established a reputation, over the years, as a place of extreme cruelty. In modern historiographic literature, Fort Delaware has been called "the Andersonville of the North" and characterized as a place similar to Dante's Inferno. Confederate reports seemed to confirm the wanton cruelty rampant on the island. The Reverend Isaac Handy, a political prisoner, and Confederate general Jeff Thompson left vivid descriptions of the day-to-day life—harsh conditions, poor rations, and sadistic behavior by Northern guards. Plainly, it was easy to draw a picture of severity at Fort Delaware.

To compound the matter, by 1863 this small island, with poor drainage and little water, had become woefully overcrowded. By early fall of that year, Pea Patch Island had a larger population than the city of Wilmington, Delaware. For a brief time, she was the largest city in the state. Of course, as in any city, in any age, a tremendous infrastructure must exist to support so large a population. Laborers, boatmen, laundresses, cooks, teamsters, persons from every stratum of the social scale came to live on this bleak spit of land. And with the high concentration of people living in such conditions, always looming ominously was the threat of disease. In 1863, as the leaves turned and the air became brisk, smallpox ran through the compound, quadrupling the death rate in a matter of one month. Hospitals were hastily erected to contain the dreaded disease. The medical staff was taxed almost to the breaking point, and all the while still more prisoners arrived. The seeming negligence on the part of the Federal government only added to the nightmare that had become Pea Patch.

At its height, six men were dying every day—the stuff of high drama! It seemed impossible to exaggerate any of the stories of horror, suffering, or injustice. The evidence of testimony, however, is not borne out by the statistics compiled for those three years. It seems that, with the compilation of the official records and a thorough examination of the original rolls, the death rate (a more accurate barometer of suffering) does not corroborate the accounts so passionately retold over the years. Over the course of three years, Fort Delaware maintained a total prisoner of war population of 32,305 and, in that time, 2,460 prisoners died.[1] While the average Northern prison camp was experiencing a death rate of 21 percent, with Elmira, New York, topping out at 24 percent, Fort Delaware's death rate was a remarkably low 7.6 percent. Having checked and rechecked the numbers, we were satisfied with the math, but puzzled by the incongruity of testimony. The narrative took a turn. True enough, Fort Delaware was a prisoner of war camp and, as such, its inhabitants certainly experienced episodes of extreme behavior and circumstances. But, the records, the eyewitness reports, and the statistics tell a startlingly different story. What we found was far more interesting than recounting one atrocity after another: The search for truth, after 135 years, sheds light on a gritty, determined group of men and women who carved out a separate peace while in the throes of war.

It is the unrelenting quest for the middle ground that forms the high drama at Fort Delaware on Pea Patch Island from 1861 through 1865. Those people, it seems, had never died, but had patiently waited for their story to be told. All suppositions, prejudices, and preconceived notions about Fort Delaware were softened or revealed as distortions. The story of Fort Delaware's Civil War years is not a story of warfare. It is a story of people whose lives are forever altered by war, and, in an ironic twist of fate, are forced to live on an island with the enemy and remain at peace. At the heart of America's most tragic conflict, we find a total of 33,000 Southern prisoners and 6,000 Northern guards bound to live out the war years on a seventy-five-acre mudflat in the Delaware River. And somehow, most of them survived. The remarkable story at Fort Delaware is how few egregiously suffered, how few died. Fort Delaware's tale is the heroic story of peacefare.

*Chapter 1*

# PRELUDE

*"Upon the Pip Ash Island, it cannot be questioned but that pass may be well armed."*
—Pierre Charles L'Enfant

The experienced boatmen handled the small rowboat with the dexterity that comes from long years of seafaring. The twelve-knot current of the Delaware River made it especially difficult to maneuver the craft close enough to the mudflat to disembark the passengers without capsizing the boat. As the crew struggled against the tide, Maj. Pierre Charles L'Enfant, chief engineer of the U.S. Army, fixed his gaze on the approaching mud and grass blot that he had come to call "Pip Ash" Island. This would be L'Enfant's first time on this mudflat.

L'Enfant had come to America in 1777 as part of a contingent of French military engineers and artillerists to serve with the Continental Army. After the Revolution, L'Enfant stayed in the service of the United States, perfecting the existing network of seacoast fortifications. L'Enfant was engaged, as well, in the design and layout of the new national seat of government. Knowing that the width of the Delaware River necessitated the erection of a battery on both the Delaware and New Jersey sides of the river, he had been studying the Delaware shoreline for a suitable position to erect a fortification. During a visit to Reedy Point, Delaware, he first spied the island at low tide. There, in the center of the river, astride the shipping channels, lay an inviting piece of property.

In May 1794 "Pip Ash" Island was used primarily by crow hunters and fishermen. As the good major surveyed the shoreline he saw a barren mudflat with scant vegetation, what appeared to be a fisherman's shanty, and little else. With one last heave, the oarsmen shoved the rowboat onto the shore, which brought all forward motion abruptly to a halt, nearly throwing L'Enfant onto the mudbank. Shaken from his reverie, L'Enfant jumped from the boat and walked toward the high ground. The accomplished military engineer knew one

1

thing instantly: This island would be ideal for a defensive fortification, if the tidal action of the river could be controlled.

On the evening of May 16, 1794, L'Enfant wrote to the secretary of war:

> As to the fortifications on the Delaware, first I went to Wilmington, Delaware, and found it well sheltered by Nature against a navy coming up river. I then went to New Castle. On my arrival at New Castle, I engaged one of the stage sloops, and in company with land owners about there and some captains of vessels, began to make soundings; went to the Pip Ash a bank forming an island opposite Eagle and Reedy Points. This pass should be well armed. The channel east of Pip Ash is very shallow. I recommend a fort on Pip Ash, and batteries at New Castle should be provided for; not because of its great commercial interest, but because of its importance when militarily viewed—that place being an essential point in the grand chain of posts for garrisons which should be combined together from the Southward to the Eastern States, all along the coast, as well as on the back frontiers. This situation—New Castle—is most happily circumstanced to be made strong and to unite all what is requisite—a grand garrison.[1]

He also noted in his report, "Upon the Pip Ash Island, it cannot be questioned but that pass may be well armed, and that proper works erected there would protect the whole river bank."[2]

❦

When the first European explorers ventured into the Delaware Bay and sailed north up the Delaware River, they took no note of any extraordinary island seven miles north of the bay. In fact, no contemporary records indicated the presence of any body of land prior to the 1760s, although local legends told a story of a sailing vessel laden with a cargo of peas that ran aground on a shoal and split in half, disgorging its cargo. The peas apparently took root and thrived along the shoal. As the pea patches grew, so did the island. Soon the locals came to call the newly formed island the Pea Patch.

The Pea Patch is one and one-eighth miles from the Delaware shore and one mile from the New Jersey shore. Just forty-two miles south of Philadelphia and seven miles from the Wilmington shipyards, the Pea Patch did not escape the eyes of the military in its constant efforts to fortify the coastline of the United States. This seventy-five-acre oval mudflat did present some difficulties in erecting a fortification, however. At an average height of only three feet, four inches above sea level, with its highest point at nine feet eight inches, Pea Patch Island was prone to tidal flooding and far from being the perfect candidate for a permanent fortification. But when the War of 1812 erupted, the island was again put forth as a viable defensive position. By 1813 the British navy had set up a blockading station at the Delaware Capes near the mouth of the Delaware Bay.

Adm. Sir John P. Beresford of the Royal Navy so threatened commerce on the Delaware that the Middle Atlantic states began to clamor for more attention from the War Department and, specifically, for the installation of more fortifications to protect the Delaware and Chesapeake Bays. Many Philadelphia residents remembered the nightmare of 1777 when the British attacked and overcame Fort Mifflin during the longest siege and largest bombardment on the North American continent. It was an experience the locals on the shoreline of the Delaware River did not want to revisit.

When Brig. John Armstrong took over the position of secretary of war on January 13, 1813, he took further steps to fortify the estuaries emptying into the Delaware Bay. Before any concrete actions could be taken by the Americans, however, Sir John Beresford decided to take the war to the population. Sir John and the British fleet sailed into the Delaware Bay, hove to at Lewes, Delaware, and demanded a tribute of twenty live bullocks with appropriate support vegetation. The citizens of Lewes refused, and Sir John was forced to bombard the town. The British fleet then continued north on the Delaware estuary, sacking and burning all the settlements as far as Reedy Point. The only force opposing the British was a ragtag flotilla of nineteen gunboats, sixteen armed barges, and two block sloops. The arrival of the American flotilla soon discouraged the British, but the U.S. government realized that should the British reinforce its squadron, the small flotilla would be overrun. Thus it was determined to place a force on Pea Patch, which might delay the enemy and give the government time to muster and organize a defense.

Commanding the 4th Military Department, with headquarters at Philadelphia, was Brig. Gen. Joseph Bloomfield. This was Bloomfield's second war with the British Empire. A New Jersey veteran of the War for Independence, he had distinguished himself in that war, rising to the rank of major. But the hardships and rigors of active campaigning took their toll, and Bloomfield reluctantly resigned his commission in November 1778. When the nation again faced peril from abroad, Joseph Bloomfield, now a venerated warhorse, accepted a commission as brigadier general on March 27, 1812. Although his age precluded active campaigning against the enemy, Bloomfield was ably prepared to wage an active campaign to strengthen the defensive system around Philadelphia and its environs.

His first act was to order the construction of a water battery near Fort Mifflin, under the direct supervision of Lt. Alexander John Williams. This young engineer came to the district with an excellent pedigree, graduating first in his class from the U.S. Military Academy at West Point in 1805. Now assigned as the district engineer, his primary task was to strengthen the weakened Fort Mifflin. Williams then turned his considerable attention to Pea Patch Island, beginning construction of a water battery just opposite Fort Mifflin in 1812. By May 1813 the work was finished. Williams then was promoted to a captaincy in the 2nd U.S. Artillery and transferred to active duty against the British. He served his country with distinction, losing his life August 15, 1814, in the defense of Fort Erie. He was twenty-four years old. The absence of Williams, the only engineer the 4th District had, was keenly felt.

The new determination of the War Department to erect a fortification on Pea Patch Island required the services of an experienced engineer, and on May 25, 1813, Capt. Sylvannus Thayer was ordered to report to General Bloomfield, with specific instructions concerning the erection of a fortification on Pea Patch Island. Captain Thayer, born June 9, 1785, in Massachusetts, received a degree from Dartmouth College in 1807 and was third in his graduating class at West Point, 1808. Thayer would go on to become the Academy's fourth superintendent and develop the course of studies that remains the heart of its academic program. Upon his arrival in Philadelphia, Thayer began his survey of the Delaware River between Reedy Point and New Castle, including Pea Patch Island. Thayer incorporated a thorough study of the area, including a determination of the nature of the soil and the depth of the channels around the island. According to the survey, Pea Patch was located forty miles below the city of Philadelphia at a latitude of 39°35'18" N and a longitude of 75°34'31" W. Thayer also noted, "The east channel at that time, while deep opposite the island, shoaled to only ten feet at high water near the north end of the island, while the west channel maintained a steady depth of some thirty as it passed the island."[3] With survey in hand, Secretary of War John Armstrong proposed in June 1813 to have a "work of earth, or of more durable materials, if found advisable, on a small island of the Delaware, called the Pea Patch."[4] Meanwhile, the government had sought to purchase Pea Patch Island from a New Jersey resident, Dr. Henry Gale, who had been using the island as his private hunting and fishing preserve for years. He was offered $30,000 for the island, but he turned it down, evidently hoping to secure more money. Rather than negotiate, the Federal government went to the State of Delaware and asked for the cession of the Pea Patch for the purpose of constructing a defensive work. The Delaware State Legislature ceded the island on May 27, 1813.[5]

Despite the recommendations of Secretary Armstrong and the strenuous advocacy of General Bloomfield, no action was taken for nearly a year. Finally, on February 19, 1814, newly promoted Col. Joseph Gardner Swift, chief engineer, sent to the War Department plans and estimates for the erection of a "Martello Tower" on Pea Patch Island.[6] Colonel Swift, West Point's first graduate, had served from 1812 as its second superintendent. Swift proposed, in the name of expediency, constructing the tower with timbers rather than the traditional masonry, citing two reasons for his decision: the perception that this work was needed immediately and not knowing if the mudflat could support a heavy masonry structure.

As with Thayer's report, Swift's proposal languished. It seemed that Pea Patch was destined to remain untouched by the United States Army, but the exigencies of war often have a way of hastening progress on even the slowest of projects. The summer of 1814 was proving to be a rough one for Americans living on the major coastal waterways. The British had implemented a new campaign, calling for coordinated attacks of the major seaports along the eastern seaboard. One force moved against the Mississippi and the seaport city of New Orleans while the other force began operations in the Chesapeake Bay, with an eye toward the capture of Washington City and the utter destruction of the United States Army. On June 25, 1814, the British sacked and burned the town of Hampton, Virginia. As the British demonstrated their power, it became increasingly evident that no major seaport was safe. The citizens of Philadelphia and their political representatives in Congress began to clamor for more forts, more protection, and more help from the Federal government. Philadelphians created the Committee of Safety for the Corporation of the City of Philadelphia, which began to set aside funds for the erection of a suitable fortification designed to protect the city.

Secretary Armstrong, eager to mollify the increasingly anxious citizens and bolster the defenses of the Delaware River, wrote to Swift and ordered him to "send on without delay an officer of your corps to erect the towers proposed by you for the defense of the Delaware River." Swift quickly selected an engineer to report to General Bloomfield in Philadelphia and "communicate with the Corporation of the City from whom he will derive his funds. When the towers are erected, (or while they are erecting, if possible) he will lay out and execute a small covering work at Red Bank on the Jersey shore, opposite to Fort Mifflin. This should be constructed against assault. Perhaps a third tower would be cheapest & best kind of work at this point."[7]

Colonel Swift had selected Capt. Samuel Babcock. Swift had served with, and was impressed by, this 1806 graduate of West Point. He had graduated second in his class and was sent directly to the Corps of Engineers, serving under the direct supervision of Swift from 1808 until early 1814 and employed in strengthening the defenses of New York Harbor. On September 20, 1812, Babcock was promoted to captain. In early 1814 Babcock had been transferred to

Fort McHenry, and he was busy at work on the fortifications of Baltimore when he received the order to report to Philadelphia. Meanwhile, on July 11, 1814, Colonel Swift had written to the Committee of Safety advising them of Babcock's assignment to Pea Patch Island to constuct works at Red Bank, New Jersey. Swift reiterated that it was his and the secretary of war's understanding that the Corporation of the City of Philadelphia would supply the funds for the proposed projects. Ten days later, Babcock, having arrived in Philadelphia, wrote to Secretary Armstrong acknowledging his assignment.

Babcock made initial inspections of the sites and felt he was "ready to proceed with the works as a regular mode is established for procuring materials." He also alerted Armstrong that it was the Committee's position that the funding for these projects was to be in the form of a loan to the United States rather than as an outright grant. Philadelphia was balking and dragging the project through a complicated paper trail, which resulted in no actual work being done. Babcock reported to Armstrong on August 20 that "the Corporation of Philadelphia had declined furnishing the Agent for Fortifications, Mr. Linnard, with funds for carrying on the Works ordered to be erected in the River Delaware."[8]

While Babcock, Swift, Armstrong, and the good citizens of Philadelphia were embroiled in their extended debate, the British invasion fleet moved up the Potomac River, captured Fort Washington, and attacked, captured, and burned Washington City. Another force had begun operations in the Chesapeake Bay, with the intent of capturing Baltimore, forcing the U.S. Army to recall her best officers to the point of conflict. Captain Babcock was ordered to the Baltimore Harbor defenses as part of Maj. Gen. Samuel Smith's command. Babcock then took part in the successful defense of Fort McHenry in September 1814. Following the repulse of the British, Babcock was employed in the erection and strengthening of fortifications in the Baltimore Harbor.

When Armstrong, acutely aware of the British threat, received Babcock's letter of August 20, he was alarmed to find that no progress had been made at Pea Patch Island. Armstrong responded to Babcock's missive in a communiqué to Swift ordering him to "as soon as practicable repair to Philadelphia and confer with the commanding General and Committee of Safety relative to the defenses of that place—you will furnish plans and give the necessary directions for erecting such works as the Corporation may require at the Pea Patch for the defense of the Delaware—you will report to this Department an Estimate of of the cost of such work as shall be agreed on by the Corporation of Philadelphia."[9] As Armstrong sent the order he was preoccupied with the defenses of Washington City, but it soon became evident that the capital's defensive forces were woefully ill prepared. The enemy simply brushed them aside. By the end of August, Armstrong was replaced by James Monroe. Swift responded to the War Department on September 5, 1814, stating that he would repair to Philadelphia immediately to make the best arrangements possible for the immediate defense of that great seaport. Those arrangements would be "quick and dirty."

But with the relative ease the British seemed to be operating on in the interior of the United States, Swift, although following the orders of his superior, felt that his mission was more properly in New York, getting ready for the inevitable attack there. Swift also chose to bring along Brig. Gen. Jonathan Williams, former chief engineer of the U.S. Army and now commander of the New York State Militia, to help with the planning of the defenses of Philadelphia. Swift and Williams arrived in Philadelphia on September 6. Swift and party then took a fast-paced tour of the immediate defensive system around the city and determined that the best defense—that is, the fastest and cheapest—of the Delaware would be the sinking of several ships across the shipping channel. They also recommended the placement of a ship of heavy ordnance with her broadside perpendicular to the channel and the erection of an earthwork battery of 24-pounders on Davis Pier, formerly Middlebank, New Jersey. The channel would be blocked by the sunken obstacles, the guns of Fort Mifflin, the earthwork battery in New Jersey, and the floating ordnance vessel. Smith and Williams expected that this would constitute a satisfactory defense.

On September 7 Swift submitted a written report to the Committee. In that report he included a set of drawings showing the plans for the tower to be erected on Pea Patch Island. Swift was careful to note that the tower would be constructed of wood, surrounded by a ditch and sodded earthwork. He also anticipated an additional defensive measure in the deploying of row galleys and sinking hulks in the channel to serve as obstacles, plans similar to those around Fort Mifflin. Swift then wrote to Secretary of War James Monroe, "I have conferred with the Commanding General of the 4th Military District and with the Committee of Defense—have been down the Delaware and have recommended plans for additional security. The Corporation will erect the towers I advised for Pea Patch and for Newbold in late Spring. Plans and drawings are furnished. The expense of erecting each tower will be $8,000. I go to New York at 2 A.M. tomorrow."[10]

When Swift arrived in New York he prepared a set of plans for the projected Pea Patch works, modifying the Martello Tower by squaring it to accommodate the construction material. This blockhouse affair was to be twenty feet high, armed with 32-pounders and mortars. Swift included flanking batteries, a dry ditch, and covering earthworks for the defensive infantry. He also included two buildings in the rear of the defenses to serve as quarters for the small garrison. Surprisingly, considering the urgency of Swift's reports, no actual physical labor on Pea Patch began until Christmas Day 1814, when Capt. Thomas Clark of the Topographical Engineers arrived at Pea Patch with a hundred soldiers and thirty workers. By the time construction was started on the first structure, a wharf, the new year had come and the war with Great Britain had ended.

⟢━⟐⟐⟐⟐━⟣

With the end of the war, the urgency to complete the fort all but evaporated. But Captain Clark and his 130 men had a mission to fulfill. When he finished the wharf in January 1815, Clark began the construction of dikes, wharves, and a new fortification. The biggest problem confronting the continued work on Pea Patch was the tidal nature of the island, and controlling the water level was the primary mission of Captain Clark. As the work progressed over the next several years, the War Department realized that a more competent engineering officer was needed to supervise the military constructions on the island. On January 13, 1819, Capt. Samuel Babcock was ordered back to Pea Patch. Meanwhile, the Corps of Engineers had reconsidered the Martello Tower and decided on a better plan. Joseph Gilbert Totten, a brevet lieutenant colonel,[11] designed and received approval for the erection of a star fort, with five large bastions extending from a regular pentagon, at the highest point of Pea Patch Island. Captain Babcock began work on the fort immediately. The exterior of the polygon was 331 feet in length, with the bastion faces measuring 157 feet. The courtings were 23 feet, and the flanks were 22 feet. The stone wall of the fort was 39.55 feet high. The entire structure was surrounded by a moat, known as a wet ditch, which was 55 feet wide and 7 feet deep. The interior of the structure included ten flights of cut-stone stairways and two masonry buildings acting as quarters and storage buildings for the garrison. The star fort was to be a masonry structure with wooden floors, beams, roofs, and window and door frames. The questionable nature of the terrain regarding its ability to sustain a building of stone was about to be answered. Samuel Babcock had come to the project from the defenses of Fort McHenry, where he had done extensive work with masonry fortifications and had witnessed firsthand the strength of those fortifications.[12]

When Babcock returned to the Pea Patch Island project, he reviewed Totten's 1815 plans and decided to change the nature of the proposed fortification. Since the war was over and the speed of the construction was no longer a factor, Babcock changed the position and the foundation of the permanent masonry structure. In 1815 Captain Clark had conducted borings in conjunction with his dike construction. Those borings revealed a reasonably solid foundation of soil and sand. Babcock based his decision on Clark's findings and proceeded with the construction of the star fort. Babcock also felt that he had been given discretionary powers regarding his ability to deviate from the Totten plans. His estimates for the star fort called for a budget of $379,509.

The first priority of the work was the erection of a temporary dike to control the flooding of the island. Babcock then prepared to bring the cut stone to Pea Patch Island by 1820. The work required to bring the materials to the island was monumental. Several tons of stone, hundreds of timbers, plus the equipment needed for the work, all had to be imported from the mainland. The preparations took several months.

Meanwhile, soldiers and workers on the island began contracting illnesses affecting the upper respiratory system. In the fall of 1823 Babcock himself became ill and was unable to supervise much of the construction. Capt. René Edward DeRussy, an 1807 graduate of West Point, was temporarily assigned as superintendent of the construction. He remained at that post through December 1823. Despite his illness, however, Babcock, who had since been promoted to major, was expected to supervise all phases of his department with especial care being taken to guard against unnecessary expenditures. The work on the star fort continued, and Babcock returned to active status in January 1824. Although the interior was yet unfinished, the fortification was deemed fit for a garrison, and Maj. A. C. W. Fanning was appointed commander of the installation. The final cost of the project was $469,704—a cost overrun of $90,195.

When Major Fanning and two companies of the 4th U.S. Artillery took possession of America's newest fortification, they found an isolated island with living quarters still under construction. The troops were forced to camp on the parade ground until the work was completed. While Fanning set about adapting his two companies to the conditions on Pea Patch Island, the workmen continued to finish the interior. Two immediate problems faced Major Fanning—there were no plans for a hospital and so none had been erected, and the foundation of the masonry fort had already begun to shift. As acting superintendent, Captain DeRussy had reported to the Corps of Engineers several deviations from Babcock's plans. The work on the interior was thought to be a short stretch to completion, but the building seemed to shift with every tidal action. Cracks and fissures developed in the quarters for the garrison. The shifts also caused cracks to open in the escarpment walls.

Reports to the War Department of the constant problems at the fort soon brought serious consequences for Major Babcock. On May 10, 1824, the army ordered an inspection of the star fort to examine the allegations that there were no proper foundations and that Maj. Samuel Babcock had improperly appropriated funds. The results of the inspection found compelling evidence against Babcock, and a court-martial was ordered. Major Babcock was relieved of duty on August 20, 1824, and, with one of his assistants, Capt. Hipolite Dumas, was accused of disobedience of orders, neglect of duty, incapacity, and conduct unworthy of an officer and a gentleman. The court-martial was set to commence on August 25, but the trial did not get underway until September 6, 1824.[13] The trial lasted for six days. Babcock's defense rested upon a solid mass of physical evidence—all his communiqués, reports, plans, and correspondence with Colonel Totten, as well as written approval from Totten and Swift giving him discretion in the erection of the fortification.

Babcock also maintained that cost overruns were a result of the unforeseen expenses incurred in arresting the tidal action on the island. Upon examination of the evidence, the board saw that Babcock did, indeed, supervise all aspects of the project despite his illness. His signature or initials were found on almost every piece of paper important to the project. On September 13, 1824, the court ruled out the first and third charges and found Babcock not guilty of two of the three specifications. The court did rule that Babcock had neglected his duty and conducted himself in an unworthy manner. The court, however, attached no criminality to his actions. By ruling out the first and third charges the court indirectly rebuked the Corps of Engineers for failing to properly inspect the construction on Pea Patch Island. Babcock was released from arrest and ordered to report to Old Point Comfort, Virginia. There Babcock soon found himself working with a brilliant young engineer by the name of Robert Edward Lee. By late 1830 Samuel Babcock was played out. Suffering from a prolonged illness, he resigned his commission on December 22. At the age of forty-six, Major Babcock died on June 26, 1831.

Garrison life continued at the star fort in the usual mundane way. In December 1827 Major Fanning was transferred and replaced by Maj. Benjamin Pierce, the brother of future president Franklin Pierce. By 1827 the fortification had been stabilized, and separate barracks for the officers and enlisted men were complete. Officers' wives and families were billeted on the island. The winter of 1830–31 was a particularly cold one. The Delaware River teemed with large chunks of ice and threatened to freeze over, clogging the shipping channel. The garrison had difficulty keeping warm, even though fires were maintained at all times. Disease, a constant companion on Pea Patch, made matters even worse. Eleven percent of the garrison were ill, including Major Pierce's wife. On February 8, 1831, Mrs. Pierce died. Her body was laid out in the parlor of the small detached building that the Pierce family used as quarters. The following day a fire broke out in the fort. Major Pierce wrote a detailed report on February 11, 1831:

> On February 9 at 10:30 P.M. a sentinel noticed smoke from the roof or under the roof which covers the walls of the fortification. Officers and men went to the left to fight it with water buckets and axes but it was soon out of control. The

powder was carried out of the magazines and thrown out the embrasures into the moat to prevent the destruction of the walls by an explosion. Finding the roof could not be saved, the exertions of the men were directed to the preservation of the platforms and quarters but the flaming shingles and rafters falling on their heads made the work futile.

My home containing my four infant children and the unburied remains of my deceased wife then became threatened. It was a small building detached from the main work. I thought there was a greater chance of saving the lives of the children by removing them through the suffocating smoke and fire that surrounded us on all sides. A number of men ascended to the roof and were able to keep this building from burning. They stayed until 8 A.M. the next day when the fire had died down sufficiently for us to leave.

It has been suggested that arson is responsible, but I believe the cause to have been accidental. The roof probably caught fire from one of the stove pipes extending through it.

The fire of February 9, 1831, destroyed all the wooden works, quartermaster stores, and ordnance on the island. The barracks for the troops, all their provisions, and all their personal property were swept away. Pierce was forced to abandon the fortification on February 10, 1831, leaving behind one officer and a small guard. The rest, along with his wife's body, were removed to nearby New Castle, Delaware. The damage was disastrous. All that remained of the star fort was the charred and crumbling cut stone.[14]

***

Very little could be done on Pea Patch. First came the simple work of getting the garrison safely off the island, then came the difficult work of damage assessment and searching for the cause. Major Pierce never backed the continuing rumors of arson. Despite his devastating losses, Pierce was able to boil it down to a minimum: The buildings caught fire because of the extensive use of wood and the deterioration caused by the inadequate foundation. Cracks had developed in the masonry as a result of the shifting of the foundation, allowing the sparks and smoldering particles to collect on the wooden roof and eventually ignite. The fort was virtually destroyed. But the United States was not through with Pea Patch Island. In 1832 a concerted effort was put forth to stabilize the existing structure, with an eye toward restoring the fortification. But as the damage parties began to file their reports, it became evident that more was needed than originally thought, and a promising young engineer, Capt. Richard Delafield, was assigned the job of restoring the fort. After several weeks of sifting through the wreckage, Captain Delafield wrote in April to Brig. Gen. Charles Gratiot, chief engineer general, requesting $10,000 to take down the fort and erect temporary quarters.[15] Capt. Richard Delafield, a New York native, was born September 1, 1789. At the age of sixteen, Delafield entered the U.S. Military Academy at West Point. Four years later he graduated first in his class, May 4, 1818, and he became the first cadet to rate a post—West Point assignment according to merit. His fifty-two-year career in the army was one of meritorious and conspicuous service, including a twelve-year hitch as superintendent of the Academy, retiring as chief of engineers with the rank of brevet major general. In Fort Delaware's early history it is important to note the caliber of the engineers assigned to the project. Delafield was one in a long line of talented young men who had their hand in the construction of the fort. It is a testament to the importance that the Corps of Engineers and the War Department placed on the project. Forty-two-year-old Captain Delafield understood the essential nature of the work at hand, and he devised plans to construct a massive fortification on Pea Patch. In his planning he would utilize the most recent advances made in the science of military engineering.

Having defeated the British in two wars, the United States was ready to show the world that it had arrived as a mature player on the world stage, and it rushed to develop bigger and better material representations of American society. The military thinking of the time was influenced by these desires, and so it was that Richard Delafield sought to erect a marvel of military architecture on Pea Patch. Every effort, vast treasuries, and determined, willful engineers worked through all hazards to the completion of the fortification. Delafield applied a vision beyond a simple military post and sought to create a symbol of a remarkable people. On April 18, 1833, Maj. Gen. Alexander Macomb issued General Order No. 32, declaring the fort on Pea Patch would henceforth be known as Fort Delaware.[16]

Having received approval of his ambitious plan, Captain Delafield set about the task of making his dream a reality. He had designed a fortification larger and stronger than any erected in North America, a fortress that would rival the largest castle in Europe, capable of withstanding a bombardment from the greatest cannon devised by man. The new plan called for a two-tier, five-sided fortification covering more than twelve acres. Delafield's fort was five times the size of the star fort and would house at least 275 pieces of seacoast artillery. Upon completion, the new Fort Delaware could host a garrison of more than 2,000 men and would boast the latest in military architectural design. The three bastions facing the shipping channel to the east were the longest sections of the fortification, with four flanking batteries—two large flanking batteries at the northeast and southwest corners of the fort and two center-post flanking batteries separating the eastern wall into three bastions. The eastern bastions, running diagonally from the northeast to the southwest along the south end of the island, would mount the largest seacoast guns. The northern bastion would run perpendicular, from east to west to the northwest flanking battery, and would house the next largest set of seacoast guns. From the northwest flanking battery, running directly south, ran the western bastion, terminating at the southwest flanking battery. The western bastion held the least artillery, mostly weapons of a smaller caliber to repel any attack from land.[17]

Much had to be done to prepare Pea Patch Island for this massive structure. Not only did the old fortification need to be razed, but preparations also had to be made for a proper foundation. Delafield was intent not to repeat Major Babcock's errors. There was also the problem of tidal flooding on the island. That spring, with a force of a hundred laborers, Delafield commenced work. Using the debris from the star fort, the men built a protective dike around the island. The dike would keep back inundations of the tide, which in turn would help stabilize the foundation. Demolition took the better part of 1833.

On July 2, 1833, an unknown civilian visited the island. Captain Delafield was in Philadelphia securing the materials needed for the fort, and his civilian assistant, Mr. Belin, was supervising the work on the island. Upon his arrival the stranger immediately asked for the person in charge. After some time, Mr. Belin approached the stranger and asked him the nature of his business. The stranger declined to answer, identifying himself only as a lawyer representing the concerns of a Mr. Hudson and demanding a list of the island's tenants. Mr. Belin refused to produce the list, no doubt causing the barrister great consternation. Realizing that he was not about to get what he asked for, the attorney made his departure, promising to return in a few days with a "writ of ejectment."[18] It seems that Mr. J. T. Hudson of New Jersey had inherited the possessions of the late Dr. Gale, and among those possessions was title to Pea Patch Island, Dr. Gale's former hunting preserve. Mr. Hudson, hoping to realize a tremendous profit from the government, brought suit against the State of Delaware, claiming legal ownership of the island. The attorney did not return in a few days with his writ, as promised, but litigation had begun, and it would have serious consequences on the construction.

As the litigants prepared their case for the eventual court date, Delafield continued his work. While demolition of the old star fort continued, Captain Delafield saw to the details of his plan, always mindful of the flaws of the old structure. Totten had alerted Delafield to be constantly aware of the foundation slippage and to produce a working plan to provide a solid foundation for the new fort. The many boring samples collected in the previous five years by the engineers revealed exactly the soil foundation of Pea Patch Island. The island was composed of mud to a depth of 46 feet, sand for the next 20 feet, and coarse sand to a depth of 96 feet, where a boulder was struck. Boring through the boulder consumed another two weeks. Once through the boulder, the borings disclosed a dark clay; after the clay a very fine, white sand was found at the depth of 143 feet; and under the white sand was water, considered not potable. Borings, to an average depth of 47 feet, were also taken at the corners of the star fort. Sand was the common element found at each boring. It was evident that a base of sand and mud would be the site for the foundation. Essentially, the construction of this massive structure was akin to building the Empire State Building on a foundation of jelly.

Delafield developed a plan for driving piles into the mud to establish a firm footing for the fort. He estimated that 6,594 forty-five-foot-long logs of white oak and pine would be required to serve as piles. The logs would be driven forty feet into the mud, and grillage would be laid out on top of the piles. Delafield also included in his inventory two million bricks; 42,000 tons of stone; and four steam pile-driving machines. The materials were ordered in 1833 and received throughout 1834–36. The work of building an adequate seawall and preparing the site for construction consumed two years. The seawall was completed in 1836, and Captain Delafield then turned his attention to the complex problem of transporting materials to Pea Patch Island. Hiring every available vessel in the area, he launched a small flotilla, beginning in July 1836 and continuing into September. After familiarizing himself with the schedule and the workings of the four steam pile drivers on hand, Delafield and the construction team commenced the work of driving piles to create the foundation for the fort.

The concept of creating a stable flooring for the building was similar to the construction of a pier. The idea was to drive each pile into the island to an equal level. Once that was accomplished, a platform, called a grillage, would be attached, covering the top of the piles with a level surface. There the engineers could place the masonry structure, with little chance that the foundation would shift. In October Delafield anticipated the completion of the pile driving and ordered the grillage timber. Even as the grillage timber was arriving, however, the singular properties of the Delaware mud and the inefficiency of the steam pile drivers slowed the progress to a virtual standstill. Fewer than one-tenth of the piles had been driven by midsummer 1837. To complicate matters, the civilian work crew was weakened by disease. Fully 25 percent of the crew were absent at any given time.

The winter of 1837–38 further hampered progress. Pea Patch Island, surrounded by the ice-choked Delaware River, had frozen, increasing the difficulties the workforce encountered. In January the frozen soil was all but impenetrable, causing damage not only to the piles but also to the pile drivers. Delafield and Belin suspended activities and devoted their energies to the perfection of the grillage plans. The construction team was ordered to arrange the necessary materials on the island in anticipation of the spring thaw. By March 1838 activity on the island was back to full bore as the work to create the foundation continued. The maddeningly slow pace continued through the summer. In late August Delafield received orders to report to West Point to become the Academy's seventh superintendent, effective September 1, 1838. Captain Delafield's five-year commitment to Fort Delaware had come to an end, and he had installed only 1,095 piles in two years.

Delafield was replaced by the Academy's sixth superintendent, Lt. Col. René Edward DeRussy, who had been a participant in the construction of the original star fort, serving during Major Babcock's illness. DeRussy, a West Indian by birth, had a long career in the Army Corps of Engineers. He had been awarded a captaincy in 1814 for gallant and meritorious conduct at the battle of Plattsburg, reached his majority for ten years' service, and in 1834 attained the rank of lieutenant colonel. DeRussy served as superintendent of West Point from 1833 to 1838. Now he was back at Pea Patch after a fifteen-year absence.

DeRussy continued the tedious work of driving piles, noting the slow progress of the operation and attempting to find a better plan to increase its efficiency. At this pace, he estimated that the construction of Delafield's forti-fication would take twenty-five years to complete. Colonel DeRussy decided to divide his force and begin the grillage construction over the existing piles, even as the driving continued. But while in the process of reordering the sched-ule, DeRussy's work came to an abrupt halt. Mr. Hudson's attorney finally had obtained his writ of ejectment, and the army was ordered to vacate the island. All work was suspended in the fall, as Colonel DeRussy, Mr. Belin, and the laborers closed down their operation and left Pea Patch Island, many of them for the last time.

The fate of Fort Delaware was now in the hands of the judicial system. The Federal government had spent more than a quarter-million dollars on the various constructions on Pea Patch and was not willing to relinquish its claims of ownership. The complicated dispute found, at its base, the boundary line between Delaware and New Jersey. The official line dividing the two states is the eastern bank of the Delaware at high tide, therefore Pea Patch Island, being in the middle of the river, fell under Delaware State jurisdiction. In 1813 the Delaware State Legislature had ceded Pea Patch Island to the United States for the purposing of erecting a defensive fortification. Dr. Henry Gale, a New Jer-sey resident, had been using the island as a hunting and fishing preserve for some years prior to 1813. Although his claim to ownership was not accompa-nied by any compelling paperwork, such as a deed, Dr. Gale had the right of first occupation. To compound the legal morass, the United States had initially offered Dr. Gale $30,000 to purchase the island. When he refused, the government approached the State of Delaware for the cession of the property, eliminating Dr. Gale's bargaining position. In 1838 Dr. Gale's heirs finally succeeded, via the courts, in repossessing the island. The courtroom battle lasted ten years.

On December 10, 1844, Delaware senator James A. Bayard introduced Bill No. S10 on the floor of the U.S. Senate, which was promptly referred to the Judiciary Committee.[19] Bayard and John M. Clayton, a future secretary of state, outlined a plan that called for the use of binding arbitration and placed the name of Supreme Court Chief Justice Roger B. Taney as the arbitrator, on the floor of the U.S. Senate. The bill never made it out of committee. The decision on ownership was left to the courts to consider. Fort Delaware's case wound its way through the judicial system. Finally, in 1847 an arbitration plan similar to the bill proposed by Senators Bayard and Clayton in 1844 was agreed upon by all the parties involved. The Honorable John Sergeant of Philadelphia was appointed as arbitrator. Sergeant conducted an extensive investigation, examining claims within a twelve-mile radius of New Castle, Delaware, some of which dated back to King James II's original grant to William Penn. On January 15, 1848, Sergeant offered a split opinion. The legality of the title held by the representatives of Dr. Gale was of dubious value. Sergeant ruled that the United States had a legitimate right to ownership of Pea Patch through the cession by the State of Delaware. Dr. Gale's claim of ownership extended from his de facto use of the island in the early nineteenth century, not from any deed of sale. Sergeant then ruled that the government had allowed the establishment of prior claim through its offer of payment for the island. Therefore, the United States was ordered to pay Mr. Hudson the sum of $1,000.[20] Pea Patch Island was once again the property of the United States and, as such, a military facility.

❦

In the ten years since the army vacated Pea Patch, nature had not been kind to the island. In 1839 an unusually high tide completely flooded the island, despite Delafield's dikes. Some of the material, especially the timbers, was washed away. Again, in October 1846 a high tide flooded the island. In fact, the oldest inhabitants of the region claimed that the 1846 tide was the highest in memory.[21] The tide had been propelled by an unusually strong storm from the southeast, which caused extensive damage to the work and washed away more of the timbers slated for use as piles and grillage. The pile drivers also were damaged.

Pea Patch Island had become a tangled wasteland. Debris was scattered everywhere, vegetation had grown over the brick and stone piles, the engines were relics, and most of the timbers were gone. Bvt. Maj. John Sanders could scarcely believe his eyes as he surveyed his new assignment. John Sanders, a war hero, was one of the finest engineers the army had in its ranks. Having graduated second in his class at the Academy in 1834, Sanders was assigned to direct improvements on the Ohio River just above Louisville, Kentucky. He had participated in the Mexican War, actively engaging in the sieges of Vera Cruz and Monterey, where he was breveted to the rank of major for gallant and meritorious conduct. He had served on the staff of Gen. Zachary Taylor and was commended by both Taylor and Gen. William Worth.

When he set foot on Pea Patch Island for the first time, Major Sanders was in his forty-eighth year. Although short in stature, Sanders appeared to others as a large man, no doubt because of his "uncommonly large head."[22] He was described by his contemporaries as an intellectual, with piercing dark eyes; a spirited conversationalist; and a religious man. Sanders brought to his newest assignment his wife and seven children. At the height of his career, Major Sanders was considered by the War Department as the very best engineer for the job of completing the "largest modern fort in the country."

The first order of business required an inventory of the implements and stockpiles left unsecured on Pea Patch. Major Sanders's March 1, 1848, inventory revealed that the four steam pile drivers required an extensive overhaul and the replacement of all the brass and the boilers. The grillage timber, piles, and six scows had rotted beyond salvage. Of the 250,000 feet of pile timber, only 42,000 feet were usable. The stone and bricks were another story. Although some of the bricks were cracked, 1.3 million were deemed usable for the construction at hand. More than 19,000 tons of stone remained and were considered in good shape, despite their exposure to the elements.

Sanders had in hand a series of drawings and plans from Col. Joseph Totten detailing exactly what was to be done. Over the course of the last ten years the War Department had begun to rethink its position regarding Delafield's fort. The sheer magnitude of Delafield's plans involved massive expenditures—money the government did not have. Still, Philadelphia remained America's seaport and needed the protection, but the funds available could not possibly pay for the erection of a fort the size Delafield had envisioned. There were some, most notably Senators Clayton and Bayard, who pushed to retain the plan developed by Delafield, despite the financial considerations. Financial objections were not easily overcome, however, and it was readily acknowledged that the cost to erect the original fort was prohibitive. The results of the recent Mexican War also played a role in reducing the size of the construction. Warfare was, and is, a very costly enterprise, thus shrinking the Treasury, which has a practical result in the amount of expenditures allocated for defense. The lessons of combat affected the plans at Fort Delaware, as well. Simply put, fixed fortifications were no longer as unassailable as they once were. A modern fortification's strength was not necessarily its size, but its position of armament.

New plans were ordered to replace Delafield's fort: The size of the new Fort Delaware would be halved. If practicable, the new edifice should be erected on the site of Delafield's massive structure. The new plans, designed by Col. Joseph Totten, with the assistance of Capt. Henry W. Halleck and Lt. Montgomery Miens, called for a two-tiered structure spanning six acres on the southeast side of Pea Patch Island. Totten presented a theory of modular construction for the erection of all seacoast fortifications. Advances in gunnery in the fifty years prior to the great fort-building efforts of the United States had forced army engineers to reformulate their plans for offensive as well as defensive uses of the larger seacoast guns. Totten's casemates and embrasures were naturally born as a reaction to the technological changes in weapons and armament. The new design would use Totten's plan incorporating casemates as the base element in all fortification construction.

Totten's fortification design called for casemates to be used as building blocks. The number of casemates used would depend on the amount of territory the structure would cover. The engineer could simply attach casemates side by side until the desired ground was covered. Totten's casemate design made it possible for the Army Corps of Engineers to preplan seacoast fortifications to be placed at strategic points around the nation's seaboard. In this manner the casemate was similar to interchangeable parts in weapons' manufacturing. The casemate design also made it possible to present much more armament to the enemy and, by extension, more firepower. The design called for two levels of casemates in which guns were mounted. The ramparts, with the breast-high wall, would serve as a third gun platform. Totten's casemates also employed a radical construction technique that allowed gunners to accurately fire their weapons at fast-moving targets. The casemates also provided excellent protection for the gun crew during hostile action. Despite the shrinkage reflected in the new design, Fort Delaware, with its capacity to mount 150 seacoast guns and room for a garrison of 800, would still be the largest construction ever attempted by the U.S. Army.

Major Sanders examined the plans and the topography of the ground upon which his work would stand. Realizing the difficulties involved in creating a stable foundation, Sanders suggested several changes involving the location of the fort. In his first report to Colonel Totten, Sanders was remarkably astute in his observations, backing up his suggested modifications with well-reasoned arguments and plans to effect his proposals efficiently and economically. His intelligence, candor, and attention to detail impressed his superior and forged a rapport that continued throughout their professional relationship.

Sanders's plan for the erection of the fort began with the clearing of the debris field Pea Patch Island had become. Much of the existing material was strewn about and resting, in many cases, on top of the proposed position of the fort. Major Sanders compared this initial work to rock excavation; the conditions, however, were far more difficult than on a fresh site. After hiring more than a hundred laborers, Sanders began the exhaustive site preparation. Temporary housing had to be erected for the workers, the stone had to be moved, the bricks had to be examined and restacked, the four steam pile drivers required extensive repair, and the Delafield site had to be strengthened, catalogued, and prepared for incorporation into the new plan.

In the course of the site preparation, Sanders had also stabilized the dike and seawall surrounding the island. This gave him complete control of the water inundating the island. Sanders had a plan to use the water to his advantage. He had noted the difficulty the Delafield crew had in driving the piles to a uniform depth and in a vertical position. Purchasing some stone but, for the most part, using the debris from Babcock's fort, Sanders surrounded Pea Patch with a high seawall. The wall protected the island from flooding but also allowed the engineers to flood or drain the island using a system of ditches and a sluiceway on the eastern side of the island.

To facilitate the pile-driving operation Sanders proposed flooding the site and driving the piles from scow-mounted machinery. It would be a relatively easy task to float the timbers into place and then, with block tackle, raise and place each timber into position for the driving operation. The forty-five-foot-long piles could easily be placed and driven with some efficiency. By October 1849 only 400 piles remained to be driven. Sanders had preplanned the entire project so each phase would dovetail neatly into the next. Confident of the speed and efficiency of his crew, he began negotiations with timbermen from the Susquehanna River–area in Pennsylvania to order the logs needed for the grillage timber. The contracts were drawn up with unusual speed, and the timber was slated for delivery in the spring of 1850. The logs were to be cut during the winter and floated down the existing waterways, through the Chesapeake and Delaware (C&D) Canal, terminating at Pea Patch Island. The War Department, Colonel Totten, and Major Sanders and his crew were overjoyed at the success of the operation and anticipated new congressional appropriations. Success, however, was a fleeting commodity on Pea Patch.

The strong and almost constant wind blowing across the island brings a dramatic change in temperatures, especially in the fall and winter. It was not uncommon to witness a ten-degree variance in temperature between the mainland and island, not including the wind-chill factor. Winter weather came early to Pea Patch Island in 1849, and the wind brought with it ill omen. The mud began to congeal; thousands of piles began to slip. Some popped up, others sank, and suddenly the level platform was not only uneven but, at times, undulating. Sanders attempted to redrive the offending piles, only to find that some required repunching to greater depths with a small volley of blows, while others sank spontaneously.

"The whole matter perplexes and embarrasses me. I wait with some solicitude for your views," wrote Sanders to Totten as he struggled with a design to curb the movement of the piles. The correspondence between Totten and Sanders at this juncture reveals the determination both these men had to fulfill their mission. They made detailed notes and constantly sought the other's opinion. Both knew that they were charting innovations that had never been tried on this scale. Their awareness that the record of their work would be the foundation for many projects of this nature in the future compelled them to detail each step of the process.[23] Finally, they decided to repunch every pile in the foundation using a procedure designed by mathematician Jean-Victor Poncelet and a pile driver of Sanders's own design, the ringing pile engine. Of the four pile drivers that remained on the island, only three could function, using a combination of existing parts and manufactured new parts, and their performance was tedious at best. Sanders's ringing pile driver was capable of delivering twenty blows per minute with a 2,000-pound ram, greatly increasing the drivers' speed and efficiency. In the course of the work 1,594 piles needed to be spliced together, sometimes as much as three deep; some piles were driven to a depth of seventy feet.

Sanders had developed a schematic of the pile placement; each pile was designed to cover an area ten and one half square feet. The tedious labor involved in respacing and resecuring each pile took an additional eighteen months. As each section of the fort's foundation was completed, Sanders assigned a crew to level the tops of the piles. Initial cuts were done with steam-driven circular saws, but the results were unsatisfactory. After some debate it was found that whipsaws achieved the uniform result needed to maintain a level grillage. Each of the total 6,006 piles had to be topped before the grillage could be assembled. Once the piles were topped, the lower-tier grillage was secured to the pile heads with oak tree nails, eighteen inches long, two and one half inches in diameter. One-foot-square timbers were added for the upper tier; each timber was notched and spiked to the lower tier at three-and-one-half-foot intervals. Earth was then packed around the pile heads and grillage timbers. Finally, four-inch-thick planks were spiked to the lower timbers, completing the smooth grillage platform upon which the masonry structure would rest.

The delivery of the grillage timber in the spring of 1850 was, by necessity, delayed until the pile-driving process was near completion. Sanders did have at his disposal some leftover grillage material and had begun the work on each section as it was complete. Throughout the winter of 1850 work continued on stabilizing the piles. Finally, several lockings of the 12" x 12" white-pine grillage logs were floated from Delaware City and delivered on June 27, 1851.

Three weeks before the arrival of the grillage timber came a promising young engineer to assist Major Sanders. A native Philadelphian, Bvt. Capt. George B. McClellan was initially disappointed at his assignment. Fresh from battlefield triumphs during the Mexican War and a stint at West Point, McClellan believed that this assignment was beneath him. George McClellan, second in the Academy's class of 1846, had distinguished himself during the Mexican War, receiving two brevet promotions to the rank of captain. He had hoped for an assignment to create a U.S. Army practical engineers' school, and he constantly badgered Colonel Totten about the possibility. Totten, in his exasperation with the young man, sent him to the most practical of engineers' schools, the construction on Pea Patch Island. Now, much to his surprise, he came to enjoy his work with Major Sanders. As the grillage timbers were delivered McClellan began to supervise the placement and eventual construction of the grillage itself. At his disposal was a large force of wharf builders, standing by to begin the work of laying the timber. The work, supervising the placement of the timber in the designated holding area on the island, was not demanding. McClellan had enough leisure time to learn German and do a lot of hunting and fishing. That summer he wrote home, "I have gone on the principle of making myself perfectly acquainted with my duties before I go to amusing myself. I shall be able to work it so as to fish & shoot without interfering with my work."[24]

On August 25, 1851, the last of the grillage timber was delivered and the work began in earnest to attach the entire platform. Captain McClellan supervised the swarm of wharf builders, divided into sectional work details. While the builders began the construction of their respective sections, another team of laborers attended to the backfill of the piles. Sanders had asked for concrete or sand to pour around the heads of the piles, leveling and further stabilizing the pile heads. As always, though, cost cutting was an issue, even with the choice of backfill. Pea Patch Island was a source of plenty of mud, and so, as the water was drained from the piles, Pea Patch Island mud was poured in. Just as the work on the platform was taking shape Captain McClellan was transferred to Washington City to write his book on bayonet exercises.

The last planks of the grillage platform were spiked into place on May 14, 1852. It had taken Major Sanders and his team three years to complete the foundation. Now the engineers began the work of laying out the lines on the substantial base platform. The five-sided fortification would present its longest bastion to the west facing Delaware, with a southwest and southeast bastion facing the Delaware Bay. The eastern bastion, which would contain a substantial portion of the armament, faced the government farm in New Jersey, while the northern bastion gaped over the north end of Pea Patch Island. As the masons and stonecutters redoubled their efforts, Major Sanders faced yet another dilemma.

When construction resumed in 1848, there was $20,000 left over from the Delafield project. Since then, Sanders, with the help of Secretary of War Jefferson Davis, was able to secure congressional appropriations at the rate of $50,000 per annum. By December 12, 1852, more than $100,000 of the $170,000 had been spent on the foundation alone. Only $9,500 remained to complete the task. It was not at all certain that Congress would appropriate more funding to the seemingly bottomless pit of Fort Delaware. Sanders closed down operations and moved himself and his family to Philadelphia. Over the winter Totten and Sanders worked to present an extensive report to Secretary Davis in hopes of renewing the appropriation. The work was impressive, and with the help of many political friends, the appropriation was passed.

By April 1853 Sanders and crew were back on the island. The immediate task at hand was to drain the foundation, as Sanders had ordered it flooded before they left in December to preserve the integrity of the piles. Thirty stonecutters attacked the Quarryville stone left from fifteen years before. The Quarryville stone worked quite readily, but 1,200 blocks of the Port Deposit stone were found to be hard as iron. One report maintained that the consistency of the Port Deposit stone was so hard that the cutters could make only a superficial cut of one foot per hour. Cement was purchased from New York and shipped in 500-barrel lots via schooners. Despite the delays work was progressing quickly. By first frost that fall, all the Port Deposit stone had been set, the work containing about 8,000 cubic feet of masonry.

Pea Patch Island had become a community. A little over 200 laborers and their families now inhabited the island. Major Sanders and his two assistants, Lieutenants Morton and Casey, labored not only on the construction at hand, but also on the maintenance of public health in their bustling village. Sanders now performed two functions on Pea Patch: superintending engineer and de facto mayor. And the problems of construction compounded the problems of the community. At the top of the list was a relatively new department regulation prohibiting the supply of military medical assistance to civilian personnel. Sanders requested that this regulation be rescinded on Pea Patch Island. He rightly pointed out that the civilian labor force was confined to the island and consequently any medical emergency would have to be handled by the military. The regulation was rescinded, and Major Sanders received approval to hire a civilian physician from Delaware City. Meanwhile, disease had been a constant companion on the island. The inadequate sources of fresh water, the poor drainage, and a lack of understanding about the necessity of sanitary conditions combined to contribute to the deteriorating health of many of the workers. Major Sanders, Dr. Hamilton, and the workers combined their resources to address the health concerns of the population. Sanders erected a four-bed post hospital, with the labor supplied by the mechanics and laborers.

The laborers also organized the Fort Delaware Employees Mutual and Sick Fund, paid for through the attachment of a portion of each employee's wages. The disbursement of funds helped to pay for medical emergencies, and even went so far as to advance money to the worker who might be a little short between paydays. Major Sanders established a scheduled workday of ten hours and a work week of six days. The labor force on Pea Patch was highly paid, receiving 25 percent more money than their equivalents on the mainland. Laborers were paid $1.00 a day, mechanics $2.50 a day; clerks and draftsmen received $80.00 to $90.00 a month. Dr. Hamilton was paid the average wage of $86.00 a month. The workers were paid time and a half for overtime. Everyone was paid monthly, the money initially being drawn from the Delaware City Bank. As the workforce increased to its maximum of 300 laborers, the payroll averaged $10,000 a month, sorely straining the resources of the Delaware City Bank. Beginning in 1855 the payroll was drawn from the Philadelphia Mint and delivered by Adams Express, at the rate of $2.00 per $1,000.

The workers took up residence on the island and were forbidden to commute from the mainland. Major Sanders had his pick of the best laborers available. Because the wages were high, competition for the jobs was extreme. German wharf builders, ships' carpenters from Liverpool, a lock builder from the Delaware and Raritan Canal, and hundreds of Irish and German emigrants completed the roll call of this polyglot crew. To ensure retention of his crack crew, Sanders created jobs that would carry the majority through the winter months. Stonecutters continued to work year-round, carpenters were employed in building new shops and residences for the influx of laborers, and smiths were employed in wheelbarrel manufacture and machinery maintenance and repair.

The construction of a military fortification, especially one of such a complex nature as Fort Delaware, required a familiarity with military terms. It was vitally important that every laborer, not just the engineers, grasped the terms used to describe the various sections of the fortification. The moat surrounding the fort was known as the wet ditch. The outside wall of the ditch was called the counterscarp revetment, with the inner wall (or the actual outside wall of the fort itself) known as the scarp wall. Each section of the five-sided structure was called a bastion. The component parts of the bastions were the casemates, or housing for the guns. Fort Delaware was a two-tiered bastion. Each tier was in essence a gun platform. The ramparts, or the top of the fort, formed a third tier to serve as an additional gun platform. The breast-high wall on the top of the ramparts was called the parapet, designed to protect the gunners serving the pieces in the open air. The rampart was covered with earth known as the terreplein. The terreplein served two purposes: to cushion the shock of recoil from the firing of the large seacoast guns and to act as a natural drainage system directing the rainfall to the front and the back of the fort, rather than draining the water down through the structure itself. Each casemate was equipped with the Totten embrasure, the window through which the gun fired. The Totten embrasure had spring-closed iron shutters, which automatically shut when the gun was being serviced, thus protecting the crew during action. The Totten embrasure also included an iron tongue attached by an iron pin to the interior scarp wall. The tongue was subsequently attached to the truck of the gun. At the breech end of the truck was a semicircular iron rail bolted to the floor, known as a traverse rail. With the pin at the front, or muzzle end, of the truck, and an iron wheel running along the semicircular track, a gun crew could easily move the gun and maintain accurate fire.

Fort Delaware also featured a remarkably modern plan for the use of indoor plumbing. Fresh water had always been a problem on Pea Patch. The wells dug over the years provided water of a brackish nature that was entirely unsuitable for drinking purposes. Totten devised a technique to collect rainwater and use it as the fort's supply of fresh drinking water. Water-collecting troughs were located strategically along the ramparts; the water was collected in the troughs and funneled through filtered pipes to a series of cisterns located underneath the fort proper. Pipes were attached to the cisterns, which had a capacity of 543,000 gallons of water, and the water was pumped into the various kitchens inside the fort. Flush toilets, known as Carr's Patent Hoppers, were installed inside privy chambers. Some of the rainwater was collected in tanks on the ramparts and directed to smaller holding tanks over the hoppers. The waste was flushed into a holding platform beneath the fort, called a privy vault, and attached directly to the moat. Through the use of the sluice gate, which attached the moat and drainage system to the Delaware River, the waste could be flushed into the river with the tidal action. Fort Delaware was truly to be the most modern, innovative fortification ever constructed.

Totten had not added features such as plumbing and flush toilets for the comfort of the garrison. These innovations were military necessities. The ability to rely on the rain for fresh water and the self-contained nature of waste management solved many of the difficulties that Pea Patch Island presented. Certainly, one contingency any defensive plan must anticipate is siege. With her massive walls and formidable wet ditch, any enemy would be hard-pressed to breach the walls and enter the fort, but the fort itself could be surrounded and reduced by siege. The siege would employ systematic approaches to the reduction of the garrison, by cutting off the water and food supply and the ability to manage waste. Eventually, the garrison would be forced to capitulate. Fort Delaware's water- and waste-management system allowed the potentially besieged garrison a longer time to hold out against such tactics. The enemy could never stop the rain and the waste flushed into the moat, the same moat the enemy must cross to gain access. The garrison of 800 could survive inside the fort, unsupplied, for a little over four months, ample time for any siege to be lifted by allied forces outside of the fort.

Sanders began to record real progress in the completion of the fort. The scarp wall, composed of granite blocks cut and positioned to form a solid wall facing the enemy, was the major undertaking of 1854. The scarp wall, also called the rubble, used all of the obdurate Port Deposit granite. John Lieper's quarries were exclusively engaged in supplying the final portions of granite blocks for the scarp wall. Sanders had his stonecutters and masons setting a course of stone per month or 1,500 running feet of wall. By the fall of 1854 the scarp wall was raised to a ten-foot height. Besides the scarp wall granite, Leiper also furnished fine, white stone for the circular staircases. The fancy white granite used in the sally port (the main entranceway) and the postern gate (the alternate entranceway) came from Quincy, Massachusetts. Quarries in Maine, Massachusetts, and Pennsylvania supplied thousands of tons of granite for the lintels, embrasures, coping, stairs, and the flooring of the fort.

Behind the rubble came the brickwork. The casemates and barracks buildings required the use of more than two million bricks, coming primarily from Philadelphia and Chester, Pennsylvania, and Wilmington, Delaware. The casemates and powder magazines relied on the use of the archway as the main feature of their construction. The arch, with its anchoring keystone, provided strength to the buildings and subsequent protection to the garrison during bombardment. The powder magazines featured a right-angle entranceway, heavy oaken doors flush with the brickwork, and an interior vented gallery. Inside the parade ground stood three three-storied brick buildings. These buildings contained the offices, mess halls, kitchens, privies, barracks, and the quarters for the officers and their families. The longest building, erected on the western curtain wall, was 279 feet long, 66 1/2 feet wide, at a height of 52 feet. This building housed the enlisted garrison, the laundresses' quarters, and the kitchen facilities.

With the completion of the scarp wall in 1855, Sanders reported that the fort would be ready for armament and garrison by the fall of 1858, depending upon the willingness of Congress to appropriate the necessary funds. At the midway point of construction momentum began to increase as the efficiency of Major Sanders's team reached full power. The tangible evidence of a massive fort on Pea Patch Island had piqued public interest. The obvious strategic importance of the post, as well as the evidence of public support, compelled

Congress to continue funding the project. By 1856 Fort Delaware was called a modern marvel. The nagging problems of the construction were, for the most part, solved. The foundation appeared to be sturdy, the water overflow on the island was under control, and the construction of the interior buildings was ahead of schedule. In November 1856 the army felt secure enough to temporarily transfer Major Sanders to Fort Taylor in Key West, Florida. Sanders, through his work on Pea Patch, had become an officer to be reckoned with. His services and advice were much sought after, and the Army Corps of Engineers used his imposing talents in problem solving on several other projects. Sanders did not return from his assignment at Fort Taylor until June 1857.

Upon his return, Sanders found a new assistant clerk in his office, a young émigré from Germany by the name of Edward Muhlenbruch. He soon discovered that young Muhlenbruch had been a military engineer in Europe; captured as a revolutionary and tortured by the Austrians, he had escaped and made his way to America in 1854. He then applied for and secured a job with the Army Corps of Engineers based on his experience in Europe. Muhlenbruch soon established himself as an invaluable assistant to Major Sanders. That summer they began to take levelings to determine if any slippage had occurred. They discovered that the southern flank of the fort had sunk nine-tenths of an inch; although not substantial, the slippage was cause for concern. Major Sanders expressed his despair in a report, complaining of "this mud island, upon which there is no stability."[25]

Increasingly, Major Sanders's role as engineer was overshadowed by his role as post commandant and community leader. More than 300 people, including women and children, now lived on Pea Patch Island. The well-being of the community—its health and supply concerns and the general appearance of the village—now called for more and more of Sanders's attention. Besides, the construction was running so well that Sanders did not need to supervise every detail. His job as post commandant soon took on an almost paternalistic role as he settled differences, sought to maintain high morale, and turned his tireless energy to the details of the community. He issued special orders regulating pets on the island and establishing a school on Pea Patch. On June 28, 1858, Miss Louisa Gibble stepped onto the wharf to assume her duties as the island community's first schoolteacher.

In 1858 Col. Richard Delafield, the superintendent at West Point, formed a group of high-powered engineers, known officially as the Special Board of Engineers and composed of the most talented engineers the army had to offer. Essentially a nineteenth-century think tank, the board was assigned to oversee the Army's engineering projects, as well as address present or potential problems with the various projects under it purview. Maj. John Sanders was selected to the board. Delafield convened their first meeting on July 21, 1858, but the meeting was postponed due to Major Sanders's ill health. Again, Major Sanders was unable to attend the postponed meeting. His constitution had been weakened by diabetes, but throughout his tenure on Pea Patch Island, Sanders worked with tireless energy and enthusiasm. In the summer of 1858 he developed a carbuncle that refused to heal. The boil became enlarged and painful, keeping Sanders bedridden for two weeks. In an age when medical science had no knowledge of antibiotics, a patient healed only if the body could resist the infection. Major Sanders had used all of his powers to complete Fort Delaware, and his weakened constitution was unable to suppress the boil. On July 29, 1858, John Sanders died in his quarters, more than ten years and five months after beginning the reconstruction of Fort Delaware. In the official dispatch to the War Department, Engineer Muhlenbruch wrote, "As Major Sanders attended to his public duties during the whole of his sickness the progress of the work was not in the least impeded, only today the workmen declined working, the sad event being expected since last night."[26] Major Sanders left behind a widow and seven children.

Lt. William P. Craighill assumed the duties of superintendent pending the transfer of a higher-ranking engineer. When Craighill took up his duties there was still considerable work to be done. The stonecutters were working on the remainder of the scarp, embrasures, gateway, steps, and flag flooring for the gun rooms and powder magazines. The stonemason was setting the flagstone in the gun rooms. The carpenters and shipwrights had just finished setting the pilings for the main gate and had commenced the laying of the grillage. The riggers and painters were constantly repairing and painting the machinery, as well as rigging the cranes to move the last of the scarp stone. In September 1858 Lieutenant Craighill reported that all the casemate arches had been turned and the flagstone flooring had been completed on the second-tier parade ground wall. There remained the nagging problems of slippage and malfunctioning cisterns, which were ignored until the entire scarp wall was in place. Then, it was felt, a realistic analysis of those problems could be made.

In October 1858 Capt. John Newton arrived to assume the superintendency. Virginian John Newton had spent his entire adult life in the Army Corps of Engineers. He had graduated second in the class of 1842 at the age of twenty. Since then Newton had been posted throughout the country on various engineering projects. His only active field service had been in the Mormon Expedition the previous winter. In fact, Newton arrived in Delaware directly from Utah. Captain Newton was considered an expert in military architecture, second only to Sanders, and in the months ahead Captain Newton was instrumental in preparing Fort Delaware for use in the Civil War and his own career spanned thirty more years. Despite his Virginia ancestry, Newton remained loyal to the Union and rose to command an army corps at the battle of Gettysburg. He retired a full general in 1886 after a distinguished career.

Newton examined the progress thus far and estimated the likely time a garrison could man the fort. He reported to the War Department that, if the appropriations continued, Fort Delaware would be in complete readiness for active duty on June 30, 1860. Newton added that, given the present state of construction, with a month's notice an emergency operation could be put in place to house up to one and a half regiments as well as mounting the fort's 156 heavy guns—91 in the casemates and 65 placed on the ramparts.

As the fort neared realization, a final decision was needed on the roofing material. The interior buildings and open surfaces on the ramparts were slated to have painted iron roofs. Major Sanders had maintained that this process would be satisfactory. But a new consideration entered the picture as the United States prepared for war. The chief engineer in New York, Lt. A. A. Gilmore, wrote to Newton suggesting that the roof surfaces be applied with asphaltic tar, which would protect the roofing surfaces during attack. An additional benefit would be the waterproofing the asphalt provided. The technique of applying "mastic," as the tar was called, worked to maintain the integrity of the roof surface. An unapplied metal roof, when struck with shot from an enemy gun, would eventually crack and splinter, showering the garrison with hot shards of iron. The mastic application, when struck by shot, would heat up and melt, acting as a cushion and making it far more difficult to break up the roof. Upon consideration, Newton determined to hire a French *applicateur* named Coeur de Vache at a rate of $60 a month. Within two months, Newton realized that de Vache needed help and hired another *applicateur* as de Vache's assistant. The work of applying mastic continued through September 1860.

Assistant Engineer Muhlenbruch was now the chief civilian engineer on Pea Patch Island and, as such, was an invaluable resource to Captain Newton. It was Muhlenbruch who filed all the engineers' reports, handled all the paperwork, and maintained the fiscal balance sheet. Because of his long association with Major Sanders and an equally evident rapport with Mr. John Whitehead, the chief foreman, Muhlenbruch provided a constancy as the project neared completion. In 1859, however, Muhlenbruch's coworkers began to notice a subtle change in his behavior. Some called it an irritable distraction, others a seeming preoccupation, but all were in agreement that the forty-one-year-old bachelor had more on his mind than work. Certainly, his change in deportment did not affect his work to any great length; he did, however, seem more concerned about the mail and would repair to his quarters as soon as the workday finished.

Edward Muhlenbruch was in love. He had been corresponding for some time with an acquaintance from Newfoundland. Sometime in 1859 Muhlenbruch decided his course of action and pursued, through the mails, the hand of Margaret Cassavina. Evidently she accepted, and early in 1860, Muhlenbruch left Pea Patch Island for the purpose of marriage. No one had ever seen Margaret, and consequently there was much speculation within the community about the woman who had so smitten the confirmed bachelor. Upon his return the wagging tongues that fueled the gossip machine kicked into overdrive. Alighting from the steamer onto the western wharf came Engineer Muhlenbruch, forty-two years old in 1860, his new bride, Margaret, and a traveling companion of Margaret's named Emma Cassaving. Margaret was twenty-four years old and Emma was sixteen! As they set up housekeeping, however, it was abundantly clear that Edward was a happy man. Equally clear was that Victorian propriety had been breached, given the remarkable age difference between the couple. And naturally gossips could only speculate about the true nature of the relationship between the Muhlenbruchs and Emma. In the end, however, Margaret Muhlenbruch proved to be a wonderful hostess, and their match was truly made in heaven. The Muhlenbruch household became the social center of Pea Patch Island's population and, once the shock was absorbed, Edward, Margaret, and Emma made a home of love and fidelity.

After only seven months on the job, in May 1859 Captain Newton ordered that all labor be directly related to finalizing the placement of the guns inside the fort. It was apparent that his forecast deadline of June 30, 1860, would not be met. The expensive nature of the construction was beginning to drain the budget at an alarming pace. To date, $950,623 had been spent on the construction, and an estimated $354,849 was needed to finish the job. With less than $100,000 at his disposal, Newton was forced to make cuts and assign the highest priority to the armament of the fort. In 1860 he forwarded a bill of ordnance requesting early completion of the project. Eventually, the money was appropriated. By January 1861 Captain Newton reported that Fort Delaware was ready to receive all guns. By then the fort had a garrison of twenty soldiers. Much remained to be done, though. Newton reported that five front cisterns continued to leak. The drainage system in the parade ground, the soldiers' barracks and officers' quarters, and the wet ditch remained unfinished. A western wharf had been proposed but not acted upon, and an additional two sluiceways were considered. But, on the whole, Fort Delaware was ready for service. So far, the entire project had cost the United States $1,305,472.

After twenty-nine years of intellectual and physical labor, the largest and most modern fortification in the history of the United States was nearly complete. As the nation stood on the precipice of civil conflagration, Captain

Newton informed the War Department that Fort Delaware was ready to be manned. Although much of the fine detail work remained, the fort could serve in the event of attack. Captain Newton, aware of impending Civil War, accelerated the schedule for mounting the armament. He hoped to have all the guns in place by spring. At last, however, the bastions, the scarp wall, the wet ditch, the ramparts, and the embrasures were in place and formidable.

Fort Delaware was a marvel of military engineering. In the years since the old fort was engulfed in flames, America's brightest engineers had been assigned to the project. From Joseph Totten to George McClellan and countless laborers, the project proved to be one of the most difficult undertakings ever pursued by the Army Corps of Engineers. The determination of the government—as seen through the actions of numerous secretaries of war, including the likes of James Monroe and Jefferson Davis—to conclude this project was as remarkable as the project itself. This American Goliath boasted indoor plumbing, modern defensive architecture, innovative gunnery platforms, and the capability to hold a waterborne enemy at bay for months. Fort Delaware was truly the locked door to the seaport of Philadelphia.

The largest bastion in the modern world was prepared for America's enemies. If they came, they would feel the power of a mighty nation! Fort Delaware could now step onto the pages of history as she served her country. And serve she did. But fate often deals the unexpected card. The titanic fortification on Pea Patch would play a major part in the nation's civil conflict, but Fort Delaware's place in that war never addressed her intended purpose. Rather than saving the lives of the garrison during a horrific conflict or dealing death to her enemies from her 156 guns, she would watch over thousands of prisoners and bear mute witness to suffering and death—death not by force of arms, but by the actions of microbes.

*Chapter 2*

# 1861

*"I understand that Fort Delaware could very promptly and economically be fitted up for 200 prisoners by simply flooring the casemates."*

—Maj. Gen. John A. Dix

As 1861 opened, life changed for Fort Delaware's twenty-man garrison. As the secession crisis heightened, the military resolved to hold onto Federal property and move troops to a wartime status. Pea Patch Island was an ongoing concern throughout 1860, and with the political crisis looming, it became imperative to finish the construction. Although the fortification was more or less complete, much work remained to be done on the interiors of the quarters and the administrative and commissary buildings. Captain Newton, believing that a war between the states would precipitate a war with a foreign power, felt it was essential that the guns be mounted and the garrison be strengthened.[1]

On February 2, 1861, Capt. Augustus A. Gibson was assigned as commandant of the fighting garrison at Fort Delaware. A. A. Gibson was a West Point man, graduating twenty-third in his class of 1839. Gibson was assigned as a second lieutenant of artillery, receiving promotion to first lieutenant in 1846 and to captain in 1853. He would make a career of the U.S. Army, retiring as a lieutenant colonel of artillery in 1870. Captain Gibson's first priority was to aid in the completion of interior buildings, but he neverthelss placed the garrison on alert. The national crisis, which began in earnest only eleven days before the new year, was bound to have a profound effect on Fort Delaware. Despite the outward appearance of normal operations, Captain Gibson was entirely unclear what his response should be in the event the government changed hands. It was easy to make ready for attack by a foreign power and equally easy to keep the garrison prepared to fend off attacks by insurrectionists. But it was not clear what the military response should be if the people voted to institute an entirely new government. After all, the idea of voting a new government in place was not a new idea; it had been accomplished only seventy-four years before, by men now revered as noble patriots. To make matters more complicated, Gibson had only twenty soldiers in his garrison; he commanded more workers than he did soldiers.

Captain Gibson was not alone in his misgivings; Maj. Robert Anderson had only recently been expressly forbidden to move his forces from the vulnerable Fort Moultrie to the newly constructed Fort Sumter. Like Fort Delaware, Fort Sumter had been constructed on an island, was finished in 1860, and boasted many of the same modern conveniences. But as late as December 1860 she remained without a garrison. By the spring of 1861 Gibson knew that the government would back him and that retention of Fort Delaware was his highest priority. Immediately following the opening shots at Fort Sumter, President Lincoln wired all Federal fortifications for a status report. In a wire dated April 24, 1861, Maj. Gen. Robert Patterson reported to the War Department: "The orders of the Lieutenant-General Commanding to secure the forts on the Delaware have been anticipated. Captain Gibson reported last week that he was able to hold Fort Delaware, but requested that the remainder of his company be directed to join him. I have detailed one hundred men (raw volunteers) to be placed under his command."[2]

By now, the realization that there was to be a war took root on Pea Patch. Since 1860 the island had become a popular tourist attraction. Folks from all walks of life, and many of the neighboring states, descended on the island to gawk at America's newest wonder. Back then there was no military garrison, just a handful of engineers and a large civilian population. When war broke out Captain Gibson and his garrison of twenty artillerists had to place the fort in a position to adequately defend the river. In April fewer than half the guns of the fort were mounted. While the work continued to mount all the guns, the recognition came that Fort Delaware had, in fact, been functioning more as a tourist destination than as a fortress of war. And while it was clear that the United States would claim the legal right to retain its property, it was equally unclear where the State of Delaware would fall as the Union began to unravel.

Delaware was a slave state, one of the four critical border states that Lincoln had to convince to stay the course. Yet the populations of Missouri, Maryland, Delaware, and Kentucky remained divided on the subject of secession. Missouri had a vast population of slave owners who had endured years of internecine warfare along its border with Kansas. Despite the bloody warfare they had endured, the population of Missouri had evolved during the five years prior to the war. The massive influx of German immigrants settling in and around St. Louis and Kansas City acted as a counterweight to the slaveholders who wanted to "go South." Kentucky's slaveholding populace, while sympathetic to Southern interests, realized that, should secession become a reality for them, the state would become a major battleground for the Union. Should that occur, Kentucky and its inhabitants would experience unimaginable devastation. As a result, Lincoln's hands-off policy toward Missouri and Kentucky was formulated in reaction to the wishes of the people of those states. It was clear that any overt action on the part of the Federal government would send those states racing into the folds of the Confederacy for sanctuary.

Maryland and Delaware were different; should those states secede, Washington would be isolated. It was a matter of vital national interest to control those states, by any means necessary. The residents of Maryland were divided on a regional basis. Baltimore and the Eastern Shore were sympathetic to the South and sought to undermine the activities of the Federal government. Western Maryland was the stronghold of Unionist sentiment but the least populated portion of the state. As the Lincoln administration began to receive the troops called for, it became obvious that the movement of those troops through Maryland could be disrupted by Southern sympathizers. Some of the first fighting of the war was endured by the men of the 6th Massachusetts Infantry as they marched through Baltimore. Attacked by an armed mob, the boys of the 6th were obliged to fight their way through the streets. The ensuing loss of life and bloodshed only reinforced Lincoln's policy and offered an excuse to call on a little-known portion of the Constitution that legally entitled the president the right to suspend the writ of habeas corpus in the face of armed insurrection. In effect, Lincoln could do almost anything he pleased, using the national emergency as his excuse. And so it was that Maryland and her divided populace were forcibly retained as part of the Union. The Federal government declared martial law and suspended the writ of habeas corpus. Suspected secessionists and political opponents were arrested wholesale. It became exceedingly difficult for those politicans of Southern proclivity to cast any ballot in the state assemby. Maryland would be held in the Union by force of arms.

Although smaller and seemingly less important, Delaware, too, felt the power of the administration in Washington. Delaware, like Missouri, had witnessed a steady stream of immigration in the five years preceding the war. Primarily of German descent, the immigrants had settled in New Castle County, the northernmost county of Delaware, finding employment in the shipyards of Wilmington and at Delaware City, the terminus of the C&D Canal. Their presence outweighed the leanings of the slaveholding population living in Kent and Sussex Counties. While Governor William Burton, Senators James Bayard and Willard Saulsbury, and Congressman William Whiteley were sympathetic to the South, the state legislature was dominated by individuals loyal to the North. It was by no means clear which direction the state would go. In June a large "peace convention" was held on the green in Dover, the capital. The convention elected as its president the former governor of Delaware, William Temple, an outspoken opponent of the Lincoln administration. The convention took on a decided pro-Confederate flavor as speech after speech denounced Lincoln's policies, and Governor Burton added fuel to the fire by calling for the establishment of the Delaware Home Guard, intended to become the state's own army. With the call for a home guard came Lincoln's decision to deal with Delaware as he had with Maryland. But because there had been no armed uprising within the borders of Delaware, there was no legal basis to send in troops. President Lincoln had to bide his time and wait for the legal opportunity to exercise his power.

In this atmosphere of uncertainty Captain Gibson had to prepare for the worst. And the worst, in his mind, was a sudden attempt to overrun Pea Patch. Since all of the guns had yet to be mounted, Gibson was of the opinion that Fort Delaware could easily fall to any organized militia. In that event, the effective loss of control of navigation would surely cripple the United States. While Newton continued to place the guns, Gibson developed a plan that would impede any hostile attempt to take the island. Gibson asked Newton to design earthen batteries outside of the fort proper, which would have the effect of slowing the efforts of the enemy during attack. With the fort as a support position soldiers could slow any amphibious force if it attempted a landing on Pea Patch. In addition, Gibson planned to utilize the complicated drainage-control system. In the event of a successful landing by the enemy, Pea Patch Island was to be flooded by opening the sluiceway, allowing the Delaware River to flow into the island. Fort Delaware, located on the highest point of the island, would be immune to the flooding, and the garrison could then pick off the enemy with impunity.

Gibson's garrison of now fifty men was soon reinforced with the Pennsylvania Commonwealth Artillery, a ninety-day company of eighty men, composed of volunteers from Philadelphia, in the first week following the bombardment of Fort Sumter. As the Commonwealth men arrived, Captain Gibson turned his thoughts to ensuring that his command was in a high state of readiness. The fifty Regular army artillerists then stationed at the fort were ordered to begin training the new recruits. Captain Newton redoubled his efforts. The work concentrated on the flanking howitzers, and the 8- and 10-inch Columbiads scheduled for placement on the second tier and barbette.

With reinforcements coming in, the engineering work proceeding at an almost breakneck speed, and the uncertainty of the politics in Delaware, Captain Gibson expanded his efforts to bring Fort Delaware to a war footing. On April 21, 1861, he issued Post Order No. 2:

> Guard by day from 4 A.M. to retreat will consist of one man
> in side arms who will walk the parapet and observe every-
> thing on the island and water. He will report arrival of boats
> and vessels. Parties of men, other than fishermen, will not be

permitted to land without permission from the commanding officer, nor will anyone be allowed to enter the work
without same permission. One non-commissioned officer
will always be in garrison to attend calls and reports of sentry and make his communication with the commanding
officer.

At night the command will sleep in their uniform and be
ready to fall under arms. If alarm is sounded, every man is to
rush to arms. The men must always be near the garrison,
quiet in deportment. No loud noise or unnecessary commotion, sure indications of bad soldiery.

Note: The garrison is in a state of war and so each man
must exercise extreme vigilance.[3]

Gibson began to organize the routine of his soldiers. Despite the continuous
labor to complete the fortification, the soldiers arriving had to be trained. On
April 29, 1861, Captain Gibson issued Post Order No. 3 spelling out the daily
schedule for the garrison as well as clearly stating the rules regarding conduct on
the post. The soldier's day began at daybreak with a police of the quarters;
breakfast began at 7:00 A.M. followed by sick call at 7:30 A.M. Morning parade
began promptly at 8:00 A.M., which was immediately followed by guard mount.
The heavy artillery drill consumed an hour and a half of the soldiers' time beginning at 8:45 A.M. After the midday meal, the garrison was assigned fatigue duty,
continuing the completion of the fort's construction as well as making preparations for mounting of the guns. Retreat was sounded at sunset and at 9:15 P.M.
the duty drummer tapped three times on the head of his drum, signaling tatoo
for the garrison. Captain Gibson also included the makeup of the guard, which
consisted of three noncommissioned officers and twelve men. There were to be
four guards posted inside Fort Delaware: the first sentry was posted at the guard
box, the second at the drawbridge on the eastern entrance, the third at the eastern wharf, and the fourth at the western wharf.[4]

In 1861 the Federal army designated two types of service in the artillery
branch—light and heavy. The light artillery, horse-drawn and highly mobile,
was intended for use in the field. The weapons of the light artillery, known as
fieldpieces and offering a variety of projectiles and the ability to keep pace with
a moving army, were designed to support the infantry. Heavy artillery was
placed in fixed fortifications, the ordnance of which consisted of large-bore seacoast guns, many of the tubes weighing more than 10,000 pounds. The big
guns were by no means mobile, but they did offer long-range firepower and
tremendous stopping capacity. The guns could throw a 30-pound ball well over
four miles downrange. Fort Delaware's total armament consisted of 156 guns.
Forty-two pieces were placed on the first tier: ten 24-pounder howitzers, three

32-pounder seacoast guns, twelve 8-inch Rodmans, and seventeen 10-inch Rodmans. The second tier contained forty-eight pieces of heavy artillery: ten 24-pounder howitzers, four 32-pounder seacoast guns, fifteen 42-pounder rifled guns, thirteen 8-inch Columbiads, one 8-inch Rodman, and five 10-inch Rodmans. The guns to be placed *en barbette* (on the ramparts) numbered forty-four pieces: fourteen 8-inch Columbiads, twenty-five 10-inch Columbiads, and five 10-inch Rodmans. Typical of the size of heavy artillery ordnance, the tube of the 8-inch Columbiad weighed 9,800 pounds, with an additional 3,000 pounds for the truck and gun carriage.

The work in mounting that much artillery was painstakingly slow. Captain Newton employed almost his entire civilian workforce, as well as the soldiers from the Commonwealth Independent Battery, to press forward in the completion of the armament of the fort. Forty tons of cannon were shipped from Boston on the steamer *Eliza Jane*, arriving on June 3, 1861. Through the months of May and June every effort was extended to place the guns in position. While Assistant Engineer Muhlenbruch reported the progress of the work on the guns, he also placed a skeleton force of workers to complete the barracks and officers' quarters.

The Commonwealth Independent Battery, Heavy Artillery, was organized in Philadelphia on April 24, 1861, to serve ninety days. Commanded by Capt. James Elginton Montgomery, the Independent Battery boasted the brightest and best young men from Philadelphia society. As they disembarked from the packet steamer onto Pea Patch Island, the men quickly realized that their stay at Fort Delaware would be a far cry from the life they had known in Philadelphia. Because the engineering work had concentrated on the mounting of the guns, very little had been accomplished in completing the soldiers' barracks located on the western curtain. A temporary wooden structure, meant to house 350 soldiers, had been erected on the parade ground and it was to become the new home of the elite, high-society boys from Philadelphia.

The citizen-soldiers of Captain Montgomery's command knew a good deal about gourmet foods but nothing about effectively defending a seacoast fortification. Captain Gibson assigned his Regular army men as drill instructors and set about the task of turning those fresh-faced young men into hardened artillerists. The troops were scheduled for two hours of drill in the morning, then used as a labor force in the afternoon. The men of the Heavy Artillery were required to master two drill manuals: *Hardee's Infantry Tactics* and *The School of the Heavy Artillery*. The business of loading, aiming, and firing those behemoths of artillery required an extraordinarily well-disciplined and well-drilled team of six men per gun. Eventually each gun crew would be expected to accurately load and fire two rounds per minute. To complicate matters, the guns were all muzzle loaders, and the crews were expected to act in concert with the other guns in battery.

But before they worked the guns, the troops had to learn the infantry drill of the time. The close-order drill that all soldiers in the Civil War learned required the full attention of the recruit and molded a team that, when perfected, could act as one and rapidly execute the complex maneuvers designed to bring the most firepower to bear on the enemy. The practice consumed many hours of a soldier's life, as much as four hours per day. As the boys learned the evolution of line—and very likely grumbled about the relevancy of infantry drill for artillery men—they also learned how to function as a team. It was this training that supplied the base for the boys to effectively operate the big guns during hostile action.

Spring had arrived on Pea Patch. The civilian work crew, under the direction of Captain Newton and Assistant Engineer Muhlenbruch, and the soldiers of the regular and volunteer forces, commanded by Captain Gibson, had little time to dwell on the beauty of the river scenery, however. The population of the island had drastically increased, approaching 550 souls by May. Provisions for the folks now residing on Pea Patch had to be secured on the mainland and ferried over. Despite the priority of the guns, storehouses needed to be erected along the wharf on the eastern side of the island. A contingent of civilian laborers, mostly carpenters, was sent to build the storage facilities. With all the work required in the spring of 1861, the island became the site of constant, feverish activity. The ten-hour workday for the civilians was extended to twelve. Work began at sunrise and often did not cease until sunset. The troops varied their time between military assignments and construction. By June 30, 1861, Captain Newton declared Fort Delaware to be "now in fighting order as far as partial armament extends."[5] Only forty-seven of the 156 guns had been mounted: twenty flanking howitzers, eight 8-inch in the second tier, five 10-inch and fourteen 8-inch Columbiads in the barbette. The permanent bridge was completed with an excellent draw, and the bakery, in the northwest bastion, was open for business. There were also plans to construct shot furnaces, but they were never realized.

The ever-present problem of medical facilities continued to be a dilemma for Captain Gibson, however. With the 33 percent increase in population, the existing hospital was proving to be woefully inadequate, still operating under Sanders's system of medical care (civilian doctors and a small cooperative hospital). Gibson now sought, through the surgeon general, to put the medical operation on a war footing. Civilian physician Dr. George Webster, who succeeded Dr. Hamilton in 1860, organized the supplies and paperwork necessary to make the transition to a military status. Dr. Webster, who resided on Pea Patch Island with his wife, Margaret, and their twelve-year-old daughter, Helen, continued to work until December 1861, when he and his family stepped aboard the steamer *Major Reybold* for their journey back to Delaware City. He would be the last civilian physician on the island; henceforth all the medical operations would be conducted by military surgeons.

On the eve of the first major battle of the Civil War, Fort Delaware was prepared in the event of an attack. But she was far from finished: 109 seacoast guns had yet to be mounted, the front five cisterns were still leaking, the drainage system in the parade ground was unfinished, the construction and fitting out of the officers' quarters and soldiers' barracks remained to be completed, and some of the copings needed to be repointed. Outside the fort proper the moat stones had not been placed in the counterscarp, the western wharf needed to be finalized and expanded, and the drainage system needed higher jetties and two new permanent sluiceways. All that considered, as Captain Newton departed the island for his new mission overseeing the defenses of Washington, he looked back with satisfaction. The largest bastion in the arsenal of the United States was prepared for war.

⚓

The gentle lapping of the waters of Baltimore Harbor mingled with the oaths of the stevedores, the creaking of the wooded deck, and the bustle of the crew as they prepared to get the steamboat *Saint Nicholas* underway. Richard Thomas stepped off the gangway and made straightaway for the ship's master; he had booked passage onboard the *Saint Nicholas* and was searching for his cabin. Thomas also noted that he was expecting several friends who had intended to make the journey with him. The master was able to provide Thomas with his cabin assignment, but could not immediately recall the assignments of Thomas's friends. Below decks Thomas found his berth easily and at once set about locating his luggage. He had brought with him a carry-on valise and several parcels. Having located his parcels, Thomas also found his friends, and together they went below decks to prepare for their voyage.

The cacophony at the dock receded, and gradually only the steady hiss of the boiler, the whisper of the breeze on the Chesapeake Bay, and the splash against the hull of the *Saint Nicholas* replaced the bustle of civilization. The steamer was bound for the Potomac on the evening of June 28, 1861, with a cargo of general merchandise and a handful of passengers. Richard Thomas was familiar with the vessel, as he had booked passage on her several times. In fact, Thomas had considerable experience at sea. Richard Henry Thomas, a native of southern Maryland, had been an admirer of the republican revolutionaries of Europe and had set passage to Europe in 1848. Immediately upon his arrival in Europe, Thomas offered his services to Gen. Giuseppe Garibaldi, fighting with the revolutionaries through the campaigns to unify Italy and bring republican government to the people of Europe. With the end of hostilities in Europe, Thomas returned to his family home in Maryland. Probably to his surprise, Thomas found that he had become a hero in his community. He was considered a daring adventurer who had fought alongside the epic hero Garibaldi. In the years since his return Richard Thomas applied himself to his family business, a little politics, and strengthening friendships with his Virginia neighbors. Undoubtedly, however, Thomas missed the adventure of his youth.

When Fort Sumter was fired on, Thomas, an ardent secessionist, began to formulate plans to capture steamships to be placed in the service of the Confederacy. On April 24, in a letter to his cousin, Thomas detailed a plot to capture the USS *Constitution*, then stationed in Baltimore Harbor.[6] Aware that the propaganda value associated with the capture of "Old Ironsides" was worth more than the antiquated ship herself, Thomas believed that her capture would be accomplished easily enough. His efforts were thwarted, however, when "Old Ironsides" was towed out of Baltimore, bound for her new home in Boston— far away from any secessionist plot. But this germ of an idea became an obsession for Thomas, and he recruited compatriots for his new covert operation. The Confederacy had no navy to speak of, and Thomas knew that a modern steamship would be a great prize. He also had a plan to organize a regiment for service to the Confederacy. He and his companions began a clandestine network of active Southern sympathizers to form a special battalion at some future date. It remains uncertain whether the Confederate authorities were aware of Thomas's activities, but clearly his calling card was to be the capture of a steamship to be given to the government in Richmond.

As night fell on the Chesapeake, Thomas and his cohorts opened their parcels. They were armed to the teeth with revolvers, pocket pistols, and bowie knives. Boldly they climbed the ladder leading to the main deck and made straight for the master's mate, at the same time seizing the ship's wheel. In a few bloodless seconds the Confederacy had her first prize of war, the steamer *Saint Nicholas*. And with that prize came the South's most colorful covert operator, Richard Henry Thomas, aka Zarvona. With his prize Zarvona made for Richmond and docked on June 30, 1861. At the same time several of his followers traveled overland to rendezvous in Richmond. Zarvona presented the *Saint Nicholas* to Governor Letcher of Virginia and was promptly rewarded with a colonel's commission in the Virginia state forces, to date from July 1, 1861.[7] His new command was designated the 47th Virginia, whose rank and file were the covert operatives he had spent the last month recruiting. Zarvona's Potomac Zouaves, as they called themselves, were now a regiment of spies.

Not content to rest on his laurels, Zarvona planned to return to Baltimore and commandeer another vessel for the Confederacy. According to plan he traveled to northern Virginia and stole into Washington. There his compatriots had made the necessary arrangements for Thomas to book passage on the steamer *Mary Washington*, bound for Baltimore. Colonel Zarvona, of fair complexion and frail build, disguised himself as a French woman traveling in the United States, hiding his weapons underneath his petticoats. It was an indispensable precaution, as the crew of the *Saint Nicholas* had been released and could easily have been onboard the *Mary Washington*. On July 8, 1861, Zarvona and four other conspirators boarded the steamer for the overnight trip to Baltimore Harbor. Their planned destination, however, was Richmond, Virginia.

The captain of the *Mary Washington* had placed his crew on alert, knowing full well that what happened to the *Saint Nicholas* could easily happen to him. In fact, several of the crew on board *had* served on the *Saint Nicholas*. They were on their way back to Baltimore after their harrowing experience. Unknown to Zarvona and his team, the crew recognized them early in the voyage. As the steamer passed into the Chesapeake Bay, the captain readied his crew, arming them and explicitly ordering them to find Zarvona and place him under arrest. As the crew began to search the vessel Zarvona must have realized his predicament and made haste to hide himself. After a protracted search, Zarvona's four henchmen were easily detained, but Zarvona's whereabouts remained a mystery. Finally, Richard Henry Thomas, aka Colonel Zarvona, aka the French Lady, was located hiding inside a dresser in his stateroom. He was taken to the main deck, and his true identity was revealed, confirmed by the eyewitness testimony of the *Saint Nicholas* crew. Zarvona and his partners were placed in irons and sent below to await docking in Baltimore where they would be turned over to the authorities. Upon arrival their detention was swift; the constable promptly turned over his charges to the Federal authorities in Baltimore. Zarvona, his four operatives, and the four witnesses were quietly and quickly taken to Fort McHenry, in custody of the United States government. Col. Richard Henry Thomas Zarvona was now the Federal government's most curious state prisoner. The following day Zarvona was charged with piracy and ordered to prison, where he would await trial.[8] The details of the arrest and imprisonment included the same treatment for operatives as well as the witnesses. All were imprisoned in Fort McHenry. Since the imposition of martial law, all the Federal properties in Baltimore had now become prisons, holding for the most part "prisoners of state." The iron fist of the Lincoln administration was making itself known in Maryland.

Overseeing the prisoners at Fort McHenry in Maryland was the superintendent of the Military District of Pennsylvania, Maj. Gen. John A. Dix. At the age of sixty-three, Dix had behind him a long career in the service of his country. He served in the Army during the War of 1812; was admitted to the bar in 1828; retired from the army; sought public office in Cooperstown, New York; served in the U.S. Senate; was appointed postmaster of New York City in

1859; became the secretary of the treasury in the last months of the Buchanan administration; and by 1861 was an outspoken and ardent Unionist. His stand as a free-soil Democrat had led to his ouster from the party, and ever after Dix espoused the ideology of the Republican Party. His spirit and indomitable will surfaced when, early in 1861, he telegraphed a harried Treasury official in New Orleans, "If anyone attempts to haul down the American Flag, shoot him on the spot."[9] Now, as a major general of volunteers, Dix was faced with a myriad of problems, not the least of which was the overcrowded nature of his makeshift prison system. In July 1861 Dix telegraphed to the War Department the following communiqué:

> You will allow me to suggest that prisoners may be divided into two classes—those who are detained for public safety and those who are to be tried for high crimes and misdemeanors. It is a delicate question whether persons held for trial can be even temporarily removed from the jurisdiction of the court, but is it not different with those detained for public safety alone and who are to be relieved when safety will permit? Of this class I judge the police commissioners to be. The charge against them is a negative one, an error of judgment or culpable inefficiency in the performance of official duty to which correct intention and incapacity would probably be a sufficient plea. (While I confidently assure the Government that their arrest prevented riot and that their detention is yet necessary I do not think that a trial for any positive crime can result in their conviction.) It admits of serious question whether Colonel Thomas, whose crime is that of piracy of the worst form and which was committed in the waters of the United States, perhaps in Maryland and perhaps in Virginia, must be detained and tried in this criminal district alone.
>
> The same question arises in relation to the four prisoners arrested yesterday. They were armed and intended crime—piracy or treason—somewhere within the jurisdiction of the United States. Must they be held and tried in Baltimore alone? The condition of the public mind may make it necessary that a trial to be impartial and just to the prisoners and the Government shall be postponed for some months. Must they be held here during the delay? Would not Fort Delaware considering the necessity of the case be sufficiently

within the law of vicinage to justify their detention there? And if such temporary imprisonment should not be within the law as it now exists ought not the attention of Congress to be called to this most important subject during the present session?[10]

It was in General Dix's effort to relieve the overcrowding at Fort McHenry that he conceived of the idea to utilize Fort Delaware as a prison. Although it is impossible to tell who first alighted on the idea, General Dix makes first mention of the possibility in the official record on July 10, 1861. Dix's first concern was about Colonel Zarvona, his notorious and popular prisoner, then incarcerated at Fort McHenry. Given the tenuous nature of politics in Baltimore, it was conceivable that citizens might try to release Zarvona from Federal custody. Zarvona had to be transferred and soon. The problems of legal jurisdiction were clearly on the mind of the jurist turned general when he wrote to Maj. Gen. George B. McClellan, by now commanding general:

Fort McHenry, which has not sufficient space for the convenient accommodation of the number of men necessary to man its guns, is crowded with prisoners. Beside our own criminals awaiting trial or under sentence we have eleven State prisoners. To this number six more will be added tomorrow. I do not think this a suitable place for them if we had ample room. It is too near the seat of war which may possibly be extended to us. It is also too near a great town in which there are multitudes who sympathize with them who are constantly applying for interviews and who must be admitted with the hazard of becoming the media of improper communications, or who go away with the feeling that they have been harshly treated because they have been denied access to their friends.

It is very desirable that an end should be put to these dangers on the one hand and annoyances on the other. If as is supposed Fort Lafayette is crowded may they not be provided for at Fort Delaware? There are several prisoners here who are under indictment. The Government decided that they should not be sent away. I concur in the correctness of the reasoning, but is there any impropriety if their safety requires it in taking them temporarily beyond the jurisdiction of the court by which they must be tried to be remanded when the court is ready for their trial? I confess I

ambitious training schedule for his company, and he planned to do the training on Pea Patch Island. The grueling training calendar was set to begin the following day. With as much as eight hours set aside for drill each day, the Zouaves had very little time to do much else while serving at Fort Delaware.

By mid-August the demand to sightsee the island had reached fever pitch, presenting some very real problems for Captain Gibson. Since visitors had to be accompanied by a resident of the island to get inside the fort, it became common for tourists to offer workmen money to go with them into the fort. Often the amounts offered exceeded the worker's daily wage. No doubt a few enterprising residents set up informal businesses as tour guides. In August, however, the top attraction was the drill of Collis's Zouaves. Even the men of the newest unit on the island, Independent Battery G, Pennsylvania Heavy Artillery, which had arrived on August 22, 1861, clamored to see the Zouave pyramid and the intricate precision bayonet drill perfected by the Zouaves. A young lieutenant of the "heavies," Charles Steck, quite taken with Captain Collis and his training, took careful notes and hoped to apply what he had learned to the training of his own troops.

The sycophancy the public showered on the Zouaves was capitalized on when Captain Collis organized a fund-raising cruise aboard the steamer *Ariel*. Hosted by Lieutenant Biddle and a squad of Zouaves, 500 sightseers stepped aboard the steamship, sailing for Pea Patch Island and a day of gaiety. It was easy to forget that there was a war while all the attention was paid to the flashy company of men stationed on the island. But the lax, carnival atmosphere on Pea Patch soon came to an end, however, when sometime in mid-September an unknown party or parties of Southern sympathizers took an excursion to the island and disabled one of the newly positioned seacoast guns. The operation, known as "spiking," was the simple act of driving a railroad spike into the vent hole at the breech of the gun. This accomplished, the enlarged vent allowed the gun to depressurize quickly, and the energy of the explosive was vented into the air rather than pushing the projectile through the tube. The discovery of the sabotaged piece forced Captain Gibson to suspend all visits to the island by unauthorized personnel, much to the consternation of the tourist industry. This act did bring quiet to the island, and a serious attitude began to take hold. By fall the number of soldiers exceeded the civilian population. The garrison totaled almost 400 officers and men.

Just as the construction seemed to proceed at a snail's pace, so the arrival of garrison troops seemed to trickle rather than flood. On September 19 the men of Independent Battery A, Pennsylvania Artillery, arrived to take up their posts, and two days later Captain Collis's colorful Zouaves boarded transports for the journey to their new posting in the Shenandoah Valley with Maj. Gen. Nathaniel Banks. Collis had used his time well at Fort Delaware. His Zouaves de Afrique served with distinction in the deadly campaigns against the brilliant Confederate general Thomas J. "Stonewall" Jackson. In less than a year Collis returned to Philadelphia with orders to expand his company into a regiment, and the Zouaves de Afrique soon became the nucleus of the 114th Pennsylvania Infantry. Their heroic record encompassed all the campaigns of the Army of the Potomac, and Collis himself earned his nation's highest honor, the Medal of Honor, for his gallant leadership as the regiment's colonel during the battle of Fredericksburg. The exploits of the regiment became legend, and in time, they were awarded the ultimate distinction—selection as headquarters guard for the commander of the Army of the Potomac, Maj. Gen. George Gordon Meade.

The Zouaves' replacement, Independent Battery A, Pennsylvania Artillery, was not as colorful as its predecessor, but the men too were destined to leave their mark on Pea Patch Island and the national roll of honor. Officered by two flamboyant European expatriates, Capt. Franz von Schilling and Lt. Stanislaus Mlotkowski, the men of Independent Battery A had been organized in Philadelphia and had signed papers to serve for three years or the length of the war. Private Meinke, brother-in-law of Lieutenant Mlotkowski, had written only a few pages in his new diary when he arrived at Fort Delaware. His description of the hero's feast he and the boys received in Philadelphia and the subsequent train and boat ride to Pea Patch revealed his youthful enthusiasm—certainly feelings shared by all the boys of the battery—and his nervous excitement as he embarked on an unfamiliar journey. In 1861 Meinke and other young men were all eager to volunteer, to "see the elephant," to prove the courage of their convictions. Private Meinke did not know what future awaited him as he climbed onto the western wharf to take up residence inside Fort Delaware. He was concerned, however, with the present as he settled into the temporary barracks inside the parade ground. Captain Gibson had posted the orders of the day and ordered all the officers and men to attend classes on military theory. The curriculum was a full plate. The officers were to take instruction in light and heavy artillery (taught by Gibson himself); the noncommissioned officers received instruction in the duties of the cannoneers; and the enlisted men were to attend a course of study on rifle tactics. Captain Gibson was determined to have his command ready for any contingency. Their day began at sunrise and continued without respite until sunset. If a soldier was not engaged in drill, he was on police or guard duty, or was studying military theory. Captain Gibson placed a high priority on education, ordering into existence the post library, which eventually held more than 5,000 volumes.

By the fall of 1861 several state prisoners and a few prisoners of war had come and gone. Gibson seems to have developed an attitude of tolerance toward the prisoners in his charge. Although he did not personally give credence to their beliefs concerning their relationships with the United States, he was committed to their right to hold those beliefs. The prisoners in the early days at Fort Delaware were treated with respect, even kindness. In November Gibson sent a note of thanks to the Honorable Elihu Jefferson of New Castle, Delaware, for his thoughtful package of materials for the prisoners then held inside Fort Delaware. Gibson personally delivered the package to the prisoners.[13]

Meanwhile, Delaware remained bitterly divided over the national crisis. Many of the finest young men of Kent and Sussex counties had "gone South," coming back only to recruit in their neighborhoods. Despite the ratio of one slave for every ten freemen in Delaware, she remained a slave state and, as such, represented many of the Southern traditions. North of the C&D Canal, however, was a hotbed of Unionist sentiment. And in accordance with administration policy, General Dix ordered the search for and the arrest of secessionists in Delaware and Maryland. Those arrested, of course, wound up at Fort Delaware. In October Dix sent the following cable to Brig. Gen. Henry H. Lockwood, then in command at Cambridge, Maryland:

> All the disunion companies in Queen Anne's County should be disarmed. I much prefer that you should do the work with your Delaware troops. Arms and prisoners should be sent here. I am trying to get a steamer to put at your disposal. If I do not succeed I must send you our tug at Annapolis. We can spare her two or three days in a week.
>
> If you can get any legitimate authority, executive or military, in Delaware to direct the disbandment or disarming of companies in that State it should be done. In that case I think the arms had better be deposited at Fort Delaware. I have been urging the Government for two months to send a force into Accomac and Northampton Counties, Va., and break up the rebel camps there. General McClellan encouraged me to believe that it would be done and I trust it will not be delayed much longer.[14]

The army would be the agent of loyalty. Henceforth, the citizens of Delaware and Maryland came to realize that the U.S. Army was an instrument played by the Federal government to enforce the political agenda of the administration in power. Or, if one were loyal to the Union, the army was merely responding to a national calamity with a mandate to restore order and peace to this once peaceful nation. Regardless of one's politics, the result called for the incarceration of a great many people.

With 1861 in wane, a vast restyling of the national landscape was in store for all Americans, and Lincoln's agenda for 1862 would have direct and far-reaching effects on the community at Pea Patch Island. Lincoln had set his policies in motion even before the new year, policies that would land directly on the drawbridge of Fort Delaware. As another year passed, the Muhlen-bruchs, Captains Gibson and von Schilling, Lieutenants Mlotkowski and Steck, Private Meinke, and the hundreds of souls living in the shadow of Fort Delaware could only speculate about the future—the future whose recipitate could never have been imagined. In late December Dr. Webster, medical bags in hand and family in tow, shuffled up the gangway to the steamer scheduled to make the run to Delaware City. As the *Major Reybold* slipped into the shipping channel, Dr. Webster gazed at Pea Patch Island with her surrounding seawall, humble outbuildings, and massive fortification. For thirty years the majority of the people who lived, worked, and played on Pea Patch were, like Dr. Webster, civilians. Although Fort Delaware was a military post, the civilians had always outnumbered the soldiers. The community defined everything on the island; pride was taken in being a resident. They had overcome impossible odds, established a progressive labor environment, and built a monument to their craftsmanship. They were fiercely proud of what they had done, and now, with war being waged all around them, they had to turn Fort Delaware over to her rightful owners. Dr. Webster was the last civilian surgeon to work on the island. Now all the doctors would be military. As the red roof of the soldiers' barracks faded from view, Webster could only shake his head and pray.

*One of the more famous prisoners of war held at Fort Delaware was Gen. James J. Archer. Archer's defiant attitude was not well suited for prison life. His plans to overthrow the Federal troops stationed at the fort were soon revealed and Archer spent most of his time in solitary confinement.*

*Trinity Chapel was constructed on the eastern side of Pea Patch Island in the fall of 1863. The structure was large enough to house 800 worshippers. Because of the variety of faiths on the island, the chapel was non-denominational, rotating ministers, priests, and rabbis.*

*This image of Confederate prisoners of war at Fort Delaware is a woodblock engraving from a Gihon photograph. Seated in the center of the group is Rev. Isaac Handy flanked on the left by Gen. Robert Vance and on the right Gen. M. Jeff Thompson. Bailey Peyton Key, Francis Scott Key's grandson, is sitting on the floor directly in front of Reverend Handy. Col. Basil Duke is standing, second from the right.*

*Attired in their finest dress uniforms, the Federal officer corps at Fort Delaware poses for this photograph in 1862. From left: Capt. John Jay Young, Capt. Franz Von Schilling, Capt. Paul T. Jones, Maj. Henry S. Burton, Capt. J. S. Stevenson, Capt. Stanislaus Mlotkowski, and Capt. David Schooley.*

*Lt. Abraham Wolf sits in the center of this group of soldiers. Wolf came to Fort Delaware as a noncommissioned officer in 1862. He earned his promotion and became second-in-command of Ahl's Independent Battery, assisting Ahl as commissary general of prisoners.*

*This Gihon image depicts the main sutler shop on Pea Patch Island, about 250 yards away on the southeast corner of the island. While the majority of the soldiers pictured are Federal, a Confederate prisoner of war is kneeling with his dog in the left foreground. Captain Mlotkowski is seated on the far right with his dog.*

*The vituperative Rev. Isaac W. K. Handy as he appeared at Fort Delaware. This Gihon image was taken inside the quarters of the prisoners of state.*

*The only known image of the temporary barracks inside the fort. The temporary structure was erected in 1861 to provide housing for the artillerists assigned to the fort. The main barracks were completed in 1862. Captains Von Schilling and Mlotkowski flank the group.*

*A temporary lager stand located behind the guards' barracks just west of Fort Delaware. The barracks are visible, faintly, behind the canvas awning. There are at least two Confederates shown, standing behind the row of seated men. The ubiquitous Captain Mlotkowski is seated on the right.*

*The Fort Delaware Concert Band, under the direction of principal musician Sgt. T. M. Todd (far left). The band performed at the fort and in Philadelphia, Chester, and Wilmington.*

*Major John Sander's ringing pile driver at work. Fort Delaware stands on a pier held steady by almost 7,000 40-foot-long logs. The process of erecting the foundation for the fort took almost as long as the masonry construction.*

*The mess hall and kitchen on the wooden prison compound on the northwest side of the island. These Max Neugas drawings depict the hustle of life within the prison walls. The mess hall, officially Division 37, could only feed 800 men at a time. It took about six hours to complete one meal for all the prisoners.*

*The grandson of Francis Scott Key, Bailey Peyton Key, was one of the youngest Confederates confined to Pea Patch. He served as an orderly to General Thompson and General Vance. Key was fourteen years old in 1864.*

*Brig. Gen. Albin Francisco Schoepf.*

*The eastern side of Fort Delaware in 1864. All prisoners were processed inside Fort Delaware and assigned quarters outside of the fort. When the POWs arrived at the wharf, they would be assembled and marched across the bridge into the processing room.*

CIVIL WAR CANNON

*The interior of Fort Delaware, looking south. The large earthen bank in the center of the image was erected to facilitate the movement of guns and munitions to the second tier of the fort.*

*The number one lock of the C&D Canal, Delaware City. This is the last sight of civilian activity a POW saw before being transshipped to Pea Patch Island.*

*The cover of the album presented to Lieutenant Wolf by prisoner-of-war artist Max Neugas.*

*Major John Sanders, the Army Engineer who built Fort Delaware. Sanders served on Pea Patch Island from 1848 until his death in 1859. He never saw the completion of his masterwork.*

*Poster advertising a concert for the Fort Delaware Band.*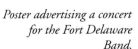

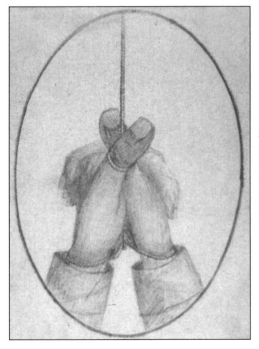

*A drawing done by a Federal soldier of the 6th Massachusetts regiment. A common punishment for infractions such as stealing rations was being hung up by the thumbs.*

*Max Neugas renderings of Fort Delaware in 1863 and 1864.*

*Gihon photo of Captain Ahl's office. Captain Ahl is leaning against the right center pillar. Lieutenant Wolf is seated in the center of the group. At his feet is the camp mascot, Bill the Cat.*

*Neugas' excellent rendering of a cannon in barbette mounted on the ramparts of Fort Delaware. This gun is facing east; in the left background are the homes of ranking Federal officials on Pea Patch Island.*

# Chapter 3

# 1862

> *"Prisoners escaped last night from Fort Delaware and were*
> *assisted by men in New Castle. Traitors from New Castle. . . .*
> *All may escape if more troops are not sent."*
>
> —A. H. Grimshaw

Captain Gibson and Engineer Muhlenbruch continued to wrestle with the problems of applying the finishing touches to Fort Delaware. It seemed that although they had made progress in 1861, the final constructions at Fort Delaware were never ending. The interior of the administration building was still incomplete in January 1862, and the post surgeon's office and the officers' quarters remained unfinished, and enlisted men were forced into a makeshift shanty in the center of the parade ground. Engineer Edward Muhlenbruch had assumed the role of supervising engineer following Captain Newton's departure in 1861, and the day-to-day operations were now under Muhlenbruch's control. He faced a laundry list of nagging problems. The drainage in the parade ground continued to be poor, the moat stones on the counterscarp had yet to be mounted, and the leaking cisterns were a particularly difficult challenge. Twenty-one cisterns, the primary source of fresh drinking water, were located underneath Fort Delaware, with a total capacity of 543,000 gallons. The front five had experienced problems with leaks ever since their construction. The cisterns were the primary source of fresh drinking water for the soldiers living inside Fort Delaware. The difficulty did not arise from the cisterns leaking out, but from the water in the moat leaking in. The moat served two purposes: to provide an obstacle for the enemy attempting to scale the walls of the fort and to serve as the sewage system. All of the hoppers inside Fort Delaware flushed onto a platform located beneath the fort and connected to the moat. At high tide of the Delaware River, a connecting sluice gate was opened, which allowed the water to flow into the moat; as the tide receded the water drained from the moat and carried the waste into the river. Unfortunately, the tidal action was not strong enough to remove all the waste, and it collected on the platform. Thus, the leakage into the front five cisterns was the backup of human waste, which then contaminated the drinking water. And as more men took up residence, the contamination increased exponentially. While it was clear that this problem presented a serious health risk to the garrison, it was not known why.

The science of medicine in the mid-nineteenth century was very different from today's. No medical professional of the time understood microbiology; in fact, the science did not exist. The existence of microscopic entities, or germs, was known, but their true nature had not yet been divined. At the time, a highly debated claim was circulating the European community that germs were indeed responsible for human disease. Most medical pundits dismissed the theory, however. Disease, they averred, was part of the atmosphere. The air that surrounds the earth was thought to have pockets of bad air and good air. Of course, the good air was considered salubrious and beneficial to one's overall health, while the bad air carried maladies of every sort. Airborne disease entered the body through the skin, and, once intruded, the individual would succumb. Plainly, people identified their environment as the source of health and developed theories pertaining to the relationship between the body and the environment. In fact, U.S. Army regulations included in the duties of the medical officer a daily meteorological observation, as weather and health were inseparable. By the 1860s, however, the world of medicine entered what came to be called the "sanitary age."

In vogue were four basic tenets: disease was airborne; disease was absorbed into the body through exposed skin; personal cleanliness ameliorated disease; and order in the environment was reflected through cleanliness, which in turn reduced disease. Medical practitioners knew that people became ill more frequently when surrounded by disorder and filth. They generally did not understand why this happened, but they knew that the effects of disease could be curtailed with the proper application of cleanliness in any given situation. As a result military regulations were specific regarding post, camp, and personal hygiene. Although regulations were not universally followed, they did indicate an understanding of the need for basic sanitation to promote the good health of the soldiers.

In the case of Fort Delaware and Pea Patch Island, authorities identified almost immediately the harmful nature of the environment. The drainage system designed by the engineers served two ends. Because the island was below sea level, the dike and the drains were necessary to prevent the daily flooding of the island. When working properly, the drainage system also removed the filth, as well as any standing water, from Pea Patch. Standing water was identified as a source of effluvial air that in turn generated disease. It was a matter of great importance to attend to the drainage. In addition, it was equally important to keep the inhabitants covered against disease. Clothing covered the skin, even in the warmest weather.

As the number of prisoners increased at Fort Delaware a schedule was set in place to ensure cleanliness on the part of those incarcerated. In Post Order No. 11, dated March 30, 1862, Captain Gibson set up regulations regarding the company police and their duties: "One non-commissioned officer and four private prisoners of war will be detailed from each barrack squad for Company Police. They will be held responsible not only for the cleanliness of the rooms but of the men and their proper deportment. Disturbances will be repressed with immediate punishment."[1] The barracks rooms were scheduled to be inspected twice a day, once before noon and once after midnight. Within two days, in Post Order No. 12, Gibson addressed the increased concern over the problems with the cisterns. "Water for *washing* and *cooking* will, for the time being, be drawn from the river, fronting 'front 5.' For *drinking* it will be drawn from the tanks.[2] The cisterns will not be used. The Officer of the Guard will see to the enforcement of this order."[3]

Gibson had good reason for concern: Fort Delaware was filling up fast. In addition to the soldiers of the regular service and Von Schilling's Independent Battery A, the political prisoners, and the prisoners of war, five companies of heavy artillery arrived in late January. Officially designated Segebarth's Battalion Marine Artillery (two companies) and Capt. Paul T. Jones's Independent Battery, Pennsylvania Marines, both were organized in Philadelphia to serve three years. Captain Jones's Independent Battery, Companies D, G, and H, arrived on the island January 9, 1862.

Segebarth appealed to the large immigrant population, while Jones's Marines seemed to be made up of the "old citizens" of Philadelphia. Both men also chose to spin their recruiting efforts by calling themselves "marine artillery"—a romantic, and possibly appealing, name for heavy artillery. Neither group had enough men to become full-fledged regiments, though, and eventually were amalgamated into large organizations: Jones's command became part of the 2nd Regiment Heavy Artillery, 112th Pennsylvania Volunteers; Segebarth's command became part of the 3rd Regiment Heavy Artillery, 152nd Pennsylvania Volunteers.

In March, with the addition of the "marine artillery" units, the entire garrison now numbered 340 officers and men, with another 258 civilians on Pea Patch Island itself. Although there remained quite a bit of construction yet to be done, the routine for the soldiers stationed at Fort Delaware was tedious at best. The number of prisoners, both state and military, was low, and guarding them was uneventful. The volunteers had, as their military mentors, the soldiers of the regular battery. The regulars were career-army enlisted men; they knew their business, and they knew how to pass the time at a lonely garrison outpost. Not only did the regulars offer formal instruction in tactics and gun-nery, but they also offered informal instructions in tried-and-true army tech-niques to pass the time. "Some men like to get killed here since pay day. They all got drunk on porter and whiskey and one man got cut with a knife but nobody knows. . . .They are playing cards all day and all night until all their money is gone, some of them poorer than before they got paid," wrote volun-teer George M. Green, a member of Capt. Paul T. Jones's Independent Battery of Pennsylvania Marines, in a January 28 letter to his sister.[4] Private Green had been in the service less than two weeks when he wrote home: "Some of the reg-ulars got put in the dungeons for getting drunk and there was an awful fuss about it. One of the sergeants got put in the guardhouse for striking a pri-vate."[5] As the reality of being a soldier dawned on the volunteers, for some it simply was not the lifestyle they thought it would be. Some eventually adjusted while others lost themselves in cards and the bottle; still others adjusted by changing their surroundings. The "French Leave," as the soldiers called it, was becoming a problem for Captain Gibson.

It now became a matter of routine to send squads to Philadelphia and Tren-ton, New Jersey, to collect deserters. More than 10 percent of the garrison was absent without permission by the end of March. Would-be deserters simply reported to the surgeon during sick call exhibiting nebulous symptoms. As yet there was no separate hospital facility, and consequently few sick beds were avail-able. Those men deemed by the surgeon to suffer from acute conditions were often sent home to recover.[6] Many did not return. Worse, Gibson's concern over the desertion rate was heightened when he learned that Fort Delaware was to become an official POW facility, and two of the three companies with Captain Jones were ordered to report to their new parent regiment, the 112th Pennsyl-vania, for duty in the defenses of Washington.

As April approached Gibson called a special session of the Post Council Administration (PCA) and issued several post orders to address the problems. The PCA, composed of several officers of the garrison appointed by the com-mander, was the official governing organ on Pea Patch Island. In many ways it was similar to a town council, with one special exception: The PCA had com-plete authority over all activities, both civilian and military, on Pea Patch. Hav-ing received communication from the War Department that more Confederate prisoners would be arriving, Gibson set up regulations regarding the treatment of POWs, as well as the activities of the POWs themselves. Quarters, subsis-tence, and daily activities were set to paper as Post Order No. 10. To combat the high desertion rate, Gibson increased the amount of drill for the troops sta-tioned at Fort Delaware. As Private Green reported to his sister, "We are drilling with the cannons twice a day and sometimes more but our living is even better than when we first came here, we get fresh beef, sometimes salt beef and pork."[7] Although the soldiers' barracks were still unfinished, the temporary barracks in the parade ground seemed to be a good substitute. But living space was rapidly becoming scarce. Newly promoted Captain Anderson, of Jones's Independent Battery, was taking two-thirds of the battery to Washington city at the end of March, which would provide some room for additional troops, but not much. Gibson also sought to floor more casemates to accommodate the expected increase in prisoners. The casemates would be sorely needed.

⁂

As manager of the Central Hotel in Delaware City, Elihu Jefferson was witness to the increased activity involved in creating a prison facility on Pea Patch Island. Jefferson and his family were Breckinridge Democrats in 1860, and, as such, were considerably distressed at the turn of events. As the buds of spring made their annual appearance Elihu and his nineteen-year-old daughter, Julia, realized that the war had begun to affect their lives. At the comfortable Jefferson home in New Castle, Delaware, Julia Jefferson could have easily distanced herself from the war. Elihu had been quite successful in the import and export business in the 1850s, and his brother, Samuel, had embarked on a successful political career and expected to be elected governor of Delaware come November. Even as the furor over the political issues involved in the war continued to be debated by Delawareans, the Jefferson family fortunes continued to rise. It simply was not necessary to be involved in disputes that, certainly, would be settled only on the battlefield. Elihu, however, was not the sort of man who waited for results. His business, indeed, his family life and views of the world, were shaped by a profound Christian ethic. Mr. Jefferson was determined to do something about the war.

From the veranda of the Central Hotel, at the terminus of the C&D Canal, Elihu saw firsthand the increasing numbers of ships transporting soldiers and prisoners to Fort Delaware. His Christian conscience compelled him to learn about the kind of treatment the prisoners were receiving on Pea Patch. He was appalled at the cavalier disrespect the Federals held for the basic rights of citizens. As early as November 1861 Elihu Jefferson sought to offer aid to those persons incarcerated as prisoners of war and prisoners of state. Initially, he prepared packages filled with blankets, writing materials, clothing, and the simple things necessary to sustain life. But Jefferson was not content to offer the occassional package for those less fortunate than himself. By March 1862 he and Julia, who had inherited and expanded upon her father's Christian zeal, were organizing the citizens of New Castle into aid societies. The Jefferson family was acutely aware, probably more so than most, that Delaware had yet to feel the true impact of the war.

In fact, there had been little military activity since the battle at Bull Run back in July 1861. The inactivity lulled many who were not directly involved in the prosecution of the war into a sense of complacency, but the seizure of the Tennessee forts Henry and Donelson in February and the increasing reports of Confederate movement in the Shenandoah Valley indicated that the war had only just begun. Elihu's brother, Samuel Jefferson, embroiled in the political race for governor, was privy to the plans the Federal government had for Delaware and was well aware of the ramifications of such policies. Surely he shared those fears with his brother and their families. As a candidate, Samuel Jefferson shared his opposition to the Lincoln administration with his constituents.

Many prominent Delawareans were opposed to Lincoln's policies in prosecuting the war, and although they did not openly advocate secession for Delaware, they did believe that Southern states had the legal option to secede. There were also those who openly identified with the South and sought to aid her. Citizens of Lower Delaware had crossed the border into Maryland and enlisted in regiments slated to joined the Confederate army. Governor Burton had, in 1861, called for the formation of the Delaware Home Guard in response to the firing on Fort Sumter. The Federals were increasingly concerned with the loyalty of the Home Guards, and their ability to hold Delaware steadfast to the Union. Meanwhile, political opposition to Lincoln's graduated emancipation bill was sounding very much like the Southern argument for separation. Delaware Democrats loudly echoed the Confederacy as they opposed the bill, buttressing their case with the contention that the Federal government, in offering funding for compensation, had violated the state's right to decide for itself when and if it would emancipate Delaware's slaves. In early 1862 the arithmetic of secession was adding up, and the Federal government was clearly concerned about the potential loss of Delaware as a loyal state.

As the legislative fight over Lincoln's bill heated up in the Delaware Assembly, Congressman George P. Fisher, the lone Republican from Delaware, reported to Brig. Gen. Henry Hall Lockwood, commanding the Eastern Shore with headquarters in Baltimore, that Delawareans disloyal to the Union were actively and openly engaged in support of the rebellion. Lockwood, a native Delawarean, had spent most of his adult life on the Eastern Shore and knew a thing or two about his home state. Armed with his personal knowledge, Fisher's letters, and a directive from General Dix, Lockwood brought martial law to Lower Delaware. The belief that the Home Guard was in fact an armed organization loyal to the South dictated the immediate need for its dissolution. He also had ample evidence that Southern sympathizers had established a reverse underground railroad for the shipment of men and material south. The route utilized the Delaware Railroad to Seaford, then the Nanticoke River to the Chesapeake Bay, and from there to Virginia's eastern shore. General Lockwood's invasion of the area was designed to sever the link to Virginia and break up the cabal of sympathizers in Delaware. Lockwood accomplished his task simply by arresting all the suspected leaders. Unfortunately for General Lockwood, one of the fish ensnared in his net was related to Sen. James Bayard.

Senator Bayard was, by all accounts, the single most powerful man in Delaware, and General Lockwood had arrested his son, Thomas F. Bayard. Lockwood had responded to a communiqué from General Dix, dated October 9, 1861, in which Dix suggested that Lockwood forcibly break up secessionists in Delaware. The old politician Dix had crafted his letter carefully with the addition of a single phrase, "*If you can get any legitimate authority, executive or military* [emphasis added]," which Lockwood apparently had failed to notice. Following the arrest of Thomas Bayard and others, General Lockwood, in blissful naïveté, forwarded his catch to Fort Delaware. The storm, however, quickly descended on Lockwood's head. A flurry of letters from the War Department, departmental headquarters, and even the White House followed. General Dix ordered Bayard's release, enclosing a further explanation of Lockwood's directives in rounding up potential traitors:

> I had yesterday a letter from the Secretary of War directing me to inquire into the circumstances attending the arrest of Mr. Bayard by Colonel Wallace, and expressing the belief that there was no just ground for such a measure. I have communicated with the colonel and instructed him to release Mr. Bayard on his parole of honor to report to me when required. The colonel advises me that he has undertaken to disarm a company of militia. This should not have been done without my order. I have never in this State ventured on so rigorous a measure without the approbation of the governor. In my letter to you of the 9th of October I said:
>
> If you can get any legitimate authority, executive or military, in Delaware to direct the disbandment or disarming of companies in that State it should be done. In that case I think the arms had better be deposited at Fort Delaware.
>
> I supposed you would understand that without such authority the measure should not be attempted unless upon specific directions from me. If any of the members of Mr. Bayard's company make demonstrations in favor of the Confederates they should be arrested and the facts reported to me. On the 27th ultimo I wrote you as follows:

If any person within the limits of your command shouts
for Jeff. Davis or Beauregard as charged in Mr. Fisher's letter,
or displays any secession emblem arrest him at once and
keep him in custody subject to my order. You will please
report to me the circumstances in each case. I will not permit where I have the power any demonstration in favor of a
political or military organization which is making war on the
United States.

I wish this course to be pursued in regard to every man
thus offending against the Government and people of the
United States no matter what his private or official position
may be. But in a State which has given no evidence of a
want of loyalty no step should be taken to break up any military organization but on full consideration and after consultation with the State authorities. Individual members of such
organizations may for open acts of disloyalty be summarily
dealt with as above directed.[8]

Lockwood's zeal in routing out the traitors had exceeded his caution. There-
after General Lockwood confined his zealotry to the arrest of those citizens
who openly shouted for Jeff Davis and the like. Despite Lockwood's misstep in
the Bayard affair, his sweep of the Eastern Shore effectively crushed any open
expression of disloyalty in Lower Delaware and brought many new residents to
the confines of Fort Delaware. By March 1862 the principal prisoner inhabi-
ting the casemates of the fort was a prisoner of state.

The precedent established in early 1862 had a twofold impact on the
future use of the military facility on Pea Patch. Lockwood's sweep of the Eastern Shore, however incautious it may have been, held a subtle lesson for anyone willing to listen and learn. Armed force had affected a political mission,
and nothing of any consequence had happened. To be sure, some of Senator
Bayard's feathers were ruffled, but Delaware remained in the Union. In fact,
the Home Guard had been turned into fighting regiments for the Northern
war effort. Four days following General Dix's release of Thomas Bayard, Maj.
Henry Bethel Judd on recruiting service in Delaware, submitted the following
report to the adjutant general:

Besides the troops at Fort Delaware and a detachment of
Maryland Home Guards which return to Maryland tomor-
row, there are between 600 and 700 men of the Third
Delaware Regiment at Cantonment Fisher, near Camden.

Thinking this might not reach Washington until you had retired from your office for the night, I addressed the message to the Secretary of War. There is but little left for detail. Colonel Wallace, with three companies of the Maryland Home Guards—by what authority I have not been able to learn—after visiting the principal towns of this State for the purpose, as I was informed, of collecting certain arms issued by the Governor to companies of volunteers called Home Guards, will return to his station at Salisbury, Md., tomorrow. His command has occupied the vacant rooms of the postoffice building in this city for the past four days.

The Third Regiment, or as it is really the fourth regiment of Delaware Volunteers, is nearly completed at the camp of rendezvous and instruction which I have established near Camden, three miles south of Dover. I have mustered in the lieutenant colonel, and about 150 men are wanting to fill up the regiment, so that the colonel may also be mustered in. I have supplied the men with clothing, subsistence, and everything necessary for their health and comfort. I have on hand in store here a full supply of tents and camp equipage, and am only awaiting the signature of the lieutenant colonel, who commands the regiment, to forward a requisition for arms, &c. The men are a quiet, orderly set, most of them from the country, and the success in recruiting, as well as the care taken of them, had nearly extinguished any unfavorable sentiments which might have lingered in a State whose loyalty has been manifested by offering so large a portion of her citizens for the service of the country. I know of no military organizations of any description in the State of Delaware, either mustered or ready to be mustered into service, other than what I have reported.[9]

The year 1862 was an election year. Regardless of the means, the Federal government now had evidence in hand that proved there existed in Delaware a strong insurrectionist sentiment. Several key seats were up for grabs, the governor's chair was available, and Delaware's lone seat in the House of Representatives was hotly contested. Congressman Fisher, if not Mr. Lincoln himself, had learned the lesson taught by General Lockwood. Fisher then alerted the Federal government of a laundry list of plots and schemes alleged to individuals alone, or in combination, set to disrupt the legitimate electoral process.

Fisher asked for two simple favors— keep Delaware troops in Delaware until after the election (in the event of a general uprising, they would come in handy) and send Federal troops to Delaware to supervise the polls on Election Day. Armed with Lockwood's evidence, President Lincoln acted without hesitation.

Congressman Fisher had created a new party, essentially to soften the negativity of the "Black Republican" image and to create a coalition of Union men regardless of their party affiliation. The Union Party ran former Democrat William Cannon, a prosperous Sussex County merchant-farmer. His opponent was New Castle's Samuel Jefferson, Elihu's brother. Fisher himself sought reelection to his seat in Congress. He was opposed by former governor William Temple. The Democrats, outraged over the administration's heavy-handedness, hammered hard on any Delaware politician associated with it. In the end William Cannon was elected governor, but George Fisher lost to William Temple by a mere thirty-seven votes, and the Union Party failed to carry the Assembly. Although the results were half a loaf for Lincoln and the Republican Party, they still deemed the effort successful, and in the future, with a little more effort and planning, the same tactics might prove more successful. Fort Delaware served throughout the election year as an excellent holding area for potential traitors masquerading as political opponents. Private Green wrote to his sister that it was a common matter to receive citizen prisoners: "Some 25 come here last night. They are citizens, secesh you know, the worst kind."[10] By the fall of 1862 Fort Delaware held 129 citizens suspected of disloyal activities.

With the wholesale round up of political prisoners in Maryland and Delaware, Fort Delaware was proving to be an effective keep. Captain Gibson was able to maintain order, and no one escaped. More important, however, was the isolation of the post. Prisoners of state were almost completely incommunicado. Whatever political ramifications might occur, it was exceedingly difficult for a rabble-rousing, anti-Lincoln man to maintain a power base when cut off from the world. And as the war dragged on, it seemed less likely that the navy of any nation, much less the Confederacy, would challenge the power of Fort Delaware. She was too large and too expensive to be underutilized.

On March 9, 1862, Maj. Gen. George B. McClellan notified Fort Delaware: "The rebel iron-clad steamer *Merrimac* has destroyed two of our frigates near Fort Monroe and finally retired last night to Craney Island. She may succeed in passing the batteries and go to sea. It is necessary that you at once place your post in the best possible condition for defense and do your best to stop her should she endeavor to run by. Anything that can be effected in the way of temporary batteries should be done at once.[11] The following day the *Merrimac*, renamed the *Virginia* by the Confederates, was checked by a new

Federal ironclad, the USS *Monitor*, and retired to safe haven on the Elizabeth river in Virginia. The Confederacy had mounted several efforts to become an effective sea power, but the vigorous efforts did not bear fruit. Following this latest reversal it was now clear to the War and Navy Departments in Washington that the South would never pose a serious threat to the Northern seacoast, including Fort Delaware. It was no quantum leap, then, to the realization that Pea Patch Island could do more than warehouse a few prisoners of state.

Captain Gibson had a find in the person of Lt. Gilbert S. Clark, Segebarth's Marine Artillery. Two hundred forty-eight Confederate prisoners of war, captured at the battle of Kernstown, were scheduled to arrive at Fort Delaware on April 1, 1862, and Captain Gibson needed all the help he could get. Trained as an artillerist, Gibson did not welcome duty as a jailor. Since February 1861 Captain Gibson had expended every effort to ready his command for war, and now he found himself preparing to make Fort Delaware a prison. The addition of 248 hungry mouths would almost double the workload of the quartermaster and subsistence officer. When Lieutenant Clark arrived as the quartermaster for Major Segebarth's Battalion, Gibson was duly impressed with his efficiency and appointed Clark as quartermaster and subsistence officer for the entire garrison.

The Quartermaster Department of the U.S. Army was responsible for "the quarters and transportation of the army; storage and transportation for all army supplies, army clothing; camp and garrison equipage; cavalry and artillery horses; fuel; forage; straw; material for bedding; and stationery."[12] In other words, Clark was in charge of everything that was not nailed down. All the materials the garrison needed to sustain life were under the direction of Clark, and now he had to increase his orders and expenditures. The complicated business of running an American army in the mid-nineteenth century was trying, even for the most experienced officer. The Quartermaster Department alone had fifty-three official forms to handle every contingency imaginable, from the monthly accounts summary statement, form number one to form number fifty-three, to the descriptive lists of persons and articles employed and hired in the quartermaster's department. All forms had to be filled out in triplicate, bound in red tape, and sent to the appropriate officer or department. The forms also had to be transcribed to permanent report books. All this was accomplished in an age without computers, copy machines, or even carbon paper.

But Clark was also the officer in charge of subsistence supplies (the rations) and of commissary property (the implements needed to prepare and preserve the rations). In Post Order No. 11 Gibson prescribed the daily ration per prisoner thus:

> 1 lb. fresh beef
> 1 lb. salt beef
> 18 oz. flour
> 10 oz. coffee
> 12 oz. sugar

Each prison room received three 12-inch candles per day. Each prisoner would consume 16 pounds of beef, 8 pounds of flour, 4 1/2 pounds of coffee, and 5 1/4 pounds of sugar per week. With the addition of 248 prisoners Clark could count on a minimum consumption of 3,968 pounds of beef; 1,984 pounds of flour; 1,116 pounds of coffee; 1,302 pounds of sugar per week. The soldiers of the garrison received a similar ration, with the notable addition of rice or beans, whiskey, and vinegar. Ration returns had to be filled out and filed with issuance of each ration. Clark had to purchase, transport, and store all the rations for everyone on Pea Patch Island, including civilian contractors. He was also charged with maintaining a stockpile of supplies, in the event of a protracted siege, however unlikely that may be. Private soldiers were then selected from each company to serve as cooks for the garrison, as well as the prisoners.

A separate orderly was selected from the ranks to serve the prisoners' commissioned officers, one private for each room. The orderlies were to fetch water, maintain order, and keep the place neat and tidy. The incongruity of this scene, Federal soldiers assigned to clean up after Confederate officers, defies description. But the society of nineteenth-century America was in a period of transition, as the mores and practices of colonial America were still in effect. While the deferential attitudes of colonial America were gone, many of the customs from that era had been retained in one form or another. The ordered social structure for the average soldier serving in either army was reflected in the civilian structure from whence he came. Generally the men in the ranks elected their officers, and the officers' responsibilities were taken seriously. But the process of election does not tell the whole story. The world was divided into two types of people—leaders and followers. Men were naturally either one or the other, and one was expected to show deference to superiors. Part of that deferential behavior was the election of those considered to be the natural leaders. In that light, the concept of officer prisoners having Federal enlisted men as waiters was taken as a matter of course.

The war had not as yet become a no-holds-barred affair. The consideration of honor and the concept of a gentlemen's fight were still very much in evidence in 1862. Although a prisoner-exchange cartel had yet to be worked out, the idea remained that these prisoners of war were men of honor being held until the contending parties agreed on a reasonable method of exchange. Both governments were, in fact, pursuing just that course. Therefore Captain

Gibson held no animosity toward his charges. They were considered to be fellow soldiers and were treated as such, with some exceptions. Gibson allowed no communication between Confederates and Federals at Fort Delaware unless it was authorized or in the course of performing one's duty, due to a fear that Confederate officers, as a result of their natural "superiority," would exert undue influence on Federal enlisted men. Considerable attention was paid to keeping these two groups separated. Gibson also realized that Confederate officers had to be separated from their own enlisted men. If Confederate officers could exert undue influence on the Federal enlisted men, then they certainly held sway over men who had volunteered to follow them. The possibilities of unrest, organized disobedience, and escape loomed large.

With the arrival of the Kernstown prisoners, Virginians mostly, Gibson faced a crisis in living space. The temporary barracks housed the Federal personnel, and using the casemates took space away from the guns. The soldiers' barracks were still under construction, but the roof was on and the guardrooms over the sally port were ready for occupation. The Federals stayed put, the Confederate officers were placed in the floored casemates, and the Confederate enlisted men occupied the guardrooms in the soldiers' barracks. The prisoners filled up the place. Quartermaster Clark even had trouble finding bunks for the prisoners; they would have to sleep on the wooden floor in the guardrooms. In a matter of days, however, wooden three-tiered bunks were constructed in sufficient quantity to accommodate all the prisoners as well as the soldiers of the garrison.

This prison business was a new wrinkle for Captain Gibson. Although Army regulations were specific regarding the treatment of military prisoners—deserters, felons, and the like—there were only three regulations regarding prisoners of war.[13] Essentially those in charge were creating the POW system on the fly, as events dictated. Without any guidelines to follow, even mundane matters, such as mail for the prisoners, were decided at the highest level.

> Headquarters, Baltimore, April 2, 1862.
> Capt. A. A. Gibson, Commanding Fort Delaware.
>
> Sir: I am directed by Major-General Dix to instruct you that the prisoners of war now under your charge may receive letters and clothing and gifts of a proper character and to be previously examined by you, but that no persons be allowed to visit them without a pass from these headquarters. The prisoners may also send letters to persons not in the States in insurrection against the United States to be examined by

you, but they should be returned to the writers thereof or
destroyed if they contain any treasonable matter or improper
reflections Upon the United States Government. Apply the
same rule to all letters sent to the prisoners.

I am, very respectfully, your obedient servant,
Wm. H. Ludlow,
Major and Aide de Camp

The influx of the Kernstown group turned everything topsy-turvy at Fort
Delaware. Engineer Muhlenbruch turned most of his attention to the buildings inside the fort, temporarily abandoning the work on the moat stones for
the counterscarp wall. The hospital remained inadequate; only two rooms in
the administration building (also unfinished) served as the surgery. The hospital could provide for eighteen patients at most. Wounded or sick POWs arriving at Fort Delaware had no choice but to stay in their bunks with the healthy
prisoners. Among those captured at Kernstown was twenty-one-year-old Lewis
Holloway, captain of Company C, 27th Virginia Volunteer Infantry. He was
assigned to the walled casemates along with his fellow officers. The Kernstown
battle, Stonewall Jackson's only defeat, was fought in a driving rain on Sunday,
March 23, 1862. Captain Holloway must have contracted a cold from his
exposure and the rigors of the campaign. When he arrived at the fort he was
already ill. His cold turned to pneumonia, and despite his youth, strong constitution, and what medical care doctors at Fort Delaware could provide, the
pneumonia overcame Holloway and he died on April 9, 1862. Holloway's was
the first prisoner death on Pea Patch Island.

Holloway's death underscored the unfinished nature of Fort Delaware.
With the Kernstown prisoners on his hands, Gibson realized that the living
areas inside Fort Delaware were entirely inadequate. Engineer Muhlenbruch
was now devoting all his crew's efforts to the completion of the quarters. His
stonecutters prepared the scarp wall for pipe fittings, and set stone in the dock
in anticipation of more traffic coming to the island. The brickmason was
building the subdivision walls for the quarters and the barracks and finishing
the repairs on the gutters. Muhlenbruch's carpenters were employed in finishing the lining of the powder magazines and laying the floors in the parlors of
the officers' quarters, as well as the third floor of the soldiers' barracks. As the
woodwork was placed the painters immediately began painting it. But only
two weeks after the Kernstown Confederates arrived, Captain Gibson received
another communiqué from Dix asking Gibson "how many more can [you]
accommodate." Gibson's reply was short and to the point: There was no more
room at Fort Delaware for anybody.

Secretary of War Stanton, upon receiving Dix's message from Gibson, conferred with William Hoffman, commissary general of prisons, to determine what could be done about Fort Delaware. Hoffman assured Stanton that there was room enough on Pea Patch Island for more prisoners. Hoffman then cabled Montgomery Meigs, quartermaster general of the army, to authorize the erection of additional barracks for more prisoners of war. Hoffman also assured Stanton that he would personally make a trip to Pea Patch and inspect the facility in June. That done, Meigs followed through with the following dispatch to his deputy quartermaster in Philadelphia: "Prepare shanties to shelter 2,000 prisoners of war at Fort Delaware on the island outside the fort but under its guns."[14]

Col. George Henry Crosman, West Point Class of 1823, had served his entire career in the Quartermaster Corps and knew a thing or two about efficiency. Upon receiving the order to erect shanties on Pea Patch, Crosman dispatched John McArthur, a civilian contract architect, to Fort Delaware to design the plans for the barracks. Once McArthur's plans were approved it would be a matter of weeks to erect the barracks. Crosman, McArthur, and Muhlenbruch soon perfected an excellent team approach and eventually would work together on all of the buildings erected on Pea Patch Island during the war. In the meantime, the barracks planned by McArthur were, essentially, long alleyways with three-tiered bunks running the length of the building. The ventilation was supplied by one row of windows, at about the height of the second bunk, running on both sides of the barracks. The barracks were wooden, yellow-washed, with potbellied stoves to provide warmth in the winter. McArthur also suggested that a privy house be erected over the Delaware River. In addition, because of the absence of wells on Pea Patch Island, McArthur designed a series of gutters connected to downspouts that emptied into large wooden troughs located strategically about the barracks. The troughs were intended to supply the prisoners with fresh drinking water. By the end of May 1862 the barracks were ready for occupation by prisoners of war.

Throughout the spring Captain Gibson was busy not only with the expansion of his post as a POW facility and the tactical instruction of his garrison, but he had to attend to the needs of his growing community, requests for permission to visit Pea Patch Island, and the increasing number of deserters. Fort Delaware now received its first batch of Federal prisoners. These men, a handful in comparison to the POWs, were Federal soldiers found guilty of various crimes—from falling asleep on duty to rape—but the most common among them were the deserters. In April and May four enlisted men deserted their post, two from Von Schilling's battery and two from Jones's battery. Soldiers had to be dispatched to Philadelphia and Trenton, respectively, to arrest the men and return them to Pea Patch Island. At the beginning of June four Federal prisoners managed to escape and make their way to Philadelphia. Lieutenant Mlotkowski and a squad of soldiers from his battery were dispatched to collect these men, as well.

Desertion was a capital crime, but it was rare for the extreme sentence to be handed down and equally rare for that sentence to be carried through. Men apprehended for desertion were court-martialed, and on Pea Patch the court was in almost constant session. Captain Gibson had at his disposal an array of punishments to mete out. A natural consequence of the unfinished armament at Fort Delaware was a diminished need for gunpowder; so Gibson set aside two powder magazines for use as solitary cells. It was not long before the soldiers began to call them dungeons. Private Green reported that the prisoners "get so sassy some times that we put them in the dungeons and feed them on bread and water until they get tame."[15]

But solitary confinement was not the only punishment available for those found guilty of infractions. Physical punishment was part and parcel of discipline in the mid-nineteenth-century American military. Men found guilty of desertion commonly had the letter "D" branded on their person. A miscreant could be "bucked and gagged," which involved the use of a long pole placed in the crook of the elbow, with the prisoner's hands tied in front of him, and a stick or a bayonet, secured by a leather thong, in the mouth. At Fort Delaware, those who were bucked and gagged were then hoisted by rope to the ceiling of the sally port, where they were suspended for the duration of the punishment. Mlotkowski often sentenced men convicted of drunkenness to wear a red flannel letter "D" on the breast of their uniform coat. Thieves had their heads shaved and were forced to wear a barrel or a placard proclaiming them thieves, then forced to march inside the parade ground for a prescribed length of time.

To further complicate matters for the post commandant, no agreement was yet in place for prisoner exchange. The official policy of the Federal government maintained that the Confederacy did not exist, and thus it was impossible to arrange a cartel with a nonexistent government. Lincoln knew that any agreement would give tacit recognition to the Confederacy as a legitimate national entity. This was a terrific obstacle in creating a permanent policy concerning prisoner exchanges. In the meantime, agents from both the North and South acted on gentlemen's agreements, allowing for the free exchange of POWs. Since there was no official policy, those who were exchanged, on a man-for-man basis, were often chosen by lots, political clout, or amiability. Naturally, the great majority of the prisoners simply stayed where they were placed.[16] Gibson, as post commandant, had to attend to all the details concerning orders releasing and exchanging POWs.

In addition, several prisoners opted to take the Federal oath of allegiance and then were freed.[17]

By the end of May the war in the east was heating up. Maj. Gen. George B. McClellan had taken the Army of the Potomac to the Virginia Peninsula between the York and James Rivers and begun a series of overland marches to assault Richmond. On May 31, 1862, Confederate general Joseph E. Johnston launched a counterattack. The resulting two-day battle, known as Fair Oaks, produced little in the way of tactical or strategic outcome, but its impact was felt at Fort Delaware within a week. "We have had over 300 more prisoners arrive and we expect more each day," wrote Private Green in a June 12 letter to his sister.[18] The new prisoners were separated by rank, with the enlisted men taking up quarters in McArthur's new barracks and the officers confined to the second floor of the soldiers' barracks inside the fort. One of Fort Delaware's newest prisoners was Lt. John Barroll Washington, the great-grandnephew of George Washington. Washington would have been an 1861 graduate of West Point if the war had not occurred. With the seccession of his native state, Washington resigned from the Academy within weeks of his graduation. He was now an aide to General Johnston, and he had been carrying dispatches from Johnston to Brig. Gen. James Johnston Pettigrew when he was captured, along with Pettigrew. Pettigrew had been wounded in the right arm and, accompanied by Washington, went to Baltimore for treatment. The two were housed in a hotel in Baltimore, but they soon were sent to Fort Delaware after citizens protested their accommodations. Arriving on Pea Patch on June 19, 1862, Pettigrew became the first general officer held at Fort Delaware, and Washington served as his aide-de-camp while the two were incarcerated. They shared a room on the second floor of the solders' barracks just over the sally port.[19]

By the end of June there were 1,260 prisoners of war at Fort Delaware, many of whom were sick or in a broken-down condition. In July, following the Seven Days battles, Fort Delaware received an additional 2,174 prisoners. By the end of the month twenty prisoners had died. The hospital had been expanded and plans were in the works to create a prison city on the north end of the island. The city was to have barracks large enough to hold 10,000 POWs and an adjoining 600-bed hospital. Colonel Hoffman had visited Pea Patch in June and he felt confident that there was enough area to create a vast POW camp. His recommendations were forwarded through the War Department, finally arriving on Montgomery Meigs's desk in late August.

But Captain Gibson's problems began to multiply with the heat of the summer. The garrison could effectively field 372 soldiers to accomplish the duties of the artillery batteries as well as guard the 3,000 prisoners. On June 15, though, Hoffman reported to Dix:

There are four incomplete companies constituting the
guard. These should be filled up to the maximum limit
immediately and a fifth company should be added, which
would make an ample guard for 5,000 prisoners. Capt. Paul
T. Jones' Independent Battery and two batteries of marine
and fortifications artillery under Major Segebarth, well
trained companies, might well be relieved to take the field
and their places supplied by three companies of infantry.
Those companies require eighty-six recruits. One company
of artillery, Captain Mlotkowski, would remain to occupy
the post.

Capt. A. A. Gibson, of the Second Artillery, is commanding and that his rank may be according to his command I very respectfully suggest that he be appointed and
mustered into service as the major or lieutenant-colonel of
the four companies of infantry, which will form the guard.[20]

Colonel Hoffman's proposal became an official request to the Commonwealth
of Pennsylvania. Captain Gibson was an artillerist, however. He took his job
seriously and was imbued with a spirit of patriotism "to the hub" as he would
say. He was not fond of being a warden in a makeshift prison, and he spent
considerable time angling for that coveted combat assignment.[21] His duty had
been to train the troops and maintain order within the prison population; he
had done that fairly well. He oversaw the final phases of construction, he set
up camps of instruction, his troops behaved themselves (for the most part)
when on leave, and the prisoners were well cared for. All of these duties were
within his sworn duty as an officer.

Gibson and Muhlenbruch expended every effort to improve life on Pea
Patch. The hard economics of warfare were being felt at Pea Patch, and the
urgency for foodstuffs brought the usual cadre of unscrupulous merchants.
Twice in the same number of weeks the beef was reported to be of inferior
quality. Before long, Gibson set up a permanent inspection team to check the
rations as they arrived. When the heat of the summer increased the chances of
drought on the island, Gibson arranged to rent barges to transship fresh drinking water from the nearby Brandywine River.

As the population increased, Gibson decided that it would be more cost
effective to make the bread on the island rather than buy it from an independent supplier. On July 3, 1862, Gibson sent a request to Colonel Hoffman:
"The necessity for clothing begins to be pressing: therefore I would suggest that
the following be furnished for future distribution: 1,000 blouses (or any substitute), 500 blankets, 1,000 shirts, 500 shoes (pairs), 300 caps (or any

substitute), 1,000 pants."[22] Kernstown prisoner Lt. Randolph Barton from Winchester, Virginia, reported Gibson had allowed his parents to visit him at Fort Delaware. While imprisoned at Fort Delaware, Barton received food and clothing and was measured for a new uniform by a tailor. "I soon received a splendid gray uniform, perhaps the only one made in Philadelphia." The only major complaint about his stay at Fort Delaware was that the water, which was carried from the Brandywine in barrels on barges, was warm and putrid. He left Fort Delaware on August 5, 1862.[23]

All in all, Gibson conducted a fairly lenient camp. To be sure, he disagreed with the prisoners politically, but he treated the prisoners as he would have wanted to be treated if the case were reversed. Unfortunately for the captain, the local citizenry interpreted Gibson's kind nature as sympathy for the Southern cause. On June 23, 1862, citizens living near Fort Delaware sent a petition to President Lincoln asking for Gibson's removal for associating with persons "known to him and to the entire community to be in active and earnest sympathy with the Southern rebels."[24] The petitioners added that, during a recent town election at Delaware City, laborers at the fort voted en masse—with one exception—for open Rebel sympathizers. The petition, signed by twenty-one residents, and seen by the president on July 1, 1862, asked for Gibson's removal and the appointment of "a friend of the government."[25] Although this action by a handful of citizens in Delaware City did not directly affect Captain Gibson's position at the fort, taken in combination with several other events, it affected how Gibson was viewed by his superiors.

Gen. Lorenzo Thomas, adjutant general of the army, was a native of New Castle, Delaware. During the first week of July Thomas had paid a visit to Fort Delaware. In the course of the visit, Thomas asked Gibson if he thought the addition of a gunboat patrol around the island would enhance the security needed to hold the POWs. Gibson replied that the gunboats were not needed and expressed confidence in his dispositions.

The night of July 15, 1862, was a moonless night, affording a perfect cover of darkness for any prisoner who might desire to escape. A summer storm had swept over the island for much of the day. With no major vegetation to break the driving rain, Pea Patch could be a miserable place during a storm and the combination of wind-swept rain and an unusual high tide led most of the residents of the island to shelter. Muhlenbruch had erected a water house over the Delaware River on the western side of Pea Patch, a stone's throw from the new prison barracks. Lumber and scraps from the construction were stockpiled nearby and offered a tempting opportunity. In fact, nineteen prisoners had been planning an escape for some time, systematically salvaging scraps from the lumber pile and building several rafts to make their way across the Delaware. Although they had not finished their second raft, concealed in a reed bank on the western shore, the conditions on July 15 offered one of the few opportunities they had to make good their plans. They decided to make the trip that night. Between watches, one by one, they absented themselves from the barracks and made for the reed break. All nineteen piled onto the raft and, using makeshift paddles of scrap lumber, silently began their trek to Delaware City and beyond. They knew it was a simple matter to contact Southerners once making shore on the Delaware side. Although General Lockwood had uncovered much of the Confederate Secret Service activities in Delaware, the reverse underground railroad had continued to operate with a terminus at Delaware City and Port Penn. Any man wishing to make his way to the Confederacy could easily find safe haven throughout southern Delaware, along the Eastern Shore, and eventually to Virginia.

With the help of Delaware City residents the nineteen made their escape. By roll call on the morning of July 16, they were already dozens of miles away from Pea Patch. The alarm was sounded; the entire guard mount was marshaled and sent out to search the island. Two squads of men were dispatched to Delaware City to locate the missing prisoners. It must have been with a deep sense of mortification that Captain Gibson telegraphed Lorenzo Thomas about the first POW escape from Pea Patch. The shock reverberated through the halls of the War Department. Thomas wired back a scathing admonishment:

> When at Fort Delaware I did not understand that you regarded additional troops as necessary to prevent the escape of prisoners or I would have taken measures to have sent them. To my question whether a guard-boat was not necessary you replied no; you had perfect control over the island. General Wool has been directed to send an additional force to Fort Delaware and a guard-boat will be sent from New York. You must allow no intercourse whatever with the prisoners and keep citizens from landing on the island except those in the employment of the Government,—must not have any intercourse with the prisoners. If boats came to the island and took the prisoners off your sentinels could not have done their duty.[26]

By the time the news of the escape had made its way through the department and back out to the field, July 17, 1862, news of the nineteen escapees was incorrectly reported as two hundred. Within two days a gunboat was delivered from New York to patrol the waters of the Delaware. The prisoners were never recaptured.

Two weeks after the escape Captain Gibson received the final blow. On July 30, 1862, William Millward, the U.S. Marshal in Philadelphia, wired Stanton: "I have just searched the house of a lady named Emley, who has four women at work making clothing for secesh prisoners. She does not deny it. Says all her sympathies are with them. There are other parties connected with her. I found two letters addressed to her from Captain Gibson, commander Fort Delaware, thanking her for her kindness. What shall I do with the parties? Strong feeling here against such parties. It operates against recruiting."[27] Stanton immediately launched an investigation. Although the War Department could uncover no wrongdoing on the part of A. A. Gibson, it was clear that his days at Fort Delaware were numbered. He had served his country at Fort Delaware since the beginning of the war. Gibson had hastened the armament of the fort, he had seen to the orderly transition from defensive fortification to prison, he had maintained order and discipline. Out of the thousands of prisoners under his charge, only nineteen escaped and twenty died. Captain Gibson had made only one mistake: He had been outwardly cordial to the enemy. Gibson was transferred to the 2nd Pennsylvania Heavy Artillery on August 5, 1862.

⚬⚬⚬

The government of the United States had no idea what to make of prisoner Richard Henry Thomas. General Dix described him as "crack brained" and considered him harmless. His concern over the prisoner known as Zarvona was more about his popularity among the secessionist element in Maryland— and what they might do—than about Zarvona's ability to do genuine harm to the government. In December 1861 Dix transferred his hapless prisoner to Fort Lafayette in New York Harbor, completely out of the reach of any friends who might attempt a rescue. Despite Dix's warning of Zarvona's renown, the authorities in New York did not consider him particularly dangerous; he was just another prisoner awaiting trial. He was officially classified as a prisoner of state, despite his colonel's commission in the Virginia State forces. Dix referred to him as a pirate and recommended that charges of piracy be filed against him in Federal court. But Zarvona was indicted in U.S. district court on charges of treason rather than piracy and ordered held in confinement until the trial date.

Zarvona maintained that he was acting under orders of the Confederate government and was therefore a prisoner of war. His health had been impaired since his detention, and he sent numerous inquiries to Secretary of State Seward to speed up the date of the trial or to transfer him to the rolls of prisoners of war. Zarvona's claims of ill health and poor conditions did little to sway Seward. By February 1862 Zarvona was still a prisoner of state.

Meanwhile, the Confederacy was exerting a great deal of energy to secure his release. Confederate secretary of war George Wythe Randolph and Virginia governor John Letcher made several official efforts to secure Zarvona's exchange.

In addition, Zarvona was receiving numerous letters and packages from loved ones in Maryland and Virginia. His mother and aunt had petitioned Secretary Seward for permission to visit. All were quite solicitous of Zarvona's physical health. But it became apparent to the Southern petitioners that the Federals were not willing to respond to their requests, and the Confederate government chose to take extraordinary action.

While the Confederacy was finalizing its plans to free Zarvona, Lorenzo Thomas received a disturbing communiqué from Edward Townsend, assistant adjutant general. Lt. Col. Martin Burke, the commanding officer at Fort Lafayette, had been systematically censoring the incoming and outgoing mail of all the political prisoners in his charge, including the voluminous correspondence of Colonel Zarvona. Burke had noticed a peculiar style to Zarvona's missives: unrelated letters of the alphabet interspersed in his writing, references to various newspaper articles, innocuous poetry, and references to individuals by letter rather than name. Of particular note was his correspondence to a Mrs. Mary Norris of Baltimore, Maryland. Burke caught similarities in her own odd writing style and realized that Zarvona had been communicating in cipher. Burke broke the code and passed along his findings to Townsend. Apparently Zarvona was planning an escape, with the aid of Mrs. Norris and probably his mother and aunt. Zarvona had requested from them on different occasions acid and files to be concealed in their jewelry. Adjutant General Thomas received this information on February 28, 1862, along with the evidence and Burke's thoughts on how the code worked. Zarvona was ordered to solitary confinement on March 1, 1862. Mrs. Norris was arrested in Baltimore on March 31.

Lorenzo Thomas had an inside man at Fort Lafayette who became friends with Zarvona and informed the government that Zarvona was "a very desperate man and very restless under his confinement, and designs escaping if he can." Thomas passed his findings along to the War Department and ordered permanent solitary confinement. Yet even then Zarvona would not be dissuaded. At 9:30 P.M. on the night of April 21, 1862, as a storm raged in New York harbor, Zarvona summoned the sergeant of the guard under Lt. Charles Wood, 9th U. S. Infantry. The sergeant saw Zarvona standing at the door to his cell and indicating his need to visit the water closet. This was a routine request, and, as the water closet was located on the seawall, the sergeant summoned one of the guards on duty to accompany Zarvona. As the pair pushed their way through the howling wind and rain, Zarvona extended the distance between himself and his guard. When he reached the water closet, Zarvona mounted the seawall and before the guard could respond, was gone. The guard sounded the alarm and attempted to locate Zarvona. Soon another guard spotted Zarvona swimming in the Hudson River, making his way to Long Island. The troop-laden barge launched to intercept the wily French Lady was almost swamped by the storm, but in the end, Zarvona's latest adventure was brought to a halt, and he found himself back in his dungeon, only now soaking wet. With this escapade Zarvona stood no chance of ever seeing the outside of his prison.

The Confederacy had not given up on Colonel Zarvona, despite his latest mishap. In order to get Zarvona back he had to be classified as a prisoner of war, which was proving to be a difficult challenge. Richard Thomas was a citizen of Maryland, a state that remained in the Union. This was a complex legal roadblock, but one that could be overcome—after all, Zarvona had a commission from the State of Virginia and orders directing him to hijack the *Mary Washington*. The existence of these papers alone should have been enough to qualify him as a prisoner of war. But beyond the legalistic battle for Zarvona was the larger issue of a prisoner exchange. Throughout the winter and spring agents had been negotiating an agreement for the equitable exchange of prisoners of war. For more than a year the contending governments had dealt with the exchange of prisoners on a case-by-case basis.

Finally, the governments of the Union and the Confederacy agreed to a cartel of prisoner exchange on July 22, 1862. It was a complicated affair. Federal major general John Dix and Confederate major general Daniel Harvey Hill had negotiated what came to be known as the Dix-Hill Cartel.[28] Under the terms of the agreement, enlisted men were to be exchanged one for one, as were officers of equal rank. The Dix-Hill Cartel created a complex scale of values: Each rank above private soldier was assigned a value in terms of the private soldier. For example, a major general was worth thirty privates, while a corporal was worth two. There also was the added factor of parole. In the beginning, prisoners of war could sign a "parole of honor," which entitled them to go home and await word when they had been exchanged. Parole, however, had two incarnations—the second parole was a signed statement by the prisoner that he would not take up arms until he was exchanged. Generally the paroled prisoner was assigned to depots such as Fort Delaware and there remained until official word was given that an exchange had been effected. The Dix-Hill Cartel also covered who was eligible for exchange, which basically assigned the status of prisoner of war to those doing the actual fighting. Guerrillas, pirates, bushwhackers, and political prisoners were not eligible for exchange.

The Dix-Hill Cartel called for the appointment of individuals to be designated agents of exchange. In the late summer of 1862, the Confederates appointed Mr. Robert Ould as the agent of exchange representing the South.

Mr. Ould was an experienced attorney who had been the solicitor for Washington City before the war. Initially the North appointed agents for different districts, causing yet another problem. With an individual agent of exchange for each district, any prisoner being transferred or exchanged and traveling through more than one district had to be processed at least twice before being paroled or exchanged. By November the Federal government had appointed Gen. Ethan Allen Hitchcock as the Union's agent for exchange.

Zarvona hoped that the Dix-Hill Cartel would be the catalyst for his exchange, but the Federals were unwilling to change his status. His deportment was different, mysterious, and secretive. Zarvona behaved as if he were a spy out of a dime novel. While Zarvona languished in solitary confinement, Confederate authorities redoubled their efforts to obtain his release. Governor Letcher of Virginia appealed directly to President Lincoln, and Robert Ould argued with Dix and Hitchcock that Zarvona was merely a colonel of infantry. All their pleas fell on deaf ears. By late 1862 the Confederates were desperate to free Zarvona. They threatened that if Zarvona remained in Federal hands after the new year, the Confederates were prepared to select seven Federal prisoners at Libby Prison in Richmond to serve as hostages.

General Dix interviewed Zarvona and determined that he was a harmless zealot who had become even more harmless from his captivity. Dix recommended that Zarvona be transferred to Fort Delaware, his status changed to prisoner of war, and his exchange be expedited. What the Federals did not know was the true nature of Zarvona and his importance to the Confederacy. Robert Ould held two positions in the Confederate government: He was the Confederate agent for prisoner exchange, and the head of the Confederate Secret Service. Zarvona's regiment, the Potomac Zouaves, had become the 47th Virginia and served the South as scouts and covert operators. Zarvona was indeed an important man to the South, not because of his effective espionage techniques, but because of the concern that his secrets might be revealed. Thus far, however, Zarvona's importance remained invisible. Within the next few months Zarvona would find himself confined at America's largest fortification, but as 1862 passed into history, Richard Henry Thomas was in his cell at Fort Lafayette.

The summer months on Pea Patch Island brought soaring temperatures and stifling humidity. Although the fortification offered some relief, the interior of the temporary quarters often peaked at 100 degrees in August. Inside the office of the post commander, Captain Gibson was finishing the last of the reports he was required to prepare for the new commanding officer. Maj. Henry S. Burton was scheduled to arrive the afternoon of August 5, 1862, to assume command of Fort Delaware. As Gibson arranged the records of the Post Council of Administration, placing the books and papers in neat piles, he likely thought back on his tenure at Pea Patch with mixed feelings. To be sure, he was a military man and there was a war brewing out there, a war he was determined not to miss. Captain Gibson had known for several weeks that he was to receive an appointment in the volunteer service as colonel of the 2nd Pennsylvania Artillery. For that he was glad, but Gibson felt that he was leaving the post under a cloud. The escape, the accusations, and his conduct had led some to question his commitment. Obviously the current course of behavior would not do; one was to pronounce one's zeal for the Union loudly and to anyone within earshot. Politics would be the mainstay of command in this highly politicized war. Gibson had sought to walk a line that had been erased, and he was unaware that it was gone. But he was a good artilleryman, so his services to the government would be played out on the battlefield. Gibson donned his dress uniform and stepped out into the bright summer sun to inspect the garrison for the last time.

Major Burton could feel the thickness of the air as his transport made for the western wharf on Pea Patch Island. Perspiration ran down his corpulent face and into his heavy blond beard. As the escort of honor came to attention on the dock, Burton mentally ran through his checklist of duties and satisfied himself that he was prepared for his new assignment. Henry Stanton Burton had graduated ninth in the West Point class of 1839 and had spent his entire adult life in the 3rd U.S. Artillery. His promotion to major in May 1861 entitled him to wear the double-breasted uniform of an officer of field grade. On August 5, 1862, the gleam of his dress uniform epaulets, with the gold oak-leaf cluster, flashed in the eyes of the guards as they brought themselves to present arms. Gingerly stepping onto the inclined gangway, Major Burton returned the salute and made straightaway for the ranking officer, Capt. A. A. Gibson. After a brief ceremony the two officers retired to headquarters to review the status of Fort Delaware.

It is likely that Gibson offered his replacement some refreshment as they got down to the work of transfer of the command. As per regulations, Burton was expected to enforce the standing orders of the post, and Captain Gibson made sure that Major Burton had copies of all the general, special, and post orders. As the career artillerists turned to the armament of the fort, Captain Gibson had to admit that Fort Delaware was not yet fully armed—only forty-eight guns were in place. The work had been delayed in order to make accommodations for all the prisoners of war. And the prisoners had become the true work of the Federal soldiers stationed on Pea Patch.

The month of July saw the prisoner population peak at 3,434. Once the Dix-Hill Cartel was signed and enforced, the evacuation of POWs was immediate, and on August 1 there remained only 355 prisoners. Captain Gibson hastened to point out to Major Burton, however, that Engineer Muhlenbruch was actively engaged in the construction of a larger POW complex on the north end of the island and in the final construction phase of the fort itself. Fort Delaware had also been designated a depot for recruits, adding a third assignment to the duties of the overtaxed garrison. Finally, Major Burton was briefed on the disposition of the 200-plus civilian employees still residing at the post. After the consultation, Gibson fondly shook Burton's hand and wished him luck. With that Gibson brought himself to attention and formally saluted Fort Delaware's newest commandant. The following day Gibson stepped aboard the packet steamer scheduled to sail to Philadelphia. Eventually, Colonel Gibson, after a brief sojourn in the defenses of Washington, took command of Fort Warren in Boston Harbor. Fort Warren would serve the United States as a POW camp, as well.

If Major Burton was distressed at the enormity of the job before him, he gave no outward indications. His first and overriding concern was the number of troops in garrison, outnumbered ten to one in July; and although there were very few prisoners left in August, it was certain more would arrive soon. Another Pennsylvania Heavy Artillery Battery was scheduled to arrive in mid-August, which was a great assurance to the new commander. The construction inside the fort was coming along well: Muhlenbruch had brought in plasterers to finish the interiors of all the barracks buildings, the sewer and parade ground drainage system was complete, the roofing and the gutters were completed, and the stonecutters were cutting the mantel pieces for dozens of fireplaces inside the three buildings. Only the third story of the soldiers' barracks remained to be finished. Muhlenbruch assured Burton that if work continued at this pace the interior buildings would be ready for occupation by the new year.

The Dix-Hill Cartel was relieving the strain that POWs caused for both governments. The exchange system seemed to be working smoothly, and prisoners left Fort Delaware at a record-setting pace. Officials from the contending governments had anticipated an agreement near the end of July and made plans to make the exchange as quickly as possible. Confederate congressman A. R. Boteler wrote to Secretary of War G. W. Randolph, on July 31, 1862:

> The cartel for a general exchange of prisoners having been agreed upon I hasten respectfully to urge to you the importance of having those of our men who were taken at the battle of Kernstown on the 23rd of March released as soon as possible. Apart from the fact that their treatment in Fort Delaware has already caused much sickness and some mortality amongst them, they were among the very best soldiers in our army and their addition to our ranks at this time will

be of more service than to have five times the same number
of recruits. Most of the prisoners referred to are constituents
of mine and I am of course naturally solicitous to procure
their speedy discharge.[29]

Congressman Boteler's wishes became reality: All of the Kernstown prisoners
were released by August 5, 1862.

In fact, by the time Major Burton assumed command, the majority of the
prisoners were political prisoners. On August 20, 1862, Burton issued Post
Order No. 77, allowing the political prisoners permission to walk the parapet
from 5:00 P.M. to retreat. Additionally, they were permitted to bathe in the
Delaware River after retreat on Tuesdays, Thursdays, and Saturdays. Prisoner
of state Robert Atkinson of Bath, Virginia, reported his activities in August:
"Bought box of apples for 5 cents, sold my watch for $30 CSA—swam in the
evening, played chess and politized with others." Atkinson was imprisoned for
refusing to take the oath of allegiance. Arrested as a spy, Atkinson was taken to
Baltimore and finally arrived at Fort Delaware on August 9, 1862. He had
arrived there after midnight and was kept in the first door to the left of the sally
port in a second-story room. "We slept on boards with no bedding," he
recorded. Atkinson took advantage of Burton's order on the day of its issue,
though, reporting, "Organized chorus and chess club. Walked on parapet."[30]

Events on the island had slowed to the sleepy routine that characterized
any peacetime army post. The cartel had done its intended job, and since the
armies were involved in maneuver rather than combat, few prisoners arrived to
take up temporary residence. Prisoner of state Atkinson wrote in his diary of
the mundane record of people with very little to do: "Made a set of chessmen
out of cigar box wood. Episcopal prays about 4 P.M. in casement. . . . Storm
raged all day—leaking into quarters. Applied for parole and was refused. . . .
August 22: Fishing in evening with Smythe. . . . Sept. 10: Watermelons from
Delaware City. Went to hospital for medicine. Supped with Jones. Feeling
ill."[31] Captain John J. Young's Independent Battery G, Pennsylvania Artillery,
spent much of its time drilling under the instruction of Lt. George W. Ahl.
Hamilton, who served as the company cook and was excused from drill, mir-
rored Atkinson when he wrote: "August 26: I took my first stroll around the
island and I find it a pretty place. . . . September 2: Nothing to note today save
the passing up river of the famous gunboat *New Ironsides*. She looks a very
monster. . . . September 10: A little fight on the parade ground, a Dutch corporal was knocked down a few times."[32]

Major Burton set about relaxing the harshness of the place through a
series of post orders. The sale of lager beer was regulated, to be sold at three
designated time slots: 8:00 to 9:30 A.M., noon to 1:30 P.M., and 4:30 to 6:00
P.M., with each enlisted man restricted to one glass of beer per time slot.

Believing that additional privileges would have a good effect on his command, Major Burton allowed both his garrison and the political prisoners more freedom. Unfortunately, the major's progressive policy backfired, and he was forced to chastise his soldiers in September:

> The Commanding Officer is extremely mortified to find that the few indulgences he has been able to grant to this command have been abused without limit by some of its members. These men bring shame upon all men. If unchecked will make Fort Delaware and its garrison in a short time an exponent of low drunkenness and unsoldierly conduct. The Commanding Officer calls upon the men of intelligence and right feeling in this command to check unmanly conduct of a few men. They can see the great necessity of having everything and every man here ready for an emergency at all times. The present state of affairs in our country indicate that this post may be called upon to act a very important part in the struggle against rebellion and anarchy now going on. Let the men of reflection among us think of this and use their influence to check this disgraceful conduct of a few.[33]

In an interesting approach, Burton called for the maintenance of discipline through force of the community, rather than through the traditional force of chain of command. There were still ways to deal with the recalcitrant among the garrison, however. Courts-martial were scheduled almost weekly. For example, Pvt. John Kevenny was convicted of stealing Captain Mlotkowski's pistol. Mlotkowski and a squad were onboard the steamer *Ericson* returning from Philadelphia, having gone there to apprehend a number of deserters. Kevenny was caught in the act of reaching through a porthole into Mlotkowski's cabin and taking his pistol. He was sentenced to one month of solitary confinement on bread and water. The judgment was reversed, however, when it was found to be an illegal sentence, and Kevenny received no punishment. In another case, Privates Martin Staublein and Peter Shrouer entered the mess hall and demanded the key to the store from cook Christopher Hey. When he failed to produce the key in a timely manner they beat him and took the key. They then stole a pound of salt pork and left. Evidently the officers of the court did not believe the entire story, as they found the men guilty of stealing the food but not of attacking the cook.

But idle time would soon be at a premium. "About 1200 Confederates arrived with 38 officers in steamer *Norwich*. Amusing scene on the wharf with

Major Marowiski,[34] officer of the day, marching to and fro gesturing about."[35] By the end of September the POW population had increased from 68 to 2,470. All of the prisoners coming to Fort Delaware had been captured during the Antietam campaign, and many of them had been marching and fighting since late June without benefit of resupply. As a result, many arrived at Pea Patch already ill.

As September closed, Burton was busy arranging the exchange of most of his new prisoners, and the system seemed to be working with some efficiency. Burton also offered parole to any prisoner—either state or war—if he took the oath of allegiance to the United States. Initially it was not clear to all the secessionists what the oath entailed, and many applied for parole in the hopes of an early release. Atkinson noted in his diary on September 28 that "101 confederates took the oath and will be released. Applied for a parole and told that I might be considered." But in a final letter home to his sister, Atkinson lamented that the oath would force him to essentially turn his back on the Confederacy, something he was unprepared to do: "I'm no fighting character, but must say I am proud of being a Southerner. I always prefer the south—my home—friends." Atkinson could not sign the oath and remained at Fort Delaware through the winter; he was released on parole in June 1863 after "taking the oath only on terms that would befit a southerner."[36] He died in a Baltimore hospital of consumption in early July 1863.

The exchange system was working at a remarkably fast pace. By the end of October, 2,298 prisoners were exchanged and another 176 were released. Only 84 prisoners remained incarcerated on November 1, 1862. Major Burton's administration thus far had been relatively uncomplicated, but he was about to make his first misstep in the service of his country.

Most of the prisoners of war had arrived legally paroled, simply awaiting the paperwork indicating that they had been exchanged. Once that was cleared the POWs were transferred to a forward post, where the physical exchange occurred. During this time a large number of politicial prisoners also were being released. Burton had dutifully processed all the prisoners of state and released only those he had been instructed to release. Many of these men were politically sensitive cases, and it was thought that they ought to be detained until after the elections in November. Among such prisoners was Judge R. B. Carmichael of the Eastern Shore of Maryland. Carmichael was a presiding judge for the District Court of Maryland and of the opinion that President Lincoln's policy of wholesale arrests in Maryland was illegal. He charged a grand jury to hand down indictments against a group of arresting officers in a case involving the arrest of men suspected of sedition. As a result, Judge Carmichael was considered a dangerous insurrectionist worthy of arrest himself. In late 1861 Carmichael was arrested in his courtroom following a brief fistfight between the judge and the arresting officers. Carmichael was incarcerated at Fort Lafayette and transferred to Fort Delaware on September 23, 1862. Evidently the intention for the transfer was the release of the judge. At least that was what Major Burton surmised when he received an order for his release in October from the War Department. A puzzling development arrived with the Carmichael release order, however: A highly placed Maryland citizen also sent a letter to Major Burton warning him that Judge Carmichael needed to be locked up until after the elections in November. Burton surely pondered the import of the contradictory communiqués, but, in the end, obeyed his superiors in the War Department. This was all fine until Stanton realized that the original order was a mistake and fired off a telegram to the naïve Burton: "You will retain Judge Carmichael in custody. The order for his discharge is countermanded."[37]

Unfortunately for Major Burton, Carmichael was gone. Although it would be a simple matter of time for Carmichael to be rearrested, the political fallout from his release reached all those concerned, not the least of which was Henry Burton. Yet another career officer had failed to recognize the political situation. Lt. Col. Delavan Perkins was on his way to Fort Delaware to relieve him almost as soon as the War Department discovered Burton's political naïveté.

⟐

B rig. Gen. Albin Schoepf, future commandant of Fort Delaware, could feel the sting of rebuke as he rode with his division. Although the incident had happened a little more than a month ago, Schoepf was unable to put the matter aside. By October 7, 1862, the challenge to his reputation as a soldier was as raw as the painful gash on his commander's leg. Maj. Gen. Don Carlos Buell, West Point class of 1841, had recently suffered a fall from his horse resulting in an agonizing laceration on his leg. The acute nature of his wound forced him to conduct the business of the Army of the Ohio from an ambulance, which was doubly difficult as Confederate general Braxton Bragg had, for the last six weeks, invaded Kentucky and was threatening the city of Cincinnati. Buell's assignment was to destroy Bragg and the Army of Tennessee, which was proving to be quite difficult. This time, though, General Buell was confident that he had finally run Bragg to the ground. Federal forces were marching with all possible speed to concentrate at the town of Perryville, Kentucky, where it was known that Bragg had bivouacked his army. If Buell gave any thought to his August altercation with Albin Schoepf, he made no note of it. General Schoepf, commanding a division of 7,000 men, realized that a fight was near and chose to put his emotions aside until the battle was over. In the III Corps of Brig. Gen. Charles A. Gilbert, a friend and supporter of Buell, Schoepf's division was marching along the Springfield Pike, moving east toward Perryville.

Brig. Gen. Albin Schoepf had come a long way since his days as a captain in the Austrian Army. After his defection to Lajos Kossuth's revolution, he had advanced in rank from private to major and become a member of General Jozef Bem's staff, and part of Kossuth's personal entourage. But Kossuth's defeat made it quite impossible for the six-foot-four major to remain in Europe. He and Bem had, by April 1850, emigrated to Syria and were employed in the Ottoman service. General Bem died in December, but Schoepf stayed on, serving as an artillery instructor. Meanwhile, Kossuth was touring abroad in an effort to drum up political and financial support for the continuation of his failed revolution. In 1851 Kossuth arrived in the United States; in all probability Albin Schoepf arrived with Kossuth.[38] Kossuth was scheduled for a speaking tour of the United States, and during his engagement in Washington, Schoepf elected to seek employment and remain in the United States. He found a home among the small community of Hungarian exiles then living in Washington. The promising young Austrian officer took a job as a porter in the Willard Hotel on Pennsylvania Avenue.

Thirteen-year-old Julie Bates Kesley, living in Washington in 1851, was excited in the extreme at the prospect of hearing the legendary Kossuth speak. Kossuth's passion for democratic government, his hatred of injustice, his flamboyance, and his heroism combined to make Lajos Kossuth the ideal romantic hero. He had become the stuff of Byronic legends and people flocked to hear him speak. Miss Kesley had been following his exploits and had made up her mind to attend his speech with her family. Kossuth's lecture was electrifying. Miss Kesley was so impressed with his performance that she declared to her family that she would marry no one but a Hungarian! Evidently appealing to more than just a young girl's heart, the Hungarian revolutionary was a much sought-after speaker in the United States. Attorney Joseph Holt invited Kossuth to speak at his hometown of Louisville, Kentucky. In March 1852 Kossuth did just that and afterward repaired to a reception at Holt's Louisville home.

Joseph Holt had met and befriended Albin Schoepf sometime in 1851. Holt took a liking to the expatriate and secured a post for Albin at the U.S. Coast Survey. Holt was also a friend of the Kesley family, having known Julie's mother since the opening of her finishing school in 1846. Holt certainly knew of sixteen-year-old Julie's obsession with Hungarians and conspired to match his protégé with the young girl. Apparently Holt's matchmaking paid off; on May 7, 1855, the thirty-five-year-old Albin Schoepf married the seventeen-year-old Julie Kesley. The following year, the first of the Schoepfs' nine children was born. Julie Magdaline Schoepf was born April 4, 1856, and a second daughter, Lydia Kesley Schoepf, was born on August 8, 1857.

By 1859 Joseph Holt was commissioner of the Patent Office and on February 1, 1859, he appointed Albin Schoepf as second assistant examiner. Although the promotion was welcome and cause for elation within the Schoepf household, their oldest daughter, Julie, had been ill for quite some time. Doctors were summoned. The three-and-a-half-year-old child was examined by at least two physicians. The diagnosis: the croup. Albin and Julie Schoepf attended their child twenty-four hours a day, following the regimen the physicians had recommended. But their ministrations were to no avail and Julie Magdaline died on April 11, 1859. The next morning the bereaved father wrote to Joseph Holt: "I am in sad affliction for an unexpected and hard stroke has smitten me down. I feel it hard—hard to communicate the fact that my lovely babe, my older infant daughter is gone and will be carried to her grave this afternoon at 4 o'clock."[39]

A great sadness seemed to overwhelm Albin Schoepf; the loss of his daughter changed the amiable young man forever. He and Julie were bound closer than ever, but his natural reserve was now reinforced. The family also indicated that his penchant for order and cleanliness became pronounced following his daughter's death. A third child was born to the Schoepfs, arriving on January 4, 1860, and was named for his father. The young boy's nickname was Frank. Schoepf continued with his work at the Patent Office while Julie managed the growing household on the corner of 6th and L Streets in Washington.

On January 18, 1861, Joseph Holt was named secretary of war in the closing months of the Buchanan administration; Albin Schoepf was immediately transferred to the War Department, where he was appointed to a position as a military engineer. Following Lincoln's ascension to the presidency, Joseph Holt lost his position. Although a Democrat, Joseph Holt proved to be a firm Union man, and his experience during the ongoing Fort Sumter crisis was invaluable to the new administration. Following the resolution of the Sumter crisis and the beginning of hostilities, Holt returned to his native Kentucky. There he was instrumental in shaping Kentucky's stance of neutrality and finally the state's resolute maintenance of her relationship with the United States. Holt's firm faith in the Union and his remarkable legal background led to his appointment as judge advocate general of the army in September 1862. He served in that capacity through the war and beyond, presiding, most notably, over the trial of the Lincoln assassination conspirators.

Holt knew of Schoepf's abilities as a soldier and sought an appointment for him in the army. On September 30, 1861, Schoepf resigned from the War Department and was appointed brigadier general of volunteers. General Schoepf, at the insistence of Holt, was ordered to Kentucky on October 7, 1861.[40] Schoepf's aggressive nature and his training as a soldier served him well in the opening campaigns of the war. His brigade, comprised of the 33rd Indiana Volunteer Infantry, the 12th Kentucky Volunteer Infantry, and the 17th and 38th Ohio Volunteer Infantries, was the first brigade of the Army of the Ohio. Schoepf's immediate commander was Gen. George H. Thomas. The next day Confederate general Felix Zollicoffer's forces attacked Schoepf's entrenched troops at Rockcastle Hills on Wild Cat Mountain. The Southerners advanced to within fifty yards of Schoepf's position before being repulsed. Albin Schoepf had not been under fire for ten years and, by all accounts, he handled himself and his troops with steadfast calm.

By the new year Schoepf was stationed just south of Somerset, Kentucky, across the line into eastern Tennessee. The fighting over this area was considered vitally important to the administration. As in western Virginia, eastern Tennessee was a stronghold of Unionist sentiment. The department commander, Maj. Gen. Don Carlos Buell, was ordered to clear the area of secessionists—a task easier said than done. The terrain was mountainous and difficult on which to mount an extended military operation. But the difficulties entailed in marching and fighting did not remain the lone cause for concern. Even the routine daily paperwork, stores, and commonplace items an army uses were troublesome to obtain. Schoepf reported that even the blank forms, so ordinary to the operation of the army, were impossible to get. That December disease took hold of his brigade, and Schoepf was forced to rent a hospital for a hundred or so of his command too ill to be moved. Meanwhile he waited for the Southerners to make a move. Schoepf, in this period of the war, was constantly being held back; his apparent attitude was to get at the enemy and offer battle, but Buell evidently did not want a fight until everything was ready. Schoepf received many reminders that he should conduct his brigade in concert with the rest of the forces in eastern Tennessee.

Thus far the forces had been playing a cat-and-mouse game in the mountains of Tennessee. Zollicoffer had been attempting to draw the Federal forces into a trap, forcing them by maneuver to attack him in a fortified position. General Thomas's agenda was to outmaneuver Zollicoffer and force him to fight the Federals on ground of their own choosing. Throughout December Schoepf sent out troops to reconnoiter and to counter movements by Zollicoffer. Meanwhile, Schoepf got into some trouble for his "lack of enterprise" in maintaining the paperwork that was so much a part of army regulations. His response was to point out that he had not been shipped any blank forms.

After nearly a month of this activity Zollicoffer was lured to Logan's Cross Road on January 19, 1862. The ensuing fight was typical of battles in the early stages of the Civil War: confused commanders, confusing commands, piecemeal attacks, and neither side gaining a clear advantage. The turning point of this engagement was the death of Felix Zollicoffer. The nearsighted former editor, whose aggression had kept the Federals off balance for so many months, galloped into a body of troops and voiced his anger at them for not firing on the enemy when they were so close. The officer on the ground replied that the close body of troops was not the enemy, and asked Zollicoffer his identity. It was only then that Felix Zollicoffer realized that he had just reprimanded an armed force of Yankees! Without answering he turned his horse to escape. The Federal officer, almost at the same moment, realized that this arrogant general officer was the enemy and blazed away at the fleeing man. Within minutes Zollicoffer was dead. The battle had raged for almost three hours, and when the men saw Zollicoffer go down, their heart for the fight wavered. A spirited bayonet assault by the Federals turned faltering into a full-fledged rout as the Confederates, with their backs to the rain-swollen Cumberland River, made a pell-mell dash for the rear. Only one regiment from Schoepf's brigade took part in the combat; in the end, Schoepf's 12th Kentucky delivered the flanking fire that broke the Confederate line.

By August Schoepf had been advanced in command, taking over leadership of the 1st Division, III Corps, in the Army of the Ohio. This was a major step for a foreign-born officer, and Schoepf was aware of his accomplishment, especially notable because he had achieved his station without the considerable help of Joseph Holt. But soon after he ascended to divisional command, Schoepf crossed swords with Buell. The Army of the Ohio was rife with distrust of General Buell, which was mutual as Buell felt that volunteers were inferior types, worthy of disdain and in need of the harshest discipline. In late August, Buell rode into Schoepf's headquarters camp, apparently for a surprise inspection. The sun had set and the lone horseman caused quite a stir. Unfortunately, the stories diverge in the retelling, but General Buell supposedly commented that he had ridden into Schoepf's camp entirely unmolested, made straight for Schoepf's tent, roused him, then ordered his arrest for the lack of an adequate guard. With that Schoepf lost his temper, drew a pistol, and threatened to kill Buell, ordering him out of his camp. According to Buell it took several staff officers to control Schoepf. Later regretting the loss of temper on both sides, Buell withdrew the charges. Schoepf's story begins with an unidentified horseman slipping past the guard and brazenly riding into camp. By the time the rider approached Schoepf's tent, his staff was sufficiently excited, and one of them had snatched the bridle of the stranger's horse and brandished a pistol in the offender's face, ordering him to dismount. Buell responded that he was the army commander. Schoepf's staff officer replied that he did not give a damn who he was, he had better dismount before he received a ball between his eyes. With that Schoepf approached Buell and reprimanded him for his behavior. General Buell then ordered Schoepf's arrest and rode away.

In the choking dust of the Springfield Pike, General Schoepf plainly did not understand how the situation had been resolved. He was eager for the court-martial that was sure to follow, but Buell had unexpectedly dropped the charges. Despite this Schoepf felt that he had not been vindicated; the matter was simply dropped. In Schoepf's mind, Buell's action only confirmed the moral cowardice of his commanding officer. In fact, Schoepf had come to the conclusion that Buell's resolve to support the Union was indeed lacking, an idea that had been floating around the White House in the past few months.

Schoepf's division was assigned the role of reserve during the upcoming fight. His corps commander, Brigadier General Gilbert, cautioned Schoepf not to commit his troops to action unless specifically ordered. As the battle of Perryville developed, the Southerners were able to make some significant gains on the poorly placed troops under Gilbert. It was Schoepf's fate to witness the mauling of Maj. Gen. Philip Sheridan's division to his front. Schoepf repeatedly asked Gilbert's permission to support the blue-clad boys then being mowed down by a determined Southern assault. Repeatedly permission was denied. Schoepf appealed directly to Buell and again permission was denied. Bridling under his enforced inactivity, Schoepf ordered dispositions be made among his division to react immediately either in an offensive or defensive posture. In the end, as the Federal lines were visibly crumbling, Schoepf was ordered to send one of his brigades forward to plug a gap between Gilbert's two divisions. By this time the Confederate assault was running out of steam. The addition of Schoepf's troops halted the Southern juggernaut. Bragg had achieved a tactical victory, but not realizing his full success, he withdrew his forces, retreating into Tennessee. The great western invasion had come to an end.

Buell wired Washington that success had been complete, and, like his counterpart in the east, George McClellan, he failed to see that he had let the quarry escape. The Lincoln administration reacted to the developing news with a frustration that was now commonplace. Despite all his entreaties Lincoln was unable to coax Buell into any kind of follow-up activity that would ensure the success of his armies. To the contrary, Buell seemed content to rest and refit, demanding more men and supplies. Enough was enough; Buell had to go. But it would not do to fire him while using the Perryville victory as propaganda to bolster the Union's resolve. By November stories of Buell's mishandling of the campaign had percolated to the White House. Certainly there was plenty of hearsay evidence against Buell, and in an alleged effort to play fair, Lincoln turned to his newly appointed judge advocate general, Joseph Holt, to instigate a Board of Inquiry looking into the activities of General Buell during the campaign.[41]

Brig. Gen. Albin Schoepf had made no bones about his dislike of Buell's generalship, and he certainly was not afraid to voice his opinion in public and it is very likely that he kept Joe Holt abreast of the entire situation. At any rate, Schoepf was the only general officer on the Board of Inquiry's commission who had served as a subordinate to Buell. Indeed, Schoepf was the inside man, the ringer, the one who had the goods on Buell. Clearly the government had stacked the deck against Buell, and Albin Schoepf was happy to oblige.

# Chapter 4

# 1863

*"Brig. Gen. Albin Schoepf, U.S. Volunteers, will repair without delay to Fort Delaware, and relieve Lieut. Col. R. C. Buchanan, Fourth U.S. Infantry, in command of that post."*
                                        —E. D. Townsend, A.A.G.

Back in December 1861, George McClellan, then general in chief of the army, had wired General Buell: "Is Schoepf competent?" Don Carlos Buell responded on December 29 that "Schoepf is not incompetent, but has not shown much enterprise at Somerset." McClellan almost never questioned a general officer's competence in official correspondence, but Schoepf was foreign-born. Examples of cultural prejudice practiced by the great and small in the United States are numerous and well documented. Men like McClellan and Buell and many more Americans were ready to believe any myth, tale, fable, or account that lessened the Irish, Germans, and African Americans as a people. In 1862 Capt. Robert Gould Shaw, of the 2nd Massachusetts Volunteer Infantry, wrote home to his mother discussing the Irish in his company:

> We have a great deal of fun with the sentinels at night for they very seldom can remember the form of the challenge & the Irishmen seem sometimes utterly unable to learn or understand anything. When more than one man approaches a sentry he must say: "Halt! Advance one & give the countersign!" So one man said: "Advance one & give the counterfeit." Another "Advance and give the consignment." Another "Advance one and count ten." And night before last when I was officer of the guard a sentry challenged Greely Curtis & said: "Coom forrad & give an account of yersilf!"

84

Shaw shared his prejudice of the Irish with an equal disdain for the Germans: "I saw Sigel (the German Revolutionary) yesterday; he is an insignificant looking man."[1]

Cultural prejudice was not limited to the elite, as Private Hamilton noted in his diary: "A little fight on the parade ground, a Dutch corporal was knocked down a few times."[2] Nor was prejudice the solely owned activity of Northerners, as Fort Delaware prisoner Capt. Henry Dickinson, 2nd Virginia Cavalry, noted, "The presiding genius of this place was a fat old Dutchman speaking English badly, by rank a brigadier general and named A. Schoepf, pronounced Sheff."[3]

Albin Schoepf was, evidently, intelligent and well educated. He was able to read and write at least three languages, was a free thinker, a Republican, and had friends in high places. But he remained a foreigner—a Dutchman, a "fat old" German, and a papist. Schoepf's Republicanism alone would have met with disfavor from lifelong Democrats McClellan and Buell. In essence, Schoepf was distrusted. When Buell spoke of Schoepf's "want of enterprise," he was referring to the paperwork problem Schoepf's brigade had experienced while on Wildcat Mountain. Yet when George Thomas was advanced in rank and command, Albin Schoepf took over his division, evidently promoted in spite of his "want of enterprise." Schoepf's letters throughout this period reveal an aggressive fighter who was constantly being checked by overly cautious commanders. This prejudice on the part of Buell could not have been lost on Schoepf, and it eventually erupted into open warfare between the two generals.

At the battle of Perryville, Schoepf was forced to stand by and observe the slaughter of hundreds of young men, when he could have stemmed the bloody work on that October day. In his opinion, many men were killed or wounded for want of an order. To Schoepf, Buell and Bragg held equal responsibility for the loss of life. And now, with an investigation of Buell begun, he had the opportunity to reveal Buell for the incompetent lout that he considered him to be.

The commission formally began on December 1, 1862, meeting in Nashville, Tennessee. Buell had been relieved of his command on October 24, 1862, and he welcomed the investigation as an opportunity to redeem himself. Buell also realized that there was an equal chance that he may be held liable for his failures.

The commission's broad interpretation led to an examination of General Buell's tenure as commander of the Army of the Ohio and covered thousands of hours of testimony. Through December and January the judge advocate,

Maj. Donn Piatt, introduced witness after witness examining the movements, planning, and logistics of the Army of the Ohio. Piatt's careful planning set up a case exposing Buell's actions, missteps, and, in some cases, refusal to obey the legitimate orders of the commander in chief. Members of the commission began to take sides as the investigation continued. Generals Dana and Ord were generally sympathetic to Buell, while Generals Schoepf and Tyler were skeptical, if not openly hostile. On several occasions Buell chose Schoepf as his principal antagonist. But in underestimating Albin Schoepf, Buell more often than not walked into traps that only reinforced Schoepf's disdain. On February 9, 1863, Schoepf and Buell clashed over the import of an order from General Halleck, which Buell claimed to have acted on. During testimony, Schoepf openly accused Buell of hiding Halleck's written order: "I desire . . . that General Buell be asked for the orders he received from General Halleck. I have asked for that letter several times and have not been able to get it, and I think the Commission should order General Buell to produce the letter or orders of General Halleck." Buell responded that "General Halleck's instructions to me in the first place were oral. I remember, however, one dispatch which had reference to the route which he deemed it best that I should pursue. As far as I am concerned I would just as lief present any instructions I have from General Halleck now as at any other time, though I had designed to bring them in with my documentary evidence, and if such instructions are not found upon the books that I have submitted to the Commission I do not believe that they can be found."[4] As Buell and Schoepf continued the duel, the exchanges between them became more and more heated. But finding himself consistently on the losing end of the legalistic arguments, General Buell began to object to any perceived slight. Buell took exception to General Tyler's questioning a witness as to his loyalty to the United States Government.[5] Soon Buell's credibility began to erode. He had been on the losing end of so many arguments that, as March approached, his frustration mounted. Buell decided to launch a counterattack on Schoepf's character.[6] Buell opened his defense with the introduction of Federal general Crittenden, who had firsthand knowledge of the incident between Buell and Schoepf. As the course of questioning continued Buell produced witness after witness declaring Schoepf's hostility toward Buell. Rather than defend himself with a thorough examination and refutation of any arguments against his conduct, General Buell chose to make the inquiry a clash of personality. Although Schoepf was not on trial, the thrust of the investigation had taken a turn away from its original focus. The inquiry was supposed to end on April 3, 1863, but because of Buell's tactic, it was in danger of continuing well beyond that date.

Schoepf, over the strenuous objections of his supporters, felt that his position on the commission was in danger of jeopardizing the original intent and he formally requested that General Halleck relieve him of this duty. The commissioners were initially unwilling to allow Schoepf to make the request, but Schoepf made the point that the aim of the trial was in danger of being lost among the contentions that he was on a witch-hunt. It already had been shown that Buell had erred in his actions on numerous occasions and had even gone so far as to tamper with the official records of his command. If the upshot of this investigation was focused on Schoepf's alleged animosity toward Buell, then the work of the last few months was for naught. Finally the commissioners agreed to forward Schoepf's request, and a complete transcript was sent to Halleck for review. The commission adjourned until a decision could be made in Washington.

Apparently Halleck agreed with Schoepf and reassigned him to duty under General Rosecrans in the Army of the Cumberland by March 19, 1863. With Schoepf's removal from the commission, Buell's only defense was useless, yet he continued into to press for an airing of witnesses showing Schoepf as a subordinate officer bent on revenge. The commission unanimously agreed that General Buell's considered course was moot. The investigation continued into May with General Buell doing little to defend his reputation. Although the commission made no recommendations, Buell's record, now in the glaring light of day, indicated that he was unable to command troops in the manner that the Lincoln administration required of its generals. Buell awaited orders that never came, and he resigned his commission on June 1, 1864.

Albin Schoepf, meanwhile, had reported to Rosecrans for duty. An effort was made to restore Schoepf to divisional command, but his health precluded that possibility. Schoepf formally resigned his appointment to field command on April 10, 1863. Maj. Donn Piatt, impressed with Schoepf's performance, lamented the loss of so valuable an officer and communicated his feelings to his superior, Joseph Holt. Brig. Gen. Albin Schoepf soon was rewarded for his loyalty with a command commensurate with his rank and ability. It was a potential sword of Damocles, but Schoepf was used to that sort of challenge.

⚜

On January 1, 1863, there were seventeen prisoners confined at Fort Delaware. The population had been on the down cycle since November and appeared to be headed for a permanent reduction in the number of prisoners on Pea Patch. As the reduction of prisoners continued through the waning months of 1862, so the reduction of the garrison followed suit. Capt. Paul Jones's and Capt. David Schooley's companies of marine artillerymen were transferred to the front, some for service aboard ship in the James River. In December Lt. Col. Delavan Perkins, now acting commander of Fort Delaware, was ordered by the War Department to have all the "rebel prisoners of war confined at Fort Delaware" sent to Fortress Monroe in Virginia. Several POWs remained at Fort Delaware, however, having taken the oath of allegiance to be released once their paperwork was processed. The evacuation of most of the POWs left only prisoners of state and some deserters sentenced to hard labor on Pea Patch Island. These deserters offered Colonel Perkins his first political challenge. Delavan Perkins interpreted his duty with blinders on: In his mind, deserters were deserters, and by the rules of engagement ought to have been shot in the first place. Perkins placed the deserters in the wet casemates, and began the liberal use of the ball and chain. Private Hamilton reported standing guard over a deserter named Palmer who was shackled with a 43-pound ball. Palmer swore he would poison the man who had turned him in.

As it happened, some of the deserters claimed to be citizens of the British Empire and, as such, had written a letter to the British proconsul in Philadelphia complaining of their barbaric confinement. Following a terrible storm on January 22, the proconsul and his entourage took an excursion to the island from Philadelphia. Apparently they did not make their identity known to Perkins, as the records show no visit by a British diplomat. Nevertheless the Brits were incensed by the "barbaric" conditions they encountered. Upon his return to Philadelphia, the proconsul formally protested to Secretary of State William H. Seward. The communiqué immediately achieved the desired effect, and Seward fired off a letter to Stanton, who, in turn, alerted the department commander, Gen. Robert Schenck. Schenck, in the traditional manner of all bureaucrats, handed the whole business to his chief of staff, Colonel Whipple.[7]

The ramifications for Colonel Perkins were hidden. An inspection was made, and on paper an investigation had taken place, although nothing changed. Perkins, however, was on informal probation, and the administration watched him closely.

With the transfer of Captain Jones's batteries, Perkins's command now consisted of Capt. J. S. Stevenson's Battery A and Capt. F. von Schilling's Battery B of the Pennsylvania Marine and Fortification Artillery, as well as Captains Mlotkowski's and Young's Pennsylvania Independent Batteries. In January the entire complement numbered 10 officers and 272 enlisted men present and fit for duty. The aggregate present and absent totaled 420, but many were sick, on leave, or had deserted. Of the 156 heavy guns to be mounted inside the fort, only 47 were in usable condition. Perkins also had on hand 6 fieldpieces in the event of an amphibious landing by the enemy. Perkins now sought to finish the work his predecessors had begun and ordered the installation of more guns. He also pressed Muhlenbruch to finish the buildings inside the fort.

As the work progressed Colonel Perkins went about the business of turning Fort Delaware into a well-disciplined post. Perkins's style of military management was quite different from Burton's, demanding strict obedience. Dress parade was held every day at 5:30 P.M., Garrison review was held the last of each month, and the gun drill was expanded and scheduled for five hours every day except Sundays. Private Hamilton grumbled that the "old man" did not please the boys so well, as they had to stand, freezing, for hours in garrison review. Perkins brooked no desertion from his post and regularly sent parties into Philadelphia to fetch those men who absented themselves from his command. By spring the garrison numbered 13 officers and 531 enlisted men, with only 5 men absent—a total complement of 539. The guns mounted and serviceable now totaled 67 heavy guns and 6 pieces of field artillery.

The absence of prisoners, and thus nothing of substance for the men to do, coupled with the colonel's strict military discipline, brought the inevitable lapses in human behavior. Perkins's administration certainly could be characterized as obsessive, even for a martinet. In one special order, for example, he specified that any dog found running loose on the island would be killed.

Private Hamilton complained to his diary that Perkins had found the soldiers' new quarters dirty and ordered the dismantling and burning of their bunks. The men were then ordered to build new ones.

The courts-martial panel had plenty of cases to try. Pvt. Abraham Knapp of Stevenson's Battery A called his sergeant, Jacques Blume, "a damned lousy French son of a bitch" and threatened to split his head open. For this offense he lost ten dollars pay and was sentenced to thirty days in the guardhouse. Private Kavenney found himself before the court for entering the mess hall and demanding his supper in an abusive manner. The sentence: a ten-dollar fine and ten days in the guardhouse. Pvt. Michael King's behavior provided the officers with an explanation of how men deserted while stationed on an island. King left his guard post at the wharf for an hour and a half to visit the saloon. While he was away several enlisted men commandeered a boat and sailed away. King then offered an excuse of sickness and managed to prove to the court that he had not visited the saloon. He was acquitted. The soldiers were nonetheless gone.

Idle time did play on the men, and they often resorted to strong drink. On March 5 Captain Mlotkowski (he had been promoted in February 1862) attended his duties as officer of the day while roaring drunk. At some point during his inspection of the soldiers on guard duty, Mlotkowski decided that a guard's rifle was loaded improperly. The young man on duty took exception to the captain's remark and informed him it was indeed loaded. The challenge thus offered, the drunken Mlotkowski ordered that the musket be discharged and reloaded. Despite the sentinel's reluctance to do so, rank prevailed and the gun was discharged. The resulting projectile found its way into the arm of the guard at the adjacent post. The general alarm was raised, and several officers attempted to remove the captain, who offered stiff resistance. He finally was removed and placed under arrest, confined to close quarters under guard, pending court-martial. Lt. Joseph Royer was then named to command Mlotkowski's battery. The guard's wound turned out to be a slight graze. Evidently, the minor nature of the wound and repentance on the part of Mlotkowski mitigated the need for punishment, as the genial captain was released from arrest on March 13, 1863, and all charges were dropped.

On March 6, Perkins was ordered to transfer the prisoners of state then in his charge to Washington for exchange. Perkins sent Lieutenant Ahl with Corporal Young and Privates Cockley and Speers and five civilian prisoners, George Shearer, Thomas Fichell, James Leauge, George Putnam, and W. H. Resin, to Washington. A number of men still remained in prison at Fort Delaware, however, and one caused Colonel Perkins considerable trouble. Capt. R. W. Baylor, 12th Virginia Cavalry, was a prisoner of war, charged with a heinous crime. He had been captured in Harpers Ferry, West Virginia, and charged with the murder of Pvt. George Rohr, who was, at the time of his murder, responding to Baylor's flag of truce.[8] Baylor was a prisoner at Fort Delaware and, with the general exchange, was held at the fort due to the serious nature of the crime charged against him. But Perkins had somehow overlooked the necessary paperwork alerting his superiors that Baylor was still in custody. When Confederate exchange agent Ould inquired after Captain Baylor, Colonel Hoffman could not locate the prisoner. After several days of searching, Baylor turned up right where he had been all along. Hoffman was perplexed as to how it was possible to lose Captain Baylor, considering the small number of prisoners confined at Fort Delaware and the serious charges against him. Perkins should have been able to account for this one. Another strike entered Colonel Perkins's record. From then on Hoffman was careful to mention Captain Baylor in any correspondence dealing with the transfer of prisoners.

The government also made some decisions regarding the use of Pea Patch Island. Because of its ideal location along shipping lanes, Fort Delaware could be an excellent holding facility and stopover for the POWs who had been exchanged and were being transshipped to the designated exchange point. If the past numbers of POWs was any indication of the future, a large temporary camp was needed on the island. Colonel Hoffman indicated to Perkins that the government desired a detention facility large enough to house 10,000 POWs, yet in the time that Perkins was commander at Fort Delaware very little progress was made on the construction of the POW complex. The colonel's single-minded devotion to the completion of the fort as a defensive site overshadowed the desired barracks construction. Perhaps Perkins, given his temperament and behavior, believed that Fort Delaware's value to the nation was her original purpose, that is, as a massive gun platform, and it was his duty to see that mission was fulfilled. Or he might have concluded that the Dix-Hill Cartel was working so well that the erection of more sheds for the POWs was a waste of money. In any event Perkins failed to grasp that the War Department had defined Fort Delaware's mission. He was soon transferred to the Provost Marshal's Department. Apparently Perkins had failed so badly that, upon his transfer, he was demoted to major and assigned to administration of the Conscription Act in Connecticut.

On April 2, 1863, Fort Delaware's newest commander laconically noted in the administrative record his assumption of command. Col. Robert Christie Buchanan was an old-line regular, having graduated from West Point in 1830. In the course of his service he had seen it all, with a distinguished record dating from the Black Hawk War in 1831. Robert Buchanan also bears a footnote in history, as he was the commanding officer who had forced Capt. Ulysses S. Grant to resign from the service as a result of his alleged drunkenness.

Perhaps Buchanan was the right man for the task of creating an efficient POW facility, or he may have been assigned to Fort Delaware temporarily pending the ascension of Albin Schoepf. Whatever the purpose of the War Department in naming Buchanan as commanding officer, his tenure was a mere two weeks. In that time the POW population increased to 595, as the spring campaigns began to heat up. Evidently the colonel took his assignment seriously and pored over the plans for barracks on the north end of Pea Patch Island and sent Colonel Hoffman suggestions for further improvements.

> As I have some little experience in such matters as building quarters of all kinds and as the health of my command is in a great degree connected with that of the prisoners I request that I may have the matter of plan as well as location intrusted to me. The present barracks are not fitted in their most essential details for the purpose for which they were built and will have to be altered. One set is very badly located and I propose to change it to another point. By so doing and altering the other so as to adapt it to the purposes for which it was constructed the additional buildings which it appears to be the purpose to erect may probably be diminished in size. We want a smallpox hospital and bake ovens, with cisterns or tanks in which to catch the water from the roofs, and other things which are essential to health or comfort. By having charge of this matter I can better take care of the interests of the Government with reference to the economy of construction.[9]

The policy of the government concerning Fort Delaware and prisoners of war had changed a great deal since the implementation of the Dix-Hill Cartel in July 1862. The provisions of the cartel were specific about the method of

parole and exchange, including the locations of the physical exchange of prisoners. But in the past few months there had been increasing numbers of parole
violations on the part of both parties. Although parole was not permitted by
the cartel agreement, to do so commanders had been accepting parole as
exchange and releasing their POWs immediately upon signature. It was soon
determined that a large number of these paroled prisoners were not awaiting
official exchange before returning to their regiments and, therefore, assuming
belligerent status illegally. The new policy clearly stated that if a man was captured, he would be paroled and held in a detention camp until a formal
exchange of prisoners could be arranged. Fort Delaware's location made it the
ideal spot for just such a detention camp.  In redefining the fort's mission, the
War Department placed the construction of the camp as a top priority. The
importance of the project was underscored by a visit on April 15 by Colonel
Hoffman. His personal inspection and subsequent recommendations regarding the creation of Fort Delaware's artificial city would imprint on the community throughout the remainder of the war.

During Hoffman's time on Pea Patch Island, he met Confederate general
Thomas James Churchill, the second only general officer imprisoned on the
island. Churchill had been roughly handled while a prisoner at Camp Chase
in Ohio, and he now seized the opportunity to complain to Colonel Hoffman.
However legitimate his claims may have been, Churchill's approach must have
annoyed Hoffman. Whatever took place between the captive and the captor,
the commissary general of prisoners considered Churchill's complaints and
chose a response that was indicative of the shaky ground upon which the entire
exchange process stood. Upon his return to Washington, Hoffman wrote to
Buchanan summarizing the meeting:

> Please say to General Churchill that his letter of the 13th
> instant complaining of the treatment which he and his offi-
> cers received on leaving Camp Chase at the hands of the
> guard is before me and in reply I can only repeat what I said
> to him personally that all such conduct on the part of any
> U.S. officer or soldier is wholly unauthorized. I need not say
> that the desire of the Government is that prisoners of war
> shall be treated with all the kindness which a proper humane
> feeling prompts and which is consistent with their position,
> for it is a well-known fact that clothing and blankets have
> been issued to the many destitute who have fallen into our
> hands. The sick and wounded have been as well and as
> promptly attended to as our own soldiers and all have been
> furnished with an abundant supply of rations, even includ-
> ing what may well be called luxuries.

But if I am rightly informed it has by no means been so with our troops when they have been captured as he may learn by inquiry on reaching Richmond. So far from receiving clothing it has frequently happened that they have been stripped of all their outer garments and then crowded into prisons inconceivably filthy, so much so that it would be shocking to humanity to confine in such a place even the most abandoned criminals. Here too were confined men of all ranks, from generals to privates, and all alike experienced the most insulting indignities and most unwarrantable harshness. So far as I have learned this has been the almost invariable treatment of our citizens and soldiers who have been held as prisoners of war at Richmond and there is scarcely room to doubt that it has been done by authority.

In this brief view of the case you will say then to General Churchill that though the indignities and outrages of which he and his officers complain are not only wholly unauthorized but are in violation of the instructions which have been given to govern in such cases yet the course pursued as it appears by his Government in similar cases takes from him all shadow of grounds for complaint. He has been made to suffer by an unauthorized retaliation for innumerable outrages which have been committed on our people if not by authority of his Government at least in its immediate presence and which have given rise to the bitter feelings he so much deprecates.

In conclusion say to the general that I trust the humane example which has been set by the Government of the United States in its care for the welfare of prisoners of war may be followed by the Government at Richmond, a course which cannot fail to greatly mitigate the hardships which must unavoidably be experienced by all who are so unfortunate as to be captured.[10]

In sharing the thoughts of Hoffman with General Churchill, Col. Robert Buchanan committed his last official act at Fort Delaware. As with Perkins, Buchanan was transferred to the Provost Marshal's Department, but, unlike Perkins, he was not demoted. In 1864 Buchanan became commander of the 1st U.S. Infantry, ending the war as a brevet major general. Following the close of the war Buchanan was rewarded for devotion and placed in command of the Department of Louisiana. As an interesting aside, after the war President Grant acknowledged that his only satisfaction in achieving high rank was the day he officially outranked Bob Buchanan.

⸺⸻⸺

According to the Revised Regulations for the Army 1863, when a brigadier general assumed command of a post special honors were to be paid to that officer, including a muster of the garrison and an eleven-gun salute. Naturally all of these prescribed activities must take place out of doors, but the predictability of the weather on Pea Patch Island in spring was as certain as catching smoke on a windy day. Brig. Gen. Albin Schoepf had been ordered, on April 14, 1863, to assume command of Fort Delaware as soon as practicable. April 17, 1863, was seasonably mild, with a slight breeze; wisps of clouds danced across the high blue sky, and the river was quiet. The general was due to arrive and Colonel Buchanan, old army as he was, wanted the ceremonies to be perfect. The garrison troops had been ordered to muster for review, the post band was ordered to play a selection of martial tunes in honor of the general, and the eleven guns were loaded and ready for their turn in the ceremony. The martial pomp and circumstance was indeed impressive. As General Schoepf and his family stepped onto the wharf at Pea Patch Island, the band struck up; the garrison, arrayed just east of the fort, snapped to attention; and an eleven-gun salute was fired. While Julie and her children, four-and-a-half-year-old Lydia, three-year-old Frank, and two-year-old Holt watched with pride, the general and his aide-de-camp, Capt. William Kesley, Julie's brother, exchanged formal salutes with Colonel Buchanan and the officers of Fort Delaware.

Following the formal introductions, General Schoepf was invited to inspect his new command. Surely he must have been impressed with what he saw. Colonel Buchanan had issued strict instructions that the men would put their best foot forward. Muskets gleamed, the sun struck and added a luster to the highly polished brass of the accoutrements, boots and leathers were blackened, and the dress uniforms were brushed and cleaned. The men flawlessly performed an abbreviated form of the manual of arms, and the new commanding officer strode down the ranks, stopping to comment on a particularly clean soldier. Albin Schoepf was an impressive-looking soldier. His height of six feet four inches, his trim figure and bright hazel eyes, his closely cropped hair and thick walrus moustache combined to create an appearance of military imperiousness. His European training added a purposeful stride and ramrod posture. Schoepf had also taken a page from his American military experience and made sure to look directly into the eyes of his soldiers. His manner calculated to create an unforgettable first impression, Schoepf made it known to the garrison exactly who was in charge. Schoepf then turned to Colonel Buchanan and congratulated him on the esprit of the command. Buchanan suggested that the general might want to attend to the personal disposition of his family, but Schoepf waved him off, asking Captain Kesley to see to Mrs. Schoepf and the children. Colonel Buchanan volunteered the services of the post adjutant, Lieutenant McConnell. While Captain Kesley and Lieutenant McConnell attended Julie and her brood, Colonel Buchanan dismissed the garrison and called for an officers' meeting in a half hour. General Schoepf and Colonel Buchanan, accompanied by the ordnance officer and former commander, Maj. Henry Burton, passed through the post turngate and onto the parade ground. From there they headed for the offices of the commanding officer.

Once inside Buchanan briefed the new commander on the status of the post, handing over the books, post council records, and all pertinent information. There were 595 prisoners housed in the prison barracks, many of whom were scheduled for exchange. The garrison consisted of 18 officers and 558 enlisted men, with a total complement (both present and absent) of 747 officers and men. Captains Young and Mlotkowski commanded the heavy artillery of the post, while several companies of the 157th Pennsylvania Volunteers, an infantry outfit, remained on Pea Patch to augment the force and serve as prison guards. Two batteries of Segebarth's Marine Artillery also remained in the garrison, although they had been reorganized as the 3rd Pennsylvania Heavy Artillery, also known as the 152nd Pennsylvania Volunteers, and the majority of the command was serving in the defenses of Washington. The two batteries of the 152nd were commanded by Capt. J. S. Stevenson and Lt. C. H. Hawkins.

Schoepf's trained eye as a military engineer now turned to the plans for the north end of the island. His engineering work had been extensive, and he swiftly noted potential problems. The nature of the soil on Pea Patch was his first concern, and he questioned Buchanan about how extensive the foundations were for the proposed barracks. Buchanan shared his concern as well, pointing to the need for a hospital, a water collection plan, a separate contagious hospital, and a thorough examination of the foundation plans. General Schoepf scheduled an inspection of the grounds for the next day. By the time they had concluded the conference, the officers had assembled for their meeting. General Schoepf was gracious and polite in meeting each of the officers. Instead of a verbose speech for the officers, Schoepf reiterated his orders from the War Department. Fort Delaware was to become a permanent prisoner holding area, and their mission was to effect those orders. Beginning April 18 the post was to be organized to make their mission a success. That evening Colonel Buchanan quietly left the post he had commanded so briefly and boarded the transport for Washington.

The general spent the next few days familiarizing himself with his command and his officers. On April 20 Schoepf began the process of reshuffling

the command and creating his official family. Evidently satisfied with Major
Burton's performance, Schoepf retained him at the post he had served under
Perkins and Buchanan. Lt. George Ahl's work training the recruits on the
island was understood to be outstanding and a model of organization. Nevertheless, Schoepf moved Ahl to command of the prisoners, replacing Lt. W. G.
Rohrman, who, in turn, became the training officer. Lieutenant Ahl was to be
assisted by Sgt. R. H. Lewis as orderly sergeant for the commissary of prisoners. Sgt. Abraham Wolf of Young's Battery became the man responsible for the
deserters. Ordered to report to Major Burton, Corporal Rodgers of Stevenson's
Battery assumed duties on board the steamboat that serviced the island. On
May 4 Sgt. J. S. Black of Young's Battery was appointed sergeant major of the
post, replacing Sergeant Browning, who was returned to company duty.
Schoepf reviewed the work of the post adjutant, Lt. John McConnell, and
decided that he should remain at that post. Captain Kesley continued to serve
as the general's assistant adjutant general, and on May 5 Lieutenant Ahl was
appointed as aide-de-camp. Lieutenant Clark remained the quartermaster and
subsistence officer. Thus Schoepf had arranged the officers of his command to
fill the positions he thought them best suited to perform.

    Once in place, Schoepf's staff began to plan the orderly construction of the
camp proposed by Colonel Hoffman. With the assistance of Engineer Muhlenbruch and Architect John McArthur's plans, General Schoepf turned his
attention to the details of the plans and the organization needed to bring the
work to a conclusion. If the War Department indeed expected to have 10,000
prisoners on the island at one time, albeit temporarily, then the highest priority
should be placed on securing large quantities of drinking water. McArthur's
blueprints called for a system of downspouts to collect and drain the rainwater
from the roofs of the proposed barracks. Some considerable discussion was
devoted to the material to be used on the roofs that would facilitate the collection of water. It was eventually decided that a felt roof would greatly enhance
the drainage. In addition, Colonel Hoffman had, during his visit to the island
in April, concluded that the present construction of the existing prison barracks
had been wanting and suggested several changes.

    Schoepf pressed Muhlenbruch to be sure the changes were reflected in the
new plans and added several suggestions of his own. Schoepf thought that the
new barracks should be physically connected to the existing structures, and he
asked Muhlenbruch to design the ground plans reflecting such a change. He
also determined that special attention be paid to the proper foundation footings, since Pea Patch was still, basically, a mudflat.

    With the receipt of approval from the quartermaster, construction of the
new barracks began in earnest in the last half of May 1863. The design called
for a five-sided wooden barracks: four of the five sides would be the new
construction, with the western side being a double-wide building to serve as

the mess hall. All the other buildings would serve as the living area for the prisoners. The original prison barracks would serve as the home for the lower-ranking Confederate officers. The higher-ranking officers would be housed in the fort on the second floor of the soldiers' barracks. The enlisted men would inhabit the remaining barracks.

Presently a water house, erected over the Delaware River, served as the privy. The water house, sarcastically named "Fort Sumter" by the prisoners, was topped by a large searchlight on a swivel, allowing the guard at that post to direct the light on any portion of the barracks, as well as the river. The water house had to be moved on two occasions prior to 1863, as a result of the changing nature of the beach just underneath the building. The concept of privies was a fairly simple one: The long buildings had seats with holes cut in them; the waste was to drop into the river, and, with the swift running current, be immediately washed away. The first construction was too close to the seawall, and the waste collected rather than washed away. Following the reconstruction of the water house, tides shifted the beach area and eroded a great deal of the foundation holding the piers that served as support for the water house and the bridge connected to it. The house had to be removed, the piles driven closer to the seawall, and the house replaced. With the new construction and the anticipated prisoner population of 10,000, it was apparent that the present privy was not large enough. Rather than expand the present structure, a second water house was planned. The second structure had one significant design change: no roof. This was decided on as a security precaution as the guards could observe the prisoners from the roof of the adjacent water house, thus discouraging any would-be escapee.

The surgeon general had received several reports from inspecting officers that the low level of the island caused considerable miasmatic air, which in turn was the breeding ground for disease. The humidity, the moisture buildup on the masonry walls as well as any wood and plaster structure, and the spongy nature of the soil all combined to create an atmosphere not conducive to good health. Now, with the proposal to house more prisoners, came the concern that the natural unhealthy disposition of Pea Patch would create a slaughter pen where the bullets would be disease. However, since the War Department was determined to convert the island into a holding camp for POWs, the only defense the surgeon general had available was to recommend the erection of a hospital. Buchanan had suggested, and Schoepf concurred, that a second hospital be erected for those with contagious diseases. Quarters for the medical staff were placed east of the general hospital and south of the contagious hospital. The general hospital was designed, on the recommendation of Surgeon General Hammond, to hold 600 patients, while the contagious hospital, or pesthouse as it was commonly called, would house 200 patients. The plan called for the hospital complex to stand on the north end of the island.

Schoepf then suggested that the government erect a third hospital on the land known as the Government Farm in New Jersey, directly across the river from Pea Patch Island. Barring that, Schoepf requested the use of the new U. S. Military Hospital in Chester, Pennsylvania. The health of the command was a top priority for General Schoepf and, after an inspection of the barracks of the post, an order was issued detailing the steps to be taken to sanitize the living quarters of both the garrison and the prisoners. The quarters for the men as well as the prisoners would be cleaned and disinfected; all woodwork, including banister rails, was to be either whitewashed or varnished. The barracks of soldiers and prisoners was ordered to be policed daily. An inspection schedule was put in place, and company officers were responsible for the cleanliness of the barracks as well as overseeing the men on fatigue duty. On May 28 Hamilton reported participation in the cleanup and whitewashing of the political prisoners' barrack located in the second floor of the soldiers' barracks inside the fort. Schoepf ordered punishment for the company that failed to maintain a proper living atmosphere; any company found wanting would be relocated to tents until the men demonstrated a proper understanding of the need for cleanliness. The existing prisoner barracks were disinfected with chloride of lime. Schoepf also ordered a regular schedule for bathing.

While the business of policing the quarters received a great deal of the general's attention, the business of the post as prison compound continued. The spring campaign had begun in earnest and more prisoners were scheduled to arrive at the fort.

As the prisoners began to stream into the facility, Schoepf lost a substantial portion of the garrison. On April 29 the remaining two batteries of the 112th Pennsylvania were transferred to the defenses of Washington. They left on the steamer *State of Maine* along with the majority of the April prisoners. With the loss of the 112th, the garrison now numbered 519 officers and men, present and absent. The reality of the situation, once the sick and the desertion rates were calculated, left Schoepf with a force of 15 officers and 250 enlisted men available for duty. As a result Schoepf was forced to cancel all furloughs until the troops could be brought up to strength. Schoepf also requested reinforcements from his departmental commander, General Robert Schenck, but Schenck was unable to send any troops as a result of the perceived emergency from the loss at Chancellorsville. Schoepf would have to wait for men, but Schenck did promise to do everything in his power to process the POWs quickly. Despite the growing concern about the numbers of men and prisoners, the everyday administration of the post claimed much of the time of the new commanding officer. In an effort to improve morale and regulate the illegal consumption of alcohol by the garrison, sutlers' stands were permitted to serve lager beer between 9:00 A.M. and 5:00 P.M., Monday through

Saturday. The daily allowance for each prisoner was increased to four glasses a day. Schoepf extended the hours to lessen the congestion around the sutlers and to increase the sagging morale of the old-timers still stationed on Pea Patch. But he admonished the garrison to exercise good judgment and discipline, and the provost marshal was ordered to locate two of his guard at the sutlers during the hours of the sale of lager beer. Meanwhile, garrison courts-martial continued to meet. Sgt. Andrew Wunder was found guilty of ignoring a sentinel and using abusive language when ordered to halt, calling the sentinel a "damned camel driver." Wunder was reduced to the ranks. Corp. Daniel Horricks was adjudicated not guilty for a similar offense. Pvt. Abraham Knapp was found guilty of drunkenness and striking his sergeant. Punishment was severe for the hapless Knapp—one month in solitary on bread and water, and loss of pay for one month. Knapp also was forced to wear a red flannel letter "D" sewn to the shoulder of his right sleeve for a period of one month following his release from solitary.

With his first month of command under his belt, Schoepf had made some significant changes in the makeup of the garrison and had redefined the mission of Fort Delaware precisely so everyone would understand what was expected of him. On the battlefront, Federal armies were engaged in vigorous campaigns on all fronts. By June Robert E. Lee's Army of Northern Virginia had begun its second invasion of the North, with Joseph Hooker's Army of the Potomac in tardy pursuit. In the West Ulysses S. Grant's troops had begun the final phases of the campaign to capture Vicksburg and open the Mississippi. The net result of these early summer campaigns was a tremendous number of prisoners, many of whom soon found accommodations on Pea Patch Island. Schoepf had been alerted to the decision to send the prisoners to his post and redoubled his efforts to prepare the garrison. In addition to the anticipated arrival of Western rebels, Schoepf was informed that his department commander, Robert Schenck, and Pennsylvania governor Andrew Curtin, would be paying a visit to Fort Delaware. The garrison was expected to look its best, with a heavy emphasis on battalion drill and formations for review. Philadelphia photographer J. L. Gihon paid his first visit to Fort Delaware, taking the likenesses of Hamilton's company. Evidently he also was hoping to take the images of the governor and General Schenck. Though the visit from the governor never materialized, owing to the imminent threat to his state by Lee's army, the first of the Western Confederates arrived on June 2, 1863. Fifty officers arrived from Fort Monroe with promise of more to come. The fifty were an advance contingent, and following close on their heels were more than 2,000 enlisted men. As the Confederates began to arrive, discipline within the Federal garrison was tightened. Minor infractions were now major transgressions as Federal soldiers were routinely bucked and gagged and placed in the sally port.

Insolent convicts found themselves hanging by their thumbs inside the guard-room, sometimes for hours at a time. The finishing touches were being applied to the soldiers' and officers' barracks—installing the washboards in the kitchens, the wall strips and woodwork, and the window and door trim of the buildings. The engineer team had also begun the counterscarp wall when they encountered a problem that would cause great difficulty for many months to come. The flush-toilet design called for the elimination of waste from the fort's water closets into a privy vault located beneath the fort. The privy vaults, plat-forms where the raw sewage collected, were connected to the moat. The sluice gate, which regulated the flow of water on Pea Patch Island's system of criss-cross drainage ditches, allowed the engineers to flush the entire moat concur-rent with the tidal action of the Delaware River, thus draining the sewage every twelve hours.

With almost 800 people living inside the walls of the fort, the waste removal system was overwhelmed. Most of the soldiers, Confederate officer prisoners, and political prisoners living inside the fort had no experience with the complicated hoppers inside the water closet. With various valves to turn on and off, and smaller pipes to increase the water pressure for a successful flush, the delicate nature of the hoppers offered a particular challenge for Muhlen-bruch. Men used to using an outhouse, where almost anything could be dis-posed of, continued with old habits and often clogged the pipes or backed up the toilets. Along with the heavy use the hoppers received came a buildup of debris inside the privy vaults. The combination of human waste and numer-ous other forms of garbage held the sewage tight inside the vaults, resistant to the action of the tide as the sluice gate was opened. Thus the privy vaults backed up, emanating vapors back into the barracks, and spilling over into the cisterns in the front five. Once Muhlenbruch identified the nature of the prob-lem, the only solution available was to physically drain the moat and clean the vaults and plumbing. The work on the moat began on June 3.

Meanwhile, the barracks on the north end had become a priority and Muhlenbruch's labor force was stretched thin. In addition to the regular employees on Pea Patch Island, the deserters assigned to hard labor and the newly arriving POWs were employed in the erection of the barracks. The wood frame buildings were relatively easy to construct, provided enough hands were available. Sixty-eight Southerners, compensated at the rate of forty cents a day, joined the workforce. The barracks walls were prefabricated by teams of car-penters while others worked on the foundation footings. When a section was complete the teams were brought together to raise the walls and fasten them together. Roofers and carpenters then swarmed over the structure and began placing the support beams for the roof, which was then placed and fastened. Once the building was erect, other teams set to yellow-washing the exterior and whitewashing the interior. Finally, windows and doors were hung and the flooring finished. Iron stoves were installed to provide heat in the winter. The work resembled an Amish barn raising. The village was beginning to take shape, and as mid-June approached three-quarters of the barracks were finished. The timeliness of this construction soon became apparent when Schoepf received word that many of the western POWs would arrive by June 10. General Schoepf had scheduled a social event for June 10, 1863. The new barracks were officially opened, and dignitaries, their wives and children, the officers of the post and their families were invited to a special performance by the post band and a reception inside the new buildings. Beverages were served, toasts made, dignitaries introduced, and speeches made. The gay atmosphere contrasted sharply with the sight of the intended beneficiaries of the new buildings. The 2,000 POWs scheduled to arrive later in the afternoon of the tenth had arrived a day early. Debarking under the watchful eyes of their Ohio guard, the Johnnies grudgingly made their way to the new buildings the night before. They were filthy, disheveled, disease ridden, destitute, and vermin infested. They had been under transport for two weeks, wearing the same uniforms in which they had been captured, and were tired, hungry, and disheartened. But their presence at the fete did not seem to have deterred anyone from having a good time. In fact, the novelty of so many prisoners only added to the excitement as visitors clamored to take a look. Schoepf was feeling expansive when he wired Colonel Hoffman: "One thousand nine hundred and ninety-four prisoners of war were received here last night from the West. Plenty of room to accommodate 4,000 more."[11]

The following day was a reality check for the general. The accomplishment of erecting the barracks in record time and ahead of schedule became meaningless with the condition of the Confederate prisoners. The sober circumstances of the prisoners glared against the background of whitewash as the first rays of daylight touched the barracks. These men were the definition of destitute. Their clothing could best be described as rags. They were not just road weary from their thousand-mile journey, they were also bone tired and sullen. Understandably, their morale was low, and to add to their misery, the belligerents had begun arguing about the wording of the cartel. Their paroles were in dispute, and it was unclear what their status was. Rumors had circulated throughout the POW population that their paroles were deemed invalid by the Yankees and they would be thus confined indefinitely. There was talk of overthrowing the guards, fomenting an uprising, and taking over Pea Patch Island. As word spread of the uprising, it became a plan with timetables and objectives, by the time Albin Schoepf heard of it. In response he doubled the guard, with additional instructions to be ever vigilant for the first sign of trouble. He also issued post orders directing the discipline and obedience of the prisoners. Any prisoner disobeying the lawful orders of the sentinel was liable to be shot "on the spot".[12]

With the completion of the barracks Confederate POWs were funneled to Pea Patch at a record pace. On June 10, 1863, the U.S. transport *Maple Leaf,* a 179-foot side-wheeler steamer, left Fortress Monroe for Fort Delaware with ninety-seven Confederate prisoners. They were scheduled to be exchanged and were being shuffled to the fort for the completion of the complicated paper trail that would lead to their release. The twelve Federal guards of the 3rd Pennsylvania Heavy Artillery believed they were paroled prisoners and would not try to escape. Sec. Lt. William E. Dorsey, commanding the detachment of guards, ordered the men to unload their weapons. Dorsey firmly held that this assignment was a routine milk run, and he allowed the prisoners to freely roam the deck.

Slipping from Fortress Monroe's wharf at 1:00 P.M., the *Maple Leaf* was making good speed north when, five hours into the journey, several of the POWs attacked the unsuspecting guards and soon overpowered them. By 6:00 P.M. the ship was in Confederate hands. The coup was brief and bloodless, with empty muskets as the only defense. Capt. Emelious W. Fuller of the Confederate ram *Queen of the West* took over command of the ship. Fuller, aware of the continued danger, determined to make for the eastern shore of Virginia to abandon the *Maple Leaf.* Upon arrival on Virginia soil, seventy of the prisoners escaped, while twenty-seven decided to stay with the ship. Of those who remained fifteen were sick and the others didn't want to go back to the Confederate army. In Federal hands once again the *Maple Leaf* continued her journey the next day and delivered the remaining prisoners to Fort Delaware. Of course, Dorsey was blamed for the escape and was dismissed from the army. On April 11, 1864, back in the U.S. service, the *Maple Leaf* struck a mine and sank in the St. Johns River near Jacksonville, Florida.[13]

The *Maple Leaf* incident highlighted for Schoepf the reality that his garrison was outnumbered, and he requested immediate relief. Accordingly 500 men of the 5th Delaware Volunteer Infantry, under the command of Col. Henry S. McComb, arrived on June 20 to augment the garrison on the island. The provost guard was increased to 100 men. Any insolent behavior on the part of the Confederate officers earned immediate close confinement. When two Southern officers attempted to return their paroles, stating that they were worthless, Schoepf had them placed in solitary. When he received word that Delawarean secessionists were planning an attack on Fort Delaware to release the POWs housed there, he halted all visitation to the island unless authorized by the general himself, in writing. Schoepf also ended the practice of discharging the weapons at the end of a guard shift, ordering the guards to empty their weapons by pulling the ball rather than firing the weapon.

But the more perplexing problem for the folks on Pea Patch was the sickness of the Southern prisoners. More than 10 percent arrived ill, many gravely ill. The prisoners were in such bad shape that three died within twenty-four hours. To make matters worse only two surgeons were stationed on Pea Patch Island. There seemed little thought given to the care of the sick. Schoepf had available the eighteen-bed post hospital and the U.S. Military Hospital at Chester. But the USMH was not authorized to care for POWs, only Federal military personnel. Schoepf had few options when he wrote to Surgeon General Hammond: "Four thousand rebel prisoners here. Too many sick for two acting assistant surgeons. Please send one or two more."[14]

With the population in such a state, immediate steps needed to be taken to solve the problem. Dr. H. R. Silliman was ordered to the post to assume the role of chief surgeon, whose first official act was to request additional medical personnel. Work began on the new hospital. The present hospital was expanded into adjacent barracks rooms, but it remained woefully undersized. The cartel was still in effect, however, and prisoners continued to ride south for parole. By the end of June it looked as if the worst was over. Schoepf and his garrison had not yet begun to realize the magnitude of the onslaught awaiting them.

<hr />

O n January 2, 1862, Virginia governor John Letcher opened another phase of the Civil War with a threat to Abraham Lincoln.

> I should inform you distinctly of the course I have taken and the policy I intend to pursue. Independent of the forces which have been contributed by this State to the armies of the Confederate States[,] Virginia has a force of her own operating under the command of Maj. Gen. John B. Floyd, by whom there have been captured 201 prisoners, most of whom have been brought to the city of Richmond for safe custody. From these prisoners I have taken two of the officers belonging to the Fourth Regiment of troops under the usurped government of Virginia, to wit, Capt. Thomas Damron and Lieut. Wilson Damron, and have ordered them to be imprisoned in the penitentiary of this State and to be kept in solitary confinement, and I have further ordered that the following privates, to wit, John W. Howe, Isaac Goble and David V. Auxier, who belonged to the Thirty-ninth Kentucky Regiment, and Samuel Pack, also from Kentucky, and William S. Dils, from Ohio, both of the

Fifth Regiment of troops under the usurped government, to be also kept in the penitentiary in solitary confinement, all of them there to remain until Colonel Zarvona is properly exchanged under suitable agreement or discharged and permitted to return to this city.[15]

With that message to the president of the United States the 1863 campaign to get Zarvona back was initiated. However important Zarvona was to the Confederate authorities, their message to the Federal government brought a new dimension to the process of prisoner exchange. Governor Letcher's opening salvo was an initiation of policy so ill considered and unwise, its use would impinge on every phase of the prisoner of war programs. The Dix-Hill Cartel was already showing signs of weakening and of probably collapsing altogether. The increasing acrimony evidenced in the official exchanges between the agents for exchange underscored the preposterous nature of the cartel. The war had gained momentum, and the governments were now, more so than ever, event driven. Because Colonel Zarvona was an important man to the Confederacy, the fear that Zarvona might be tortured into revealing what he knew of the Confederate espionage network led Letcher to select hostages to be held until Zarvona was returned to them. Citing the failure of the cartel, and at the same time using the cartel as a legal force to highlight the illegal behavior of the Yankees, Letcher concluded that he had no choice but to hold men in solitary confinement until Zarvona was returned to the Confederacy. The desired effect, of course, was to convince the Federals that they had violated the cartel by insisting Zarvona was a prisoner of state and should reconsider their mistaken opinion.

Instead the Yankees realized that they had something in the person of Zarvona, and he was watched with more zeal than ever before. A solitary cell, censored letters, no visitors, interrogation, and any number of indignities now became Zarvona's fate. But a more important result grew from Letcher's avowed course in winning the release of his spymaster. American law has as its parentage English common law, which was based on precedent. The act of holding men hostage and declaring conditions for their release opened a Pandora's box of actions, reactions, and retributions.

It was a calculated and extralegal move. Letcher knew that prisoners captured by his Virginia State troops were not subject to exchange under the provisions of the Dix-Hill Cartel. Thus he had in the same hand seven men that would have remained in a bureaucratic limbo in any event; and, of those prisoners, some would be classified as prisoners of state, bringing into sharp focus the very issues inhibiting the exchange of Colonel Zarvona. With his missive to Lincoln, Letcher also made sure to contact members of the U.S. Congress with the Zarvona story. By January 28 the Senate resolved to inquire into the allegations that Zarvona had been held illegally for twenty months and was now made insane by his imprisonment. In February the House received a report concerning the hostages, accompanied by a letter by the hostages themselves pleading for their exchange with Zarvona; seven for one seemed a fair trade.[16] The administration was now under pressure to do something about this case. Secretary Stanton was forced to respond to both houses of Congress not only with reports concerning Zarvona's treatment and mental health, but also with the official justification for keeping him in the first place. The problem for the War Department was not easily overcome.

Now that Zarvona was a case before Congress, Stanton had to be careful. He knew that Zarvona was a spy, but, thus far, had been unable to get much out of him. The dilemma for Stanton and the army was that the evidence against Zarvona was largely circumstantial. They indicted him for piracy, but no trial date had been set. His spying was in many ways preposterous, and no one in Congress was taking it seriously. As the political escalation continued, Stanton assigned Judge Advocate General Holt to conduct an investigation into the entire affair.

Joseph Holt set about determining the facts of the case and was appalled to find that the witnesses had been imprisoned since July 1861—some twenty-one months—and they had only witnessed Zarvona's piracy. On March 18, 1863, Joseph Holt, an accomplished civil attorney, regarded the detention of witnesses by the military authority as wholly unprecedented and illegal. Holt focused on this illegal act and warned the secretary of war that, regardless of the crimes committed by Zarvona, the act of detaining material witnesses against their will was illegal in civil as well as military law. And if Mr. Secretary wanted to pass through this spotlight politically unscathed, the War Department might want to consider reparations for the illegally held witnesses and pray that they remained quiet.

The political pressure on the War Department concerning this matter was proving to be more than Stanton was prepared to handle; still in March he was disinclined to allow the exchange of Richard "Zarvona" Thomas. Somehow, he hoped, Zarvona would break and tell the Federal government all he knew about Confederate covert operations. Thus far the Federals had been privileged to Zarvona's opinions regarding the right of any state to secede and little else. After almost twenty-two months in solitary confinement Zarvona had not revealed anything. The fact remained, despite all the harsh treatment he had received, that the French Lady was not likely to crack any time soon. Perhaps he was as he appeared—a crackbrained zealot who truly knew nothing. Or he may have been a hard-nosed, well-disciplined covert operator who was not about to break. Another consideration became manifest as Stanton had to evaluate the situation; Zarvona had been incommunicado for so long that the value of his dated information was negligible. Anything the Federals might obtain in the future from Zarvona could not now outweigh the continued public detention of Federal hostages. The dilemma for Stanton was now a matter of saving face; the government must find a way to exchange Zarvona without appearing to give in to the Confederates. As the leaders in the War Department puzzled over their options, Zarvona offered the government their face-saving gambit. On March 19 Colonel Burke wrote to Lorenzo Thomas that Zarvona was ready to fold:

> I have to report that Colonel Zarvona (the French lady), now in close confinement at this post, wishes to give the following parole, viz: That he will not escape from the fort or hold communication with any one except through the authorities of the post and that there shall be no secret meaning to any communication so held. He wishes to give this that he may be released from close confinement and allowed the privileges of exercise in the parade of the post. I would respectfully recommend that his request be granted.[17]

Zarvona then offered something even more enticing: He would leave the country altogether, if offered parole, and not return until all had been played out.

Zarvona's offer gave the War Department an opportunity to bow out of this potentially embarrassing situation with some grace. Stanton decided to exchange Zarvona. Colonel Hoffman promptly notified all the parties involved in the exchange process. Zarvona left Fort Lafayette, in chains, on April 15, 1863, and set foot on Pea Patch Island, almost two years after this transfer to Fort Delaware had been requested by General Dix. He arrived, along with a batch of POWs waiting to be exchanged, on April 25, 1863. General Schoepf had been warned by the War Department of Zarvona's wily nature and was prepared to meet him with a squad of guards to ensure that the man remained in custody. Schoepf took a personal interest in the matter, as this particular prisoner represented some important political considerations and was his first important mission at Fort Delaware. He was on hand as the prisoner disembarked from the steamer and shuffled to the entranceway. The general accompanied Zarvona through the process, eventually placing him in close confinement until notification of his official exchange.

Col. Richard "Zarvona" Thomas had finally arrived on Pea Patch. He was on his way to freedom after almost two years in solitary confinement. His health had suffered and he considered himself a broken man. General Schoepf ordered Zarvona's continued isolation. They would await word that he was officially exchanged and then send him to Fort Monroe, where the formal exchange would take place. It was an ironic twist of fate that Zarvona would physically touch the site that had figured indirectly in the planning for his imprisonment. Zarvona had collided with Fort Delaware from the instant of his arrest, directly and indirectly. It was Dix's thought to make Pea Patch Island Zarvona's home, thus planting the seed that would eventually take root. Unknown to the authorities, Zarvona's Potomac Zouaves had been instrumental in the creation and maintenance of the secret passageway to the Confederacy, the path used by Rebels escaping from Pea Patch Island. Zarvona was to stay on the island a short time, and on May 6 he was sent via steamer to Fortress Monroe and was legally exchanged. Although his stay was abbreviated, his case had yet to be played out at the fort. Fort Delaware had not heard the last of the fearless Zarvona.

<hr />

We reach Fort Delaware just about daybreak and after landing we are marched to an open space near the Fort where we are formed into a square, the command is then given to lay everything we have in our knapsacks, haversacks and pockets out on the ground. When we had done this an officer, accompanied by several men, proceed to search our baggage. They take several fine Colts repeaters from our men. Also, pocket knives of a large size, they find a lot of calico clothing and on one person a side of leather, which they take, they have relieved several of their greenbacks and gold and silver.

After the searching is through with, we are marched into the new barracks which have been built expressly for our accommodation. The barracks are built on the plan of a ten pin alley with a row of bunks on each side, three teirs on the side. There is one row of windows on each side of the alley, and those who happen to get a position on the top teir of bunks will ceretainly have a very warm place, as the window does not extend higher than the top of the middle bunk.

I am fortunate enough to get the middle, so I may get enough fresh air, to keep life in.[18]

So ended the journey of Confederate private Thomas Jenkins, one of the first POWs sent to Fort Delaware following the battle of Gettysburg. Jenkins was in the 4th Georgia Infantry and had been captured on July 5.

The Federal victory in Pennsylvania had a profound impact on the residents of Pea Patch. Beginning within days of the battle thousands of captured Confederates were sent to Fort Delaware. By the end of July the POW population had swelled to 12,595, the highest concentration of prisoners the island had ever experienced. A typical journey for a captured Confederate began with a march from Gettysburg south to Frederick, Maryland. Following a short stay in Frederick, the prisoners were transported by rail to Baltimore and thence to Fort McHenry. At Fort McHenry the rolls of the prisoners were transferred to paroles, and once the necessary paperwork was completed the prisoners boarded a packet steamer for the journey into the Chesapeake Bay to the Chesapeake and Delaware Canal, then through the canal to Delaware City, and finally to Fort Delaware. For Private Jenkins, the conditions aboard his transport steamer were intolerable. Evidently the boat had been used to haul animals, the hold being foul with animal refuse. The prisoners were packed into the hold so closely spaced that it was impossible to sit down and the twelve-hour journey from Baltimore presently overwhelmed many of the men. Jenkins, seeking relief from the fumes below decks, was able to make his way to the open deck. The first two weeks of July saw this journey repeated for thousands of Confederates as all the captured men from Gettysburg were transferred to Fort Delaware.

With the additional prisoners the entire population on Pea Patch Island grew to more than 16,000 people; the island had become the largest city in the state of Delaware, eclipsing the population of Wilmington by a few hundred. No one had planned for such an influx, and General Schoepf and his staff were hard pressed to handle the masses coming to the island on a daily basis. The new barracks had begun to sink with the added weight of the prisoners. Schoepf was furious.

Schoepf was flabbergasted to discover that Engineer Muhlenbruch had neglected as simple a matter as making a foundation strong enough to support a building when it was full. Several of the barracks' foundations could not bear the weight of the prisoners and sank to the floorboards. Schoepf wired the conditions to Colonel Hoffman, who, in turn, wired Miegs, who wired Colonel Crosman in Philadelphia. Crosman repaired immediately to inspect the sagging barracks. Sure enough, several structures were shifting and sinking into Pea Patch mud. Repairs were necessary, but the population was so dense there was no place for the prisoners to go while repairs were made. Repairs would have to be delayed until some of the prisoners were exchanged.

The size of the prison population versus the size of the garrison—Confederates now outnumbered Federals ten to one—was not lost on Schoepf who requested immediate aid from his department commander, Gen. Robert

Schenck in Baltimore. Schenck dispatched Col. Samuel Graham's Purnell Legion to augment the garrison at Fort Delaware. The transfer would take time, however, and there were others who had not failed to notice the disparity between jailer and prisoner. As the prison filled with inmates the threat of an escape or prisoner uprising became acute. When Confederate general James Archer arrived at Fort Delaware after his capture in the railroad cut on July 1 at Gettysburg, he took notice of the dearth of guards and began to plan both insurrection and escape. Frustrated and angry over his capture, Archer had determined to make an escape as soon as possible. Ranking Confederate prisoners were routinely processed in the officers' quarters building on the eastern side of Fort Delaware. On July 5, 1863, Gen. James Jay Archer stepped through the post turngate and grudgingly submitted to the paperwork necessary for the proper documentation of a prisoner of war. Once the procedure was complete, Archer, along with several other officers, was escorted across the parade ground, into the sally port, and up the granite stairway to his quarters on the second floor of the soldiers' barracks. The sally port, with the adjacent guardrooms and the rooms on the second floor above it, were originally intended to be stations for the garrison guard and relief guard. By 1863 several of the rooms on the second level were in use by Confederate officers, but the relief guard was staged in the sally port. Members of the relief guard often passed the time waiting for their shift engaging in a relaxed game of chance, chatting with each other, or simply sleeping. All the while their muskets were set in racks lining the granite walls of the sally port. As Archer made his way among the lounging Federals, he took notice of their relaxed state and the number of weapons within his easy reach. Upon his arrival in his new quarters, he employed the same mathematical formula Schoepf had used. And Archer's conclusions were the same as Schoepf's; the Federals were seriously outnumbered. He soon planned to seize control of the weapons of the relief guard and foment insurrection. Archer believed it would be a rudimentary matter to overcome the resistance of the indolent guards he had seen. But his well-laid plans were doomed to failure inside the community of prisoners. Somehow, through an informant or loose talk, the Federals got wind of Archer's plan and Schoepf ordered his arrest and assignment to close confinement. General Archer was taken to an empty powder magazine where he was housed for the remainder of his incarceration at Fort Delaware.

James Archer was not the only prisoner with escape on his mind. But unlike Archer's bold plan to seize control by violence, the enlisted POWs were content to plan a more straightforward approach to ridding themselves of their bothersome confinement. They planned to build a raft, swim, stow away, or utilize any other device that might carry them away from Pea Patch. On July

28, 1863, the conditions seemed perfect for a successful escape from Pea Patch. "Several prisoners made an attempt last night to escape. One was shot dead by the guard and the rest returned to the barracks.[19] Confederate diarist Joseph E. Purvis noted the escape with a laconic reference, "One of our men was killed last night attempting to escape by swimming the river.[20] Thomas Jenkins noted the aftermath on August 3: "They are becoming more strict on us, owing to the fact that several of our men have succeeded in making their escape from this place. There is great sickness and death every day. Oh how hard it is to die in such a place as this after escaping so miraculously many bloody battle-fields."[21] Although the Federals attempted to stem the tide of escapes, they were simply outnumbered. Hamilton reported the transfer of the 5th Delaware and noted that no replacements arrived, leaving 300 men to guard 10,000! Despite the reinforcements in the form of the Purnell Legion, escapes continued. On August 12 a large number of men attempted escape, as the *Richmond Dispatch* reported:

> Yesterday five Confederate prisoners, including A. L. Brooks and C. J. Fuller of Co. G, 9th Georgia; J. D. Marian, 9th Georgia; William E. Glassey, 18th Mississippi and John Dorsey, Stuart's Horse Artillery, arrived here from Fort Delaware having escaped the night of the 12th. They tied four canteens, well-corked, as life preservers around each one. They swam off the back of the island towards shore. It was a dark night. Three of them swam four miles and landed two miles below Delaware City. Two, who did not know how to swim, floated 16 miles and landed at the mouth of the Christine Creek. Another soldier drown[ed] a short distance from shore.

The three at Delaware City lay in a cornfield all night. The next evening they started south. A farmer gave them supper. They then traveled twelve miles and stayed in a barn. In Kent County they were given clothes and money. They took the train to Dover and joined five others who had escaped from Fort Delaware. At Quantico, Maryland, the three took a canoe to Virginia, then the railroad to Richmond. "There was no difficulty experienced in either state in finding generous people of Southern sympathies who would give them both money and clothing and put themselves to any trouble to help them on their journey."[22]

Following the discovery of the drowned man and the recapture of some of the prisoners, orders went out disallowing the retention of canteens by the

POWs. More than 8,000 canteens were confiscated by the Federals at the end of August 1863. Some of the prisoners found a way out of the prison through legitimate means: They volunteered for the Federal service.

Pvt. Thomas Jefferson Price of Company D, 12th Mississippi Volunteer Infantry, was both a prisoner and a guard at Fort Delaware. Earlier in the war Price had been wounded during the Seven Days battle. After recovering from his wounds Price continued to serve with the 12th until the battle of Gettysburg, when he was captured on July 5, 1863, near Waterloo, Pennsylvania. Following a lengthy trip and an extended stay at Fort McHenry, he arrived at Fort Delaware on August 30, 1863. He took the oath of allegiance to the United States and enlisted in Company G, 1st Connecticut Cavalry. In September Company G performed duties at Fort Delaware, while continuing to recruit. Eighty-two prisoners were recruited at Fort Delaware for Company G, 1st Connecticut Cavalry. Price made corporal before being mustered out on November 16, 1865.[23] Needless to say, those soldiers who chose to take the oath were not well liked by the remaining Confederates. It was difficult to concede that a true Southerner would sign "the yellow dog contract." Purvis observed that "a great many of our boys are taking the oath of allegiance and I am sorry to see it, but we can do without them."[24] Jenkins, too, noted in his diary; "I can say that those who have deserted our country are generally men of Northern birth, whose heart never was with our cause and who only have been waiting an opportunity to desert us. They are known as Galvanized Yankees."[25]

George W. Ahl sought permission to form a battery of artillerists who could man the guns of the fortification, which would free other troops to serve as prison guards. His plan was to offer the POWs a way to freedom through galvanization. On July 26, 1863, Ahl's Independent Battery was mustered into Federal service. Of course, this battery of former prisoners could not serve as guards, so they manned the guns, which made available the men of Mlotkowski's and Young's batteries for service as guards. The men of Ahl's battery served through the end of the war.

The convicts imprisoned on the island also had an opportunity to relieve themselves of the boredom of prison life. Captain Ahl, in addition to his command of his Independent Battery, had organized a company composed entirely of deserters. Company Q, as it came to be called, was assigned some of the more onerous tasks about the post, but the men's duty was light compared with the work of the convicts. Still, it was not uncommon to witness the punishment of one of these bounty jumpers on any given day at Fort Delaware. Shackled with the ball and chain, bucked and gagged, or hung for hours at a time by their thumbs, the criminals' confinement on the island were a rough ones at best. Reverend Handy reported the progress of seven of the deserters attached to a plow as they pulled their device through the hardened summer earth in preparation for the construction of a new gravel pathway. Members of Company Q were often given the task of guarding the convicts, on the theory that it took one to know one.

Even as the prisoners conspired to escape, the Dix-Hill cartel ensured that the period of imprisonment would be relatively brief, and the overcrowding of the prison barracks as a result of the Vicksburg and Gettysburg battles was somewhat relieved by August. General Schoepf notified the War Department, through his departmental commander in Baltimore, that the population of Fort Delaware had peaked, and there simply was no more room. By the end of July Schoepf had been able to relocate some 3,600 of the 12,500 total prison population. More than 2,400 prisoners were exchanged, 297 were released outright, 743 men were transferred to other stations, and 111 had died. Although the transfer of so many men offered some relief, the prisoner population still hovered close to 10,000. And they had very little to do. Private Purvis undoubtedly summed up the feelings of the majority of the prisoners when he penned in his diary, "I'm still confined at this wretched place. God grant they may send us away very soon, for this is the last place on earth to me."[26]

A typical day for the POW revolved around the scheduled two meals a day. Beyond the acquisition of food, the POWs had time on their hands—time often spent socializing, writing, reading, or tending to their personal needs. Contact with the Federal guards was limited to their initial processing and the constant observation by the Federals, since the guards were under strict orders to avoid communication with their charges.

Following acclimation to their new surroundings the prisoners were left virtually on their own. "We have a nice view of the river and bay," noted Joe Purvis. "There is always ten to twelve vessels in sight. Some of the boys are catching a great many fish this morning."[27] With an abundance of water, many of the boys took to fishing as a way to supplement their diet and pass the time until their exchange. Thomas Jenkins noted a typical day in his diary: "I arose early this morning and stir around, I find that (in such a crowded place as this is) if a person wishes to be enabled to move about, to wash and to bathe himself, the best plan is to rise early. After a wash in the river, I return to my quarters and read a chapter to two of my Bible. . . . I wonder how many more Sabbaths I shall have to spend in Fort Delaware."[28] And just as the guards were charged with observing the prisoners, many of the POWs spent their days in hard observation of their jailers.

> I learn that General Schoepf is in command of this post, he
> is a Dutchman as a matter of course. They being better qual-
> ified for this duty, than any other nationality of people. The

garrison is an intermixture of Dutch, Irish and Yankee. I hear that Gen. Schoepf is very kind to our men, especially to some of them who were there at work or detail near his house.

The 5th Delaware Regt. is stationed at this place. We get two meals per day, the first about 11 A.M. and the second about 4 P.M. The following is the bill of fare: forenoon, three crackers (sometimes a piece of light bread), a small ration of beef or pork, and a half a cup of coffee. Afternoon, three crackers (sometimes a ration of beef or pork) and a cup of soup. . . .

The fort is surrounded by a canal, which is full of water, our barracks are outside of this canal; then outside of us is another canal and outside of this and extending around the island is an embankment to prevent the overflowing of the island. This embankment is used as a guard line, which is doubled at night. There is a guard posted through the yard, in order to keep the yard clean. The principal parts of the washing is done in the outer canal, and the water is kept very filthy.[29]

The boys found diversion in many ways, from gambling to gossiping, and a community was developing within the confines of the prison yard, known as the Bull Pen. The opportunity to earn some money was also made available to the men. The need for laborers was constant: the engineering projects, general maintenance of the barracks, and the ongoing battle with the tides of the Delaware River offered employment for many prisoners. The pay scale was 75 cents a day to dig ditches. Carpenters earned 25 cents a day, and carrying lumber was done for a small piece of tobacco. The rate of exchange for Confederate currency fluctuated between $5 to $30 Confederate for each Greenback.

The prisoners were a cross section of Southern society, from the tenant farmer to the plantation owner. The youngest prisoner was nine-year-old John Rudd, captured at the battle of Gettysburg while tending to his father's corpse. Although he was technically a noncombatant, the young boy was herded along with 700 other prisoners. When the Federals at Fort Delaware realized his youth, John was offered his freedom, but he maintained that he had no place to go and insisted that he remain on Pea Patch Island with his "family." Pvt. James McGown, 5th Virginia Infantry, referred to Rudd in his diary: "The boy is a general pet among all the men on the island and he seems perfectly contented and happy. He has learned to play all sorts of games with cards, swears and feels much a man as anyone. . . he being the only one who can abuse the

Yanks and they rather seem to enjoy it and to their credit would do a good thing for him. They seem to like the boy."[30]

For General Schoepf the second most pressing problem, after escape attempts, was the health of the population. The implementation of a regular schedule for whitewashing and disinfecting the barracks had become difficult, if not impossible, with the large population. Most of the schedules Schoepf had ordered were disrupted. Even the meal schedule was altered. The mess hall in the prison barracks held 1,000 prisoners at one time, and with the huge population, it took nearly six hours to feed everybody the simplest of meals. The prisoners were fed by division, and each group filed into the mess hall where the individual ration was set up on the mess table, with a Federal sergeant stationed at each table. The prisoners took their places, each man in front of a ration, and at the signal, the men took their rations and filed out of the mess. The process was then repeated.

The Dix-Hill cartel had made it possible to plan a reasonable schedule, however, because it was estimated that the average prisoner would remain at Fort Delaware for a little over two months. The exchange made it possible to rotate the use of the barracks and schedule a thorough fumigation and cleaning. But with the place full to the seams, even the cleaning schedule could not be maintained. Prisoners were remaining at Fort Delaware for longer than the prescribed two months, and the biggest concern was the likelihood that overcrowding would lead to an exponential increase in disease. One hundred and eleven men had died in July; August saw an increase in deaths despite the decrease in population. More alarming, however, was the spike in the number of sick, increasing by another fifth in August. General Schoepf gave Dr. H. R. Silliman, post surgeon, permission to employ the Confederate surgeons in the fight against disease, and by mid-August it seemed that the crisis had passed, as Schoepf noted in a report to Secretary Stanton:

> From my own observation I consider the prisoners of war at this post in as good condition as it would be possible to keep them at any other place.
>
> The mortality is less at the present time, considering the number of prisoners (about 10,000), than in any city of the same population, taking the fact into consideration that the months of July and August are most fatal to exhausted men, as was the case especially with those from Vicksburg.

The surprising influx of vast numbers of POWs had passed with relative ease. The barracks were completed just in time; even the guard situation was a trifling problem. Few had escaped, disease appeared to be under control, and the death rate was low. The operation was running as the general had intended. Schoepf was so pleased with the conditions of the post, especially when compared with April, when he had assumed command, that he invited Governor Cannon out for an inspection at the end of August. What the governor saw was impressive indeed. The north end of the island was now a sprawling military base, with whitewashed fencing, yellow-washed barracks, and a hospital under construction. On the south side, Mrs. Patterson's Inn and Boarding House was thriving, the sutlers were doing a land-office business, and, there were plans for the erection of a house of worship. General Schoepf invited the governor to return to Pea Patch Island in September to participate in the laying of the cornerstone for the new chapel. Governor Cannon readily accepted.

Fall was in the air, and the crisp feeling that seemed to inhabit the very atmosphere buoyed the spirits of the residents. A bright sun shone high in the sky, and the humidity had diminished significantly. Private Hamilton and the rest of the garrison were busy preparing for yet another military ceremony; brass was polished, boots blackened, uniforms brushed, muskets brightened to perfection. The hustle and bustle along the wharves increased as dignitaries and invited guests alighted from their vessels. It certainly was to be an impressive show. The Episcopal bishop, the Right Reverend Alfred Lee, D.D., was greeted on the dock by post chaplains William H. Paddock and E. J. Way. Way, who had been post chaplain since November 24, 1862, had lamented the lack of a suitable site to conduct worship services almost from his arrival. The Reverend William H. Paddock had just recently arrived, taking his post as hospital chaplain in June 1863. Way now had a ready ally in the quest for a suitable chapel on Pea Patch Island. The Reverend Mr. Handy's incarceration there had led to a steady upsurge of religious activities, from baptism to communion, and with the population base hovering at 15,000 souls it seemed a logical need. Way's request met with the approval of General Schoepf, and a fund-raising effort was put forth. Within six weeks enough funds had been accumulated to build the chapel, and at 2:00 P.M., September 12, 1863, the garrison was assembled to witness the beginning of the work their generous contributions had wrought.

As the drums sounded assembly, Colonel Graham's Purnell Legion formed ranks outside of the fort in the open space east of the newly constructed barracks, and the artillery troops formed inside the parade ground. The troops then marched to the site on the eastern edge of Pea Patch in the shadow of the fort. Handy noticed the formation but opted not to attend, thinking it to be just another military ceremony. As the troops took their positions in line of battle, flags snapping in the breeze, the dignitaries took their places, front and center, just opposite the granite cornerstone. General Schoepf had prepared some documents for a time capsule that was to be placed inside the cornerstone. The ceremony began with an invocation by Bishop Lee. His sermon, marking the dedication of what was to be called the Trinity Chapel, addressed what undoubtedly was on the minds of many in attendance. Lee alluded to the religious foundations that all Americans shared, even in the midst of civil strife, and he fervently prayed that the foundation they were setting would be a symbol of the foundations that war had ravished. The Trinity Chapel was to be a Union chapel in every sense of the word. Lee pointed out that people of all religious creeds were welcome in God's chapel and the 800-seat edifice would serve as a symbol of peace and reunion for all who worshipped there. Despite the formality of the military program, the troops and other attendees took comfort in the thought that this symbolic act offered hope, forgiveness, and peace.

Unknown to the participants the time was rapidly approaching when the faith and prayers of every living soul on Pea Patch would be needed. The day before the ceremony, twelve coffins had been placed on the same wharf where Bishop Lee had disembarked. The dead were being transshipped to New Jersey for burial, and although it had become commonplace to see coffins set aside for shipment, the large number was the forewarning of times to come. As Private Purvis turned to his faith to transcend his passage on Pea Patch Island, his observation of the fate of many of his comrades underscored the need for salvation. "Our boys are dying fast, but I don't wonder at it, the way we are situated here. I have formed a Christian Society in our barracks or rather a union prayer meeting."[31] Disease had been the most pressing problem facing all the military commanders at Pea Patch Island since the first garrison landed in 1818. Now, with the explosion in population it was particularly so. Since April, General Schoepf had been aware of a few cases of the dreaded smallpox among prisoners. Those with the disease had been moved to the U.S. Military Hospital in Chester, Pennsylvania, where it was thought the surgeons were better able to deal with it. Since August, however, reports began to surface that prisoners transferred from Fort Delaware were also infested with smallpox. Twenty-six alone had arrived at Point Lookout, Maryland, near the end of August. On August 14 Private Purvis reported in his diary: "I heard that smallpox has broken out amongst us. I hope it is not so, but we may look for that and other diseases of a more fatal kind such as colra [sic] and yellow fever. God grant that we may soon get away from here. August 15: Sickness increases every day I believe and so does wickedness. I never saw the like in my life before and I hope I may never witness it again. August 31: Eight or 9 of us die every day and night."[32] By the time of the dedication of the Trinity Chapel, smallpox had risen to epidemic proportions.

By the end of September 327 prisoners had died, up from 169 in August, the great majority of whom had succumbed to the pox. A little over 8,800 men were imprisoned on Pea Patch Island through the month of September, and a separate hospital had to be erected to quarantine those infested. The contagious hospital was built northeast of the general hospital. Eventually that hospital acquired a grisly reputation among the prison population; the adage became the only exit from that hospital was in a box. The pesthouse, as it was called, took only those patients who were ill with highly contagious diseases. Meanwhile, the military hospital in Chester, Pennsylvania, continued to take prisoners sick with smallpox. Many of those that recuperated at Chester were paroled and never returned to Fort Delaware. Since the sick did not routinely return to the island, the POWs mistakenly assumed that they had died.

In a letter to his wife Sarah, Dr. Washington George Nugent, one of the contract surgeons at the post, apprised her of the seriousness of the situation. "It is a first rate place to see every type of disease. . . . There are at present 660 sick, 156 cases of smallpox, and a case of about every disease ever heard of. There is a very good supply of medicine." Having a good supply of medicine, or a brand-new hospital, or physicians with best intentions was no guarantee that the smallpox could be contained, however. Because the distribution of the smallpox vaccine had been a matter of routine in the North for almost four decades, none of the prison guards became ill. But the Southerners had no such immunity. This crisis was a direct threat to the Confederate prisoners.

In consultation with Dr. Silliman, Schoepf put into effect a new plan. Even the most militant of prisoners, recognizing that the medical force was composed of doctors and nurses, not Yankees and Rebels, agreed that something had to be done quickly. The war was suddenly not between North and South but against an unseen enemy, one more deadly than any man. Orders went out to cleanse each barrack on a rotating basis; the POWs were deloused and vaccinated. From that time to the end of the war any individual coming to Pea Patch—guard, POW, or civilian—had to take the smallpox vaccine. By the end of October the epidemic was over. Schoepf's report noted, "I have 130 cases, mostly of a mild character. The disease is decreasing." In November he added:

> When I assumed command of this post I found fourteen
> cases of smallpox here and it has been prevailing more or less

constantly since that time. The remedies adopted by Dr. Silliman will not only prevent its spreading, but will lead to its
extinction. It is an important fact that within the last two
weeks very few cases have been brought out of the barracks,
the majority having come out of the hospital, and the deaths
reported are not caused by smallpox alone, but by a combination of diseases. The deaths are rapidly decreasing as fol-
lows: The number of deaths on the 5th were 6; on the 6th,
5; on the 7th, 3. This is out of 700 sick in hospital.

Schoepf included in his correspondence Dr. Silliman's report, which explained
the high death rate earlier in the year and outlined the plan he and Schoepf had
put into place to stamp out the epidemic.

> In accordance with instructions received, I have the honor
> to make the following report, viz: There are now under treat-
> ment in the contagious hospital 126 cases of smallpox and
> its modifications. Of these 110 are of the true type and 16 of
> the modified or varioloid. The deaths have averaged about 2
> per diem, but it may be observed that this mortality is not
> due to the character of the disease, but to the existence of
> other exhausting affections, such as chronic diarrhea, &c.,
> prior to its onset. The disease is evidently decreasing, and has
> been doing so for the last fifteen days. On the 15th day of
> October eight cases were admitted, on the 4th day of
> November none, and on the 5th one. . . . The measures
> which have been taken and are still being taken to prevent
> the spread of the disease are as follows, viz: The barracks
> have been cleansed and whitewashed; chloride of lime and
> the Ridgewood disinfecting powder have been freely sprin-
> kled through them; the prisoners are each day turned out in
> a body and kept moving about in the fresh air for several
> hours; vaccine and instruments have been furnished to the
> Confederate surgeons, and they have been sent into the bar-
> racks to vaccinate all they can. I can say every man who has
> not been vaccinated within the last twelve months has had
> the operation performed for him here. In addition to this,
> each man who comes to the post is compelled to suffer vac-
> cination as well as each patient who enters the general hos-
> pital. Under Providence, I think these measures are having
> their effect.[33]

By the end of November every individual on the island had been inoculated against the smallpox. The period of July–December 1863 proved to be the worst for the inhabitants of Pea Patch Island. Almost one-half of all the deaths in the POW population occurred in that time period—1,222 from disease. The average monthly death rate was 3 percent, approximately 203 per month, the average daily rate was six. The dead were interred at Finn's Point in New Jersey, their names and units burned onto the coffin lids.

# Chapter 5

# 1864

*"The sentinel must enforce his orders by bayonet or ball."*
—Gen. Albin Schoepf

The evidence that a new kind of war was in the offing was apparent for anyone willing to pay attention to the turn of events in the last three years. With the opening of 1864 America was entering the third year of civil strife. Millions of men had been committed to the conflict, millions of dollars had been expended, property had been destroyed, and countless lives had been lost. The war, in short, had taken on a life of its own. And life on Pea Patch, however grim and difficult it had been in 1863, faced a new challenge that eclipsed any problem heretofore endured. With the grim, unflinching reality of total war came a transformation of the mission assigned to Gen. Albin Schoepf and the inhabitants who lived in the shadow of Fort Delaware.

In 1864 the prison would remain full; there would be no more fluctuating prisoner population. The mission was no longer to hold men until they were properly exchanged. With the new rules came a forced change in the structure of the population on Pea Patch.

The city on Pea Patch Island required the same organizational techniques that the newly dominant military was using to great effect in the prosecution of the war. The changing fortunes of the war, the collapse of the Dix-Hill cartel, and the increased debilitation of the POW before his arrival at Fort Delaware placed uncompromising demands on Schoepf and his staff. The daily average number of POWs hovered around 9,000. These men were consuming 1,125 pounds of meat, 18,000 pieces of hardtack, and 9,000 small loaves of bread per meal; and 300,000 gallons of water per week. Tons of vegetables, beans, and fruit also had to be privately purchased. "At another time I saw hundreds of men, clad in butternut suits, rolling barrels of pork across the Island toward the prisoners' barracks. My curiosity was again satisfied with the information that was 10 days rations of mess pork for the prisoners. To make a long story short, I wish Jeff Davis and company would only starve our captured boys after the same fashion we starve theirs."[1]

But rations were not the only concern when 1864 saw the end of the Dix-Hill Cartel. With the abolition of exchanges the prison population remained stagnant. The impact on Fort Delaware was profound. Now diseases that had manifested themselves over the long term became acute, with scurvy being the principal culprit. Stephen F. Nunnalee of Co. K, 51st Alabama Cavalry, wrote: "The hospital is neatly kept, and . . . its apartments are as good as we could expect. Rebel ward masters and nurses are retained [and] our sick received pretty good attention; but for six weeks in early summer there was little or no medicine for the hospital, and our men died rapidly."[2] By 1864 the island population had again grown to 16,000. The prisoner of war complex itself, a pentagon-shaped affair, was able to house only 12,000 prisoners. The prisoners' enclosure was hastily constructed of rough boards. A difficult one-and-one-eighth mile swim was all that separated any potential escapees from safe passage to the South through Delaware and down the Eastern Shore. In July 1864, however, few prisoners were in any condition to make the swim.

The spring and summer campaigns of 1864 brought to Pea Patch Island increasing numbers of Confederate prisoners. As the prison population continued to increase, the line between military and civilian life blurred. The monotony of prison routine brought into sharp focus the absurdity of maintaining the discipline required of a military force. With only sergeants as their leaders, young Southern men chose to make their society a reflection of their civilian past rather than of their military. A chess club, a debating society, a theatrical club, and a poetry society all flourished within the prison. Artisans set up shop to sell their wares, and gambling provided entertainment for the sporting man. Jewelers were jewelers once again. The services of a watchmaker were in much greater demand than the services of a gunsmith. Barbers set up shop and offered the latest in European hairstyles. In fact, the only intrusion of military discipline came in the form of the Federal guards.

Early July always brought heat and humidity to Fort Delaware. Although the location on the river brought refreshing breezes, the very nature of the island kept everything damp and musty. The crowded conditions, a lack of natural cover, poor rations, and the misunderstanding of basic sanitary precautions added to the widespread suffering among the prison population. Two hospitals had been erected on the north end of the island to deal with the increasingly sick community of prisoners. Although the smallpox vaccine had resulted in a noticeable decline of the disease, intestinal disorders, fevers, malaria, and common childhood illnesses continued to take their toll on the prisoners. And because so few survived a trip to the hospital on Pea Patch, many deliberately chose not to seek treatment, causing yet more illness.

⟨⟩

The weeks leading to July 7, 1864, brought a great deal of excitement throughout the compound. A rumor had spread among the prisoners that many would be exchanged for Union soldiers. In late June the Federals had begun to collect a list of prisoners for transportation South and possible parole, deciding that fifty Confederate officers would be shipped to Charleston, South Carolina. On June 24, 1864, Col. William W. Ward, 9th Tennessee Cavalry, wrote: "Morning very warm. . . . The List comes. My name among others to go to Charleston. Cols. Duke, Morgan, Tucker & myself, Maj. Steel, Weber & High of our old crowd go. Gens Archer, Stuart, Thompson (Brigds.), Johnson & Gardner [(] Maj. Gens [)] go. Those who are to go to Charleston come up to our quarters. All the rest of our Mess & the crowd who were in the fort go to barracks. . . . Everything is pel mel this evening."[3]

As the fifty Confederates readied themselves for departure, it became unclear if the exchange was to occur or if the Federals had other plans for the prisoners. The selected officers nevertheless readied themselves for their departure and, on June 26, disembarked for Charleston Harbor. With the departure of the "First 50," as they came to be known, life did not return to normal on Pea Patch Island, however.

The demand for able-bodied soldiers became excessive after the 1864 spring offensive. Casualties in the Army of the Potomac alone exceeded 50,000 in the month of May. When the Federal government suspended the prisoner exchange policy, veteran troops at Fort Delaware, once used as guards, were ordered to the front, and 100-day militia units replaced them. On June 6, 1864, the 157th Ohio arrived at Pea Patch Island to replace the 5th Maryland Infantry, which had been ordered to the front. The 157th, raised in Jefferson County, Ohio, had been in the Federal service one month prior to its arrival at Fort Delaware. A diarist with Battery A of the 1st Pennsylvania Artillery noted on June 7, 1864, of the 157th Ohio: "The Ohio Militia are just one Dutch Guard. They are very green. One of their officers was on guard, got so drunk he was put on confinement."[4]

The regiment, commanded by Col. George Wyeth McCook, was green indeed. With barely two weeks of training the Ohio boys found themselves traveling by rail to their first assignment. Colonel McCook, of the famous fighting McCooks, had little time to devote to serious training. With little knowledge of even the manual of arms, the regiment was ordered onto troop transports. The men then set sail across the Chesapeake Bay through the C&D Canal to Pea Patch Island. The lack of training and discipline would contribute directly to the reputation the 157th earned during their short stay in the Union army.

The behavior of the raw militiamen at Fort Delaware was easily distinguished from the discipline of veteran soldiers. Confederate prisoner Lt. McHenry Howard of the 1st Maryland Infantry recalled it as "the difference between bad and good weather." Howard had ample opportunity to observe the demeanor of the 157th Ohio and wrote of their conduct toward the prisoners as "atrocious, devilish in their apparent desire to insult and practice small cruelties." Howard also reported that the 157th regularly confiscated the prisoners' personal property and fired upon them with only the slightest provocation.[5]

As conditions worsened on Pea Patch, the threat of escape or general uprising became more pronounced. On July 7, 1864, Pvts. William Douglas, William Huscroft, Edmund Huntsman, James Adams, and the rest of the members of Company C, 157th Ohio stood at attention and listened as Capt. George W. Ahl read Special Order No. 157. The order, intended by General Schoepf to bring more military discipline to the camp, in effect gave the guards limitless discretion to treat the prisoners as they saw fit.

> The Officer of the Guard must read and explain these orders to each relief of his guard regularly before having it posted:
>
> I. No sentinel must communicate nor allow any person to communicate with any of the prisoners, nor permit any of the prisoners to go outside the limits of their barracks without permission of the commanding general or the officers in charge of the prisoners.
>
> II. It is the duty of the sentinel to prevent the prisoners from escaping; or cutting, defacing, or in any way damaging any of the Government property, or from committing any nuisance in or about their barracks, or from using any abusive or insolent language toward them, and from any violation of good order. Should the sentinel detect any prisoner in violating these instructions, he must order him three distinct times to halt, and if the prisoner obeys the order the sentinel must call for the corporal of the guard and have the prisoner placed in arrest; but should the prisoner fail to halt when so ordered, the sentinel must enforce his orders by bayonet or ball.
>
> III. The sentinels are required to exercise the utmost vigilance and to exact from the prisoners a strict compliance with these instructions, and must always be duly impressed with the nature and extent of their responsibility.[6]

The special order was subject to the various interpretations of the guards, despite the required explanation from the officer of the guard. One private noted, "Our regiment has to guard 11,000 Rebs that are here so we have enough to do as they are pretty stuffy our orders are pretty strict. If the Rebs give us a word of insult, just blow there brains out, or if they stick their heads out of the window why blow their brains out."[7] Captain Ahl spent some time explaining the meaning of the order. He informed the relief guard of their duty should an emergency occur. If a sentinel found himself in a situation where he required assistance, he was to call for the corporal of the guard. The corporal was to assess the situation and, if needed, call for the sergeant of the guard. The sergeant had at his disposal a company of the relief guard to offer reinforcements and bring order to any dangerous situation.

Once the orders were read, the relief sentinels marched to their posts, and a formal changing of the guards took place. In accordance with the 1863 U.S. Army regulations, the regimental adjutant, the officer of the guards, and the guards themselves proceeded, at the quick time, from guard post to guard post. At each post they halted, inspected the relief, and exchanged the guards. Private Douglas was assigned to post number 20. Private Huscroft took up his duties at post number 19 1/2, Private Huntsman manned number 19, and Private Adams was posted at number 21. By 7:00 P.M. the exchange had been completed. Captain Ahl returned with the relieved guards and dismissed them. He then made the rounds on foot, checking each of his guards to ensure that they faithfully carried out their duties.

❧

As July 7, 1864, drew to a close, Pvt. William Douglas prepared to take his guard post. As Douglas was performing his four-hour tour of guard duty, Lt. Col. E. Pope Jones of the 109th Virginia Infantry was making his way to the privy. Jones had been suffering from complications of a battle wound. In fact, his foot had been badly swollen for some time; he could not even put his shoe on his injured foot. With great difficulty, Colonel Jones and a group of Confederate officers made their way toward the water house.[8] During the trek they passed Captain Ahl, who was making his rounds of the guard posts. Ahl mentally noted this assembly of Southern officers as he approached post number 20. Captain Ahl reiterated Special Order No. 157 and asked Private Douglas if he understood his orders. With Douglas's acknowledgment, Ahl proceeded to post number 21.[9]

Colonel Jones emerged from the privy only moments after Captain Ahl had gone. Stopping about thirty feet from its entrance, Jones began a conversation with several of his comrades. The group of Confederates remained in animated conversation for about ten minutes before Private Douglas ordered them to move on. Fully confident that his order would be obeyed, Douglas turned away to adjust a light located on the roof above his guard post. As Douglas turned the large beacon with its reflecting mirror and magnification lens, the beam came to rest on the Rebels, illuminating them in an unnatural yellow glare. Douglas again ordered the group to move on. While they grudgingly walked away, Colonel Jones began lagging behind. Douglas focused his attention on Jones and again ordered the wounded Confederate officer to move on. Jones muttered a reply, stating that he was doing the best he could.[10] Meanwhile, quiet had settled over Fort Delaware. Lights were extinguished and the general noise of the crowded prison had settled into the enforced silence the Federals demanded after 8:00 P.M.

The crack of a single shot and the cry of Colonel Jones broke the stillness at 8:30 P.M. Struck one time just below the right shoulder, the colonel collapsed, conscious but badly wounded. The bullet had passed through Jones's body, entering from the back, striking bone, and passing out through his chest. A small piece of fractured bone also exited his body, causing a smaller wound in his chest. As Jones fell, someone called for the corporal of the guard. The commotion became general as prisoners rushed to attend to their wounded comrade. Immediately upon his arrival the corporal of the guard called for the sergeant of the guard, and the long roll was sounded. Within minutes after Colonel Jones fell, Federal guards arrived en masse, restoring order and sending all the prisoners back to their barracks. The wounded Colonel Jones was taken to Surgeon W. G. Nugent for treatment and admitted to the hospital on the north end of the island.

Doctor Nugent found Jones's wounds to be serious but not life threatening. By 9:00 P.M. the routine of prison life was back to normal. The sentinel's shout of "all's well" punctuated the summer night's air as the prisoners drifted off to sleep. Nugent took personal charge of his patient and was hopeful that Jones would recover. Jones did not rally, however, and died on July 9.

The sensational nature of the case demanded an explanation, and General Schoepf ordered an inquiry. The boys of the 157th already were suspect, given their lack of training, and were perhaps trigger-happy. The 157th surgeon, Dr. William Eames, had reported an incident where one of the men of the Ohio regiment had staved in the head of a prisoner for refusing to obey a legitimate order. With this less-than-sterling record, and because the victim was an officer, a court of inquiry was formed to determine the facts of the case. On July 10 General Schoepf reported to William Hoffman, however, that Douglas had acted appropriately under Special Order No. 157: "As a justification of the act I submit the report of the court of inquiry, which clearly exonerates the sentinel from any blame. Many of the prisoners have been accustomed to insult and trifle with the sentinels because they are militia, and this shooting is one of the results of it."[11]

Although the War Department regarded the vague wording of Schoepf's special order as unfortunate, its overriding concern was the maintenance of order within the prison. Special Order No. 157 remained in force throughout the remainder of the war. There were other matters pressing the general. In Charleston Harbor another hostage crisis was playing out, and the men of Fort Delaware would be the principal participants.

⚜

On the evening of August 13, 1864, Pvt. Alexander J. Hamilton, Independent Battery G, Pittsburgh Heavy Artillery, stood guard over the Rebel prisoners. He was aware of a rumor circulating through Fort Delaware that the next day, 600 Confederate officers would be sent to Charleston, South Carolina. That same rumor circulated among the Confederates, but many believed they were destined to go to their homeland to be exchanged for Union prisoners of war. "What hope! What buoyancy!" wrote the imprisoned Rev. Issac Handy. "How anxious are the thousands here imprisoned, to get back once more to friends and home!"[12]

Four days later the 600 selected officers were still at Fort Delaware. Their spirits were sinking, and the depressing summer heat on Pea Patch Island was not helping matters. Finally, on August 20 Hamilton wrote in his diary that he was "very busy in the forenoon hunting up shoes and packing up things. . . . At 3 P.M. we fell in and marched up to the barracks and by 5 were on board the Crescent and under way."[13] The *Crescent City* was a converted cargo freighter that sailed from New Orleans to Galveston, Texas, before the war.

The refreshing rain of the summer's day at Fort Delaware transformed into a raging storm within twenty-four hours of their departure. "It was raining and blowing briskly and some of the boys take their first lessons in seasickness, among the prisoners below decks it is absolutely horrible. . . . At about 1 P.M. the gunboat Admiral reported herself as convoy and were soon underway enjoying all the ecstasies of Sea Sickness." At 5:00 A.M. on August 22 Hamilton was awakened and "witnessed the beauties of the raging sea. At 9 there was a strong south wind blowing and a good prospect of a storm (This is a most miserable ship to rock.) Our blow ended soon and we had a pleasant run until evening. When we got into Hatteras country we had a little blow. Have not yet been seasick."[14]

The bad weather was the least of Hamilton's worries on August 24. At about 3:30 A.M. the boat's pilot ran aground off Georgetown Courthouse on the coast of South Carolina. "We all believe that the Rebels bribed them to do so," Hamilton wrote. "When daylight came we found our position rather an unpleasant one as we were hard aground almost within rifle shot of the enemy's coast and distant not more than 15 miles from one of his strongholds. . . . The

Johnnies might at any time bring a small battery to bear on us and knock us into a cocked hat. I was very strongly tempted to shoot the pilot but was restrained by Captain Prentice, who told him he would give him until noon to get the board off or he would have been shot. . . . Our Johnnies previous to our getting of the bar were in such a good humor over the thing that they offered to give us our parole for our good treatment of them."[15]

Indeed, the Confederate officers believed the time was right to take over the *Crescent City*. A plan was quickly formed and Col. Van H. Manning of the 3rd Arkansas took command, but the plan failed and the ship was floated and returned to sea. Hamilton's tour of duty with "The Immortal 600", as they were called, ended two days later when he was sent to New York on board the *Truxton*.

The 600 Confederates had been sent to Charleston Harbor in retaliation for the standing of Union prisoners under fire from Union ships. Union major general John G. Foster, commander of the Department of the South, notified Maj. Gen. Samuel Jones, Confederate commander in Charleston, on September 4, "I demand the removal from under our fire of any prisoners of war who might be held by you in confinement at Charleston. . . . I have therefore to inform you that your officers, now in my hands, will be placed by me under your fire, as an act of retaliation."[16] Jones denied that Union prisoners were being held in harm's way.

On September 7 the 600 officers landed at Morris Island in South Carolina. With their hopes for exchange extinguished, those of the Immortal 600 that remained were returned to Fort Delaware on March 12, 1865, where their immortal journey had begun.

⌥⧫⌥

On Dec. 20, 1864, Pvt. John H. Bibb, Charlottesville Artillery, Cutshaw's Battalion, was shot and killed by John Deakyne, 9th Delaware Volunteer. After warning prisoners for throwing water from their windows, Deakyne fired into the barracks and struck Bibb, who had just risen from his bed. After the shooting of Bibb, General Schoepf ordered another inquiry. His report the following day reveals the rising hostility between prisoners and guards.

> I have the honor to transmit herewith the report of a court of inquiry appointed to investigate the fatal shooting of Private John H. Bibb, Charlottesville Artillery, Cutshaw's Virginia battalion, prisoner of war, by Private John Deakyne, Company F, Ninth Delaware Volunteers, sentinel on post. Special Orders, No. 157, from these headquarters, a copy of which is inclosed, has been posted up in all the divisions of

the prisoners' barracks, and as these orders are perfectly
explicit, the prisoners have no excuse for violating them. It
has been a very common and annoying custom with them to
urinate in a tin cup or bucket and throw it out of their windows, creating a very offensive odor about their barracks.
During the last two months two men were shot at, without
fatal result, for urinating at their doors, and this has resulted
in their using the cups and buckets within their barracks and
throwing it out of the window.[17]

Special Order No. 157 was designed to bring order in the prison compound
and to cut down on the spread of life-threatening diseases. The nebulousness
of the order, however, had resulted in the deaths of at least two prisoners.

# Chapter 6

# 1865

*"Our barracks a miniature world is not so much of a misnomer
as it might seem to be at first to the uninitiated."*
—Capt. J. W. Hibbs

The new year dawned clear and bright on Pea Patch Island, offering hope to the residents. The night before had been the scene of a terrible winter storm with a strong wind forcing all except the guards indoors. The nation now entered its fourth year of warfare and, it seemed, an end was in sight. Private Hamilton rejoiced in the knowledge that his enlistment would end in August, regardless of the outcome of the war. Sgt. Bishop Crumrine continued to despair over his inability to obtain a transfer to the fighting front. Meanwhile, the Yankees were hard-pressed to maintain the barest of guard shifts. Part of the 9th Delaware was replaced by the 11th Maryland Infantry, but the number of men assigned to Fort Delaware barely compensated for the number of prisoners to be guarded. In January there was a complement of 7,600 prisoners with a total garrison of a little more than 500 officers and men. The Federals were almost constantly standing guard.

Winter was always a cruel time on Pea Patch Island, but January 1865 was especially difficult. In January a snowstorm developed, followed a few days later by an ice storm. The drafty barracks were difficult to weatherproof and both the Federals and the prisoners suffered. The severe cold weather had disabled one of the two sloops used to fetch clean drinking water from the Brandywine River, and at time the ice-choked Delaware River could not accommodate any traffic. By early 1865 both the prisoners and the Federal soldiers began to see things as a matter of common interest. The prisoners' plight of disease and hunger became the same plight that the garrison faced. Although the guards were not permitted to engage in any intercourse with their prisoners, the commonality of experience hastened an informal arrangement where each helped the other defeat the difficulties involved in staying alive.

Although the community was beginning to come together by 1865, the roles of jailer and captive remained intact. The Federals' primary focus was still maintaining order and guarding prisoners. The jailers, however, were sometimes less than honorable in exercising their authority. Capt. Robert E. Park of the 12th Alabama arrived at Fort Delaware on February 3, 1865. Observing some of the interaction between the POWs and their jailers he remarked:

> "Brig. Gen. A. Schoepf, a Hungarian, is in command and has two unpopular and insolent officers, Capt. G. W. Ahl, Lt. Woolf [sic] as his assistants. The uniformed plebeians delight in exercising petty tyranny over their superiors in prison. Woolf [sic] is generally drunk, boastful and boisterous. Ahl is more genteel in speech and manners but less obliging and more deceitful and cruel. Gen. Schoepf is disposed to be lenient and kind but is terribly afraid of Secretary Stanton."[1]

Lieutenant Wolf was not alone in his fondness of the bottle. Indeed, alcohol had become the routine for the Federal officers on Pea Patch. The boredom and stress of the job tended to turn otherwise well-meaning men to drink to pass the time. This in turn often led to excess on the part of the officers entrusted with the care of both the enlisted men and the POWs at Fort Delaware. The Federal enlisted men frequently found solace in liquor in their off-hours. Payday at Mrs. Patterson's Inn often led to confrontation between drunken soldiers.

Although the prison community had its share of roughhousing and drinking, for the most part, the Federals quietly went about their business, walking the guard, cooking the rations, cleaning their barracks, and in their off hours writing home and dreaming of the day when the war would end. S. W. Hardinge, husband of the notorious confederate spy Belle Boyd, was captured and assigned to Fort Delaware. He noted that prayer meetings and readings were held nightly, conducted by a chaplain or Confederate officer and that "a Young Men's Christian Association was organized some time ago."[2] A community had taken root and it was through participating in this community that many men managed to survive the ordeal of prison. In 1865 Cap. J. W. Hibbs, 13th Virginian infantry, a Richmond newspaper man, organized and developed the *Fort Delaware Prison Times,* a four-page handwritten newspaper. Copied by prisoners, the *Prison Times* contained two pages of advertisements and charged 50 cents to advertise in a square. Barbers, tailors, laundrymen, engravers of rings, and shoe repairmen all offered their services. The *Prison Times* also included news of prison organizations. In his first editorial Captain Hibbs described the community that had developed at Fort Delaware:

A glance at our advertising columns will show that to our barracks a miniature world is not so much of a misnomer as it might seem to be at first to the uninitiated.

True it is that we have not the genial presence of charming women and the very few babies we have here are too old and too large to awaken that sympathy and interest we might have taken in them at an earlier stage of their existence. But excepting the want of these two grand essentials to a perfect world, women and little babies, our prison world is quite a good abridgement of the 'great world' outside.

We have here 'men about town,' 'gentlemen of elegant leisure' many of whom play the games of chess, draughts, etc. with great proficiency and skill. There are also accomplished musicians, vocal and instrumental, who occasionally enliven and charm us with the concord of sweet sounds. The Prisoners Benevolent Association has lately earned and received the thanks of our community by their generous efforts in the behalf of the sick and destitute of our number as will be seen from the statement we give in another column of the receipts of concerts given in the Mess Hall for this purpose.

Owing to the difficulty in procuring the necessary material the next of the fine arts are not so extensively cultivated. But we have nevertheless several artists who display considerable skill in drawing and sketching.

The learned professions Theology, Law, and Medicine have their representatives and though Othello's occupation's gone so far as the practice of Law and Medicine is concerned (our law and physic being imported ready made at present) we have students pouring [*sic*] over the musty tomes of Blackstone or Aesculapius. There are also debating clubs in Divisions 22 and 32. Every Thursday night these clubs hold meetings open to the public and some questions of public interest are discussed.

Then we have the Christian Association for the relief of prisoners. We have time and space to present simply to direct attention to the directory of this most excellent institution which will be found in our issue of today. The list of the standing committees there given will afford some faint idea of the noble objects and plan of operations of the Associations.

We have also in our midst, busy at work, shoemakers, tailors, barbers, washers and ironers, engravers, machinists, jewelers, and ring and chain and breast pin makers. We have seen many specimens of work that reflect credit upon the patience, ingenuity and skill of the workmen.

Thus much for some of our public institutions. We have others which we expect to notice Entemps et lieu.[3]

Later that winter, news that the Federal government had reinstated the Dix-Hill Cartel and exchange of prisoners had resumed broke the monotony of barracks life. In February Private Hamilton accompanied 1,018 POWs to Virginia for exchange. The Federal guard of thirty men under Lieutenant Lewis was accompanied by Dr. Stovall and Hospital Steward Guy Cunningham on board the steamer *Cassandra*. The trip took eight days altogether.

In addition to exchange, the Confederates were also offered release through the oath of allegiance. From the beginning, the oath had been the customary measure by which an individual could gain his freedom. But the mistrust that existed between the belligerents resulted in the allegation that freedom did not, in fact, await those who signed the oath. It took a brave man to step forward and accept the United States government as they were shunned by the Confederates in their community. General Schoepf ordered three Confederate officers to be "thrown in a blanket" in retaliation for their part in doing the same to a Confederate who had signed the oath. In spite of the small numbers of those who took the oath, the Federals continued to offer it as a means of release. On March 19, 1865, Captain Park wrote of a negro slave, Abe Goodgame, in Fort Delaware who refused to take the oath of allegiance to the U.S. government, insisting that he was a good Confederate who was "suffering the same indignities as his Confederate masters."[4]

As spring approached the news that reached Pea Patch was cause for elation or sadness, depending upon the cause one espoused. The war was surely winding down. The fall of Wilmington, North Carolina, and Charleston, South Carolina, indicated only one thing. The North was winning the war. With each victory Schoepf ordered an artillery salute announcing in no uncertain terms the might of the Federal government. Only the most committed of the prisoners entertained the notion of success against the overwhelming Federal forces. Just as the Federals realized that the end was near, so most of the POWs acknowledged that only a miracle would allow them to sustain the battle for another year.

One of the last remaining hopes of the Confederacy was Robert E. Lee's Army of Northern Virginia. Many of the POWs on the island had served in the ranks of that beloved and much publicized force. By March "Lee's Miserables," as they had come to call themselves, had been under siege outside of Petersburg, Virginia, for almost nine months. The conditions for Lee's soldiers had become far worse that the conditions endured by the average prisoner on Pea Patch. The difficult winter had devastated the ranks of the Confederacy's premiere army. If they hoped to survive until summer, this army had to successfully complete a daring maneuver against the Federals. Lee's only chance was to break out of the trenches and to fight the Federals in the open. In late March he attempted just that in a surprise morning assault on a Federal stronghold known as Fort Stedman. Early in the day, surprise had overwhelmed the defending Federals, and the élan of the old Army of Northern Virginia seemed to have returned. But the strength of the Federals was more than the Confederates could bear, and, by nightfall, Fort Stedman was once again in the hands of the Federal host. The last great act of aggression on the part of the South was the harbinger of things to come.

⸙

The long winter of America's discontent was rapidly giving way to spring and rebirth. On the later afternoon of April 3, 1865, the telegraph wires were singing with news of events in Virginia: news that was cause for celebration. General Schoepf, as was his custom, had worked through the midday meal. As his staff toiled over the unending paperwork that had become the lifeblood of organization at Fort Delaware, Schoepf was quietly reviewing the latest communiqués from the War Department. The General had been in the process of preparing a list of prisoners to be forwarded to Cairo, Illinois, for exchange. These mundane details were usually handled by his staff, but this particular exchange involved a case of a highly sensitive nature and Schoepf felt it necessary to review all the particulars before the exchange took place. Walter Pierson had been held in close confinement since being charged with espionage in June 1863. Although in uniform when taken prisoner, Pierson had on his person incriminating documents. Thus he was charged and imprisoned as a prisoner of state and was therefore ineligible for parole or exchange. In late March when Grant ordered the exchange of any person in similar circumstances, Colonel Hoffman ordered that a complete history of Pierson's incarceration be prepared to be included with the necessary paperwork to affect the exchange.

While organizing the rolls and morning reports, the general received the latest dispatches from the Delaware City telegraph office. Without a word, Schoepf abruptly stood up at his desk. His manner, evidently, expressed great excitement, as his staff stopped and stared at their commanding officer. For a moment Schoepf was speechless, simply handing the telegram to Captain Ahl who, on reading it, let out a shout. The very air inside the room seemed electrified as each man read the now much-handled dispatch. Richmond had fallen! Although thoughts were unspoken, each man privy to this astounding message knew that the war was all but over.

Schoepf gathered his emotions and sought to control the flurry of thoughts that seemed to set his brain on fire. He asked his staff into his private office, sliding the pocket doors shut behind them. The general wanted to inform the prisoners of the news in a manner they would never forget. Turning to Captain Ahl, Schoepf asked that the officers of the garrison be summoned to his office, regardless of their state of duty. Ahl saw to the details, sending for the officer of the guard and a squad of soldiers. Once they arrived at the staff office, Captain Ahl, without revealing the nature of their mission, ordered the guard to bring the officers of the garrison to headquarters. It was clear to the soldiers assigned to the task that something of import had occurred.

It was well past six o'clock as the officers arrived at headquarters. With all seventeen members of his officer corps present, Schoepf again closed the pocket doors and proceeded to inform them of the fall of Richmond. Then, in his soft Austrian accent, General Schoepf outlined for each of his officers the details and responsibilities incumbent upon them to successfully accomplish his mission. Within the hour the thousands of prisoners would be alerted to the news with the deafening roar of all 156 guns at service. Following this unusual salute, a copy of the dispatch would be read to each division as well as in the hospital. Schoepf ordered that the Oath of Allegiance be offered to any who were now ready to renounce the Confederacy. In addition, the Pea Patch community would celebrate the glorious news with a cotillion and the band was ordered to play throughout the remainder of the day. Surgeon Silliman was even given permission to open some of the hospital's whiskey stores for distribution. Schoepf told his officers not to repeat the information they had received, the broadside must come as a surprise to the population on the island. The officers were given half an hour to return to their posts and ready the garrison.

Some minutes after 7:00 P.M. the long roll was sounded and the entire garrison scrambled to their posts inside the casemates. The battery commanders had alerted the gunners to prepare the guns for a formal salute. Each gun crew loaded a charge of gunpowder and signaled to the battery commander upon completion of its task. General Schoepf, accompanied by his staff, stepped confidently to the center of the parade ground and watched for the signals from the battery commanders that all was in readiness. Satisfied that each gun was manned and shotted, the General raised his right hand over his head and shouted "Batteries, make ready!" With a last glance around the fort, Schoepf sharply snapped his hand down to his side. In a searing, deafening, acrid moment, all 156 guns discharged their sulphurous contains, and Fort Delaware belched the terrible flame and choking white smoke of war. To the west, the setting sun was eclipsed by the billowing white smoke of the simultaneous explosions. For a long minute the smoke clung to the granite walls and hung over the moat as if the fort were engulfed in a peculiar fogbank. April 3 was a bright, mild day, and had, up to this moment, been uneventful. The sudden eruption of a sheet of flame and billowing smoke, coupled with a thunderous deep-throated boom, demanded the attention of the prisoners. Heads turned, some ducked, others gaped, and still others thought to organize a defense against the attacking Yankees. Even to the least sophisticated, the knowledge that the Yankees had something to crow about, struck each prisoner almost at the same instant the shock wave from the concussion of the guns swept over them like an angry, hot wave.

The dispatch announcing the fall of Richmond was soon read aloud in the divisions of the prison compound. Shock and disbelief gave way to melancholy and resignation as the gallant young men of the South returned to their routine. For the Federal soldiers the day now was far from routine. An impromptu party gathered momentum and rolled from fort to barracks to hospital and back. There had been nothing like it on Pea Patch Island. Happiness and celebration replaced the salute and report. If any Federal officer had attempted to create military order from this evening of chaos, his efforts were ignored.

In the heady hours of celebration that followed the announcement, surely no one appreciated the irony of Fort Delaware's military activities on April 3, 1865. From the beginning she was designed to be a powerhouse, a defensive fortification bristling with the world's most advanced armament. Fort Delaware's sole mission was to rain death and destruction on the heads of her enemies while protecting the garrison that served her. But her state-of-the-art engines of destruction had never been used with hostile intent; no enemy had been able to mount a fleet strong enough to seriously challenge the brick and granite walls. After four long years of civil war the purpose of the military on Pea Patch Island had evolved into the creation and maintenance of a vast POW camp. Now, with the end of the war in sight Fort Delaware's massive weaponry was finally employed, symbolically, to signal the beginning of the end.

But the war was not over. Despite the Federals' elation or the Confederates' dejection, the war continued on its course. The next day, the routine of daily life superseded events, although for the Federals, the fatigue, hangovers, and headaches, stood in stark contrast to the intemperate events of the day before. While their comrades outside of Farmville, Virginia, continued to slug it out against Grant, the Confederate prisoners at Fort Delaware turned their thoughts to their eventual release. Some debated the advisability of taking the "Oath," while others marked time waiting to see what the Federals would do next. On April 10, Fort Delaware was notified that Robert E. Lee had surrendered the Army of Northern Virginia to the overwhelmingly superior forces of Ulysses S. Grant. General Schoepf ordered a 225-gun salute to be fired at intervals throughout the day. So now it was official, the war, as far as the volunteer guards and prisoners were concerned, was over. But it was not over; Lee's army was not the Confederacy. President Davis remained at large, an army under Joe Johnston still defiantly faced Sherman, the Confederacy west of the Mississippi—known as Kirby Smithdom—was bowed but not broken, and small pockets of Southern defenders remained a very real threat to the Federal government.

On April 15, 1865, the Delaware City telegrapher was dozing at his key. He had arrived early to work, noted that the weather promised another fine spring day, and proceeded to organize his day's work. Since the surrender of Lee, his key was not nearly as busy as it once had been. Around 8:00 A.M. the clackity-clack of the telegraph startled the telegrapher from his reverie. The message from the War Department indicated some urgency. The operator was shocked to read the news and immediately summoned the dispatcher to take the message to General Schoepf. The president of the United States of America had been shot and mortally wounded the previous night while attending the theater. Abraham Lincoln died at 7:30 A.M. in a rooming house across the street from Ford's Theater. The tragic news was delivered to Pea Patch Island within two hours of the actual event. Schoepf was visibly shaken when he received word of the assassination, but his duty drove him to respond professionally. He placed the garrison on alert, ordered the flag to be lowered to half-mast and a signal gun to be sounded at intervals throughout the day. A formal announcement was made to the garrison and prisoners of war, but the word had already spread.

Reaction to the news varied, but most were greatly disturbed by the news. In the prison barracks, however, a few Confederates began to organize a celebration. The Federal response to such rejoicing was immediate and unconditional. On board the *Oceola,* a longtime deckhand and ardent Democrat made the mistake of revealing his feelings about the assassination to anyone who would listen. He exclaimed that Lincoln "was a God damned, nigger loving, son of a bitch who ought to have been killed a long time ago."[5] As soon as one of the officers heard him the deck hand was promptly arrested and taken to General Schoepf's office. When he and his guard arrived, they were led into the staff office and told to wait. Inside the general's private office, Schoepf was informed what the culprit had said and, in a moment of anger, he took two strides toward his intended victim and slapped him across the face. Turning to his staff, Schoepf ordered that the prisoner be shaved, placed in irons, and rowed by two black laborers to Delaware City.

Aside from the immediate emotional impact of the assassination upon the residents of Pea Patch, an indirect and unknown connection existed as well, although the facts relating to the case would remain undiscovered for more than a century. Prior to his arrest and imprisonment, Colonel Zarvona, né Richard Thomas, had been instrumental in organizing a regiment known as the Potomac Zouaves. This unit, composed of men from the Eastern Shore of

Maryland and Virginia, never took the field as a combat unit. Eventually they were amalgamated with the 47th Virginia Infantry, a regiment that played a vital role in Lincoln's assassination. Although Zarvona himself was a physically broken man upon his exchange from Fort Delaware, his legacy of covert operations lived on through the war. An elaborate Confederate espionage network operated on the Eastern Shore. A system of safe houses was in use to transport escaped prisoners, spies, and matériel to the Confederacy. Several homes in Delaware City marked the northern terminus of the network. From there, traveling by night and concealed by day, the escaped prisoner would make his way to the Virginian eastern shore and thus into the Confederate States of America. Despite repeated attempts by the Federal authorities to crush the network, the system was remarkably successful. As Albin Schoepf was striking the deckhand of the *Oceola,* John Wilkes Booth and David Herold were using this network to evade capture.

The previous year the Confederate government had set in motion a plan that would have appealed to the commander of the Potomac Zouaves. The breakdown of the Dix-Hill Cartel had created a severe manpower shortage for the Confederate armed services. Thousands of able-bodied Southern soldiers were in POW camps throughout the North and they would not be rejoining the active field armies. While the Federal government could afford to lose thousands as POWs, the Confederacy could not. As the Confederacy's continued existence relied on the fighting man, the loss of exchanged prisoners was a crippling blow. It was determined, at the highest level of Confederate government, that a covert operation should be initiated with the aim of kidnapping President Lincoln. Holding the President as hostage could effect the release of hundreds of thousands of Confederate POWs. The success of this complicated operation was placed in the hands of the actor/spy John Wilkes Booth. Booth had been employed by the Confederate Secret Service since at least 1863. The covert operation relied not only on the skills of Booth and his operatives, but also on the services of Zarvona's Potomac Zouaves. A methodical, phased plan was designed to ensure success. Booth and his henchmen would carry out the actual kidnapping, while the others would carefully select and guard the escape route.

The Confederates knew that the Federals would pursue the prize, Abraham Lincoln, with vigor and resolution. Once the government realized that Lincoln had been kidnapped, the army would very likely target the Eastern Shore, the safest route to the South. Confederate troops would have to be close by to fight off the Yankees and the 47th Virginia was poised to be just such a force. The only glitch was that the Federals controlled the Eastern Shore. Zarvona's men could not be sent to the area as an organized body of troops, but they could be sent home in twos and threes. The 47th would wait at home, with orders to assemble at a prearranged location should the need arise. Booth and his team, along with the captured Lincoln, would make use of the safe houses, while an organized force protected their rear. The complicated nature of the planning, including distribution of money and the transfer of men, delayed the execution of the plan. Booth's initial attempt at the kidnapping was aborted at the last minute. Although his first attempt failed, Booth resolved to try again. The men of the 47th would remain in place, awaiting developments as the Booth team regrouped.

The events of the war abruptly changed the nature of Booth's mission. Following the surrender of the Army of Northern Virginia, members of the 47th Virginia surrendered en masse. Without the manpower to support a risky kidnapping attempt, Booth decided to attempt an assassination. The Booth team would strike out at the heads of the Federal government, targeting Lincoln, Johnson, and Seward. As Jefferson Davis and the remains of the Confederate administration fled south, evading Yankee pursuit, John Wilkes Booth shot Abraham Lincoln in the back of the head. The other members of Booth's team failed in their missions to execute the vice president and the secretary of state. Booth and his companion, David Herold, used the network and managed to evade capture until they were 150 miles south of Washington.

Col. Richard Thomas, alias Zarvona, alias the French Lady, had set in motion a series of events that had now come full circle. By conceiving the idea of a covert operations battalion, Zarvona had established the links needed to possibly kidnap and ultimately assassinate the head of state of his enemy's nation. The impact of the assassination on Fort Delaware cut deep. The initial elation of the POWs was crushed and, as the days moved forward, it was apparent that the murder of Abraham Lincoln served only to lengthen the stay of the prisoners.

At the beginning of April the prisoner population of Fort Delaware was 7,676 with an additional 899 arriving after the assassination. By the end of the month 88 had been exchanged and 120 had been released. With the deaths of 106 prisoners, Pea Patch Island's POW population stood at a staggering 8,261 in May 1865. The United States of America may have been made whole by force of arms, but the legacy of warfare was distrust and suspicion. Even the long-standing policy of unconditional release upon taking the oath of allegiance was altered until officials cleared the Confederate government in Lincoln's murder. With Jefferson Davis and most of his government still at large and desperately in need of manpower, a general release of POWs was far too risky. So it was that the majority of the prisoners remained in place, enduring the monotony of life on Pea Patch Island.

Spring brought welcome news to the occupants of the prison compound. The collapse of the Confederacy was all but complete, and with the seizure of the Confederate State documents, it was determined that there was little evidence to implicate the leadership of the South in the assassination. The War Department had conducted a thorough study of the data, searching for a link to Lincoln's murder. They had overlooked, or perhaps misunderstood, references to a covert operation called "Come Retribution"—the plot to kidnap the president of the United States. In any event, authorities in Washington concluded that the Confederacy was not responsible for the assassination. With that obstacle cleared, the fiscal impropriety of holding thousands of men as prisoners of war, after the war was over, became evident to the government. Accordingly, on May 8, 1865, all POWs below the rank of colonel were declared exchanged and ordered to be released. The U.S. government would also assume the responsibility of transporting the former prisoners to their homes. Orders were prepared and sent to the various prison camps in the North.

General Schoepf had anticipated such an order and had Captain Ahl and his staff at work preparing the rolls for the release of his charges. The physical release of Fort Delaware's 8,000 prisoners would be a complicated task. Aside from the paperwork involved, Captain Clark had to arrange transportation for each prisoner. Clark was also in competition with all the Federal stations in the Northeast for the necessary transports. Arranging these details took time, and while most prisoners were content to wait, some had run out of patience. The vigilance of the Federal troops posted at Fort Delaware had become lax; they too were waiting for orders that would release them from service. Many of the men had concluded that since the war was over, they were free to behave as civilians and, in a few isolated cases, seek redress for grievances they held against their officers. Captain Young was the notable victim of what amounted to teenage rowdyism. The boys had felt, from the beginning, that Young had taken a high-and-mighty air with them. With their impending release from service, they took offense at Young's continued military demeanor. Scoffing, ridicule, and behavior bordering on mutiny became Captain Young's lot as the month of May passed. Eleven POWs decided to avoid the red tape altogether. The preoccupation of the Federals with their own circumstances and the relaxation of the strict military regimen made it easy for them to escape. They were the last prisoners to escape from Pea Patch Island.

On May 10, 1865, President Jefferson Davis and his entourage were apprehended in Georgia, marking the true end of the Confederacy. Against impossible odds, Davis had led an infant nation through the inferno of war, armed with what at times seemed to be only his determined will. Davis was defiant to the last, attempting to rush an armed cavalry trooper who was aiming his carbine at him. Davis's defiance and will would find a source of oxygen to keep the embers glowing in the ashes of his government. Davis's entourage was split up: Jefferson Davis and Clement Clay, now prisoners of state, were ordered to Fortress Monroe; Burton Harrison, his private secretary, was ordered to Old

Capitol Prison in Washington; Vice President Alexander Stephens and Post-master General John Reagan were ordered to Fort Warren in Boston Harbor (now under the command of Maj. A. A. Gibson); General Wheeler and his staff, Colonel Lubbock, and Colonel Johnston were remanded to Fort Delaware.

As the first batches of POWs were being released, those of Davis's group arrived at Pea Patch on May 22, 1865. No specific orders arrived with these important prisoners, so Schoepf quartered them together on the second floor of the soldiers' barracks. The following day, the War Department wired General Schoepf with orders placing his new prisoners in solitary confinement. The prisoners were not to be permitted to communicate with one another. Upon receipt of this communiqué the prisoners in question were thus confined. Joining them was Maj. Henry Kyd Douglas, formerly on the staff of Stonewall Jackson. Douglas had been arrested in his native Maryland for wearing his Confederate uniform after the surrender of Lee's army.

Meanwhile, the tedious job of processing the POWs continued. On the last day of May the contingent of the 11th Maryland infantry, then serving as guards, was replaced by Col. T. Asbury Awl's 201st Pennsylvania Volunteer Infantry and Col. Francis Wister's 215th Pennsylvania Volunteer Infantry. More than 1,100 prisoners had been released, some taking the oath of allegiance, others simply opting for the status of exchanged prisoner. Initially confusion over the status of those incarcerated created additional delays. The problem stemmed from a misunderstanding of the wording of the War Department order that classified those prisoners who had been paroled as exchanged. It was unclear if the newly exchanged prisoners had to wait for the paperwork to be processed before they were released or if it was only necessary to arrange transportation for them to the South. Eventually their status was set as exchanged and they were released as soon as transportation could be arranged. Delays in processing backed up the release of the ex-POWs and it was not until June that the majority of the Southern soldiers were able to leave the island.

The soldiers of Fort Delaware's garrison were also among those leaving Pea Patch. Captain Young's Battery G was ordered to Harrisburg for discharge on June 8. As they boarded the transports for their trip home, Private Hamilton, Sergeant Crumrine, and the other members of the battery made their final military formation on Pea Patch and offered three cheers for the officers who had been there since August 1862. General Schoepf followed the frenzied and heartfelt huzzahs with a speech thanking them for their faithful service to their country. Schoepf wished them godspeed and bade them farewell. Captain Mlotkowski's Battery A, which had been at Fort Delaware since August 1861, mustered out of service on June 30, 1865. A similar farewell occurred on the dock east of the fort.

By the end of July almost all of the 8,200 Southerners had been released and transported to their homes. Major Douglas and the members of Davis's entourage, with the exception of Frank Lubbock, were released on terms granted in General Johnston's surrender. In mid-July, as thousands of men waited at the wharf to begin their long journey home, a solitary prisoner of state arrived from Washington. Burton Harrison, the private secretary to President Davis, had been remanded to Fort Delaware for safekeeping. As Harrison was climbing onto the well-trod wharf, thousands of his countrymen were making their way onto waiting steamers for the journey south to freedom. By July 28, 1865, all able-bodied prisoners had been processed and released. Only Harrison and the sick remained in the care of the U. S. Government. Among the sick was Thomas Jowers, a nineteen-year-old South Carolinian who had joined the Confederate service in the 1st South Carolina Infantry, Company H, on May 23, 1863. He had been captured at the Battle of Bentonville in North Carolina on March 19, 1865. Jowers had been ill when he arrived at Pea Patch and was quartered in the post hospital in April. On July 30, 1865, despite the best efforts of the surgeons, Jowers died. He was the 2,460th prisoner to die while incarcerated at Fort Delaware and the last POW to die on Pea Patch Island.

<hr />

With the release of the prisoners and the mustering out of the volunteer forces, General Schoepf turned to his last remaining responsibilities. The administration and paperwork of his department had to be put in order, decisions had to be made regarding the hundreds of now-empty buildings on Pea Patch, and final accountings had to be prepared. Fort Delaware was now what she had been meant to be, a defensive fortification guarding Philadelphia. Captain Ahl's Independent Battery, composed mostly of galvanized Confederates, was on duty manning the guns of the fort. Evidently, some of the soldiers became embroiled in a dispute with the citizens of Delaware City. In August many of them had threatened vengeance on the more prominent citizens upon their release from Federal service. The town authorities complained to General Schoepf about this plot, naming the offending soldiers in their complaint. Schoepf responded by sending the soldiers in question to Wilmington and mustering them out of the army. The remainder of Ahl's battery was mustered out within a week. The 201st and 215th were discharged at the end of July, replaced by the 196th Ohio Volunteer Infantry in early August. They were detailed to guard the fort's only remaining prisoners, Burton Harrison and Frank Lubbock.

Harrison remained an inmate simply because he was the private secretary of Davis, Lubbock because of his intimacy with the Confederate president. The government was entirely unclear in its course of action regarding the former president of the Confederacy. While President Johnson vacillated on the propriety of a trial for Davis, Harrison and Lubbock continued to be kept in close confinement on the second floor of the soldiers' barracks. The War Department made clear that Harrison be permitted no privileges, not even the use of the post library. It was a universal opinion on the part of the Federal soldiers stationed at Fort Delaware that Harrison's treatment was unjust and uncalled for. Small kindnesses were afforded him, but little could be done to bring Burton Harrison comfort. In the course of his incarceration Harrison was engaged in many conversations with the commanding general. Schoepf had come to respect Mr. Harrison's stoic demeanor, characterizing him as the perfect gentleman. But even the general's good opinion could do little for the release of Harrison.

Frank Lubbock, too, remained in close confinement. Lubbock was permitted no communication with Harrison. Lubbock took his meals in his cell. There were no charges against Colonel Lubbock and his role as companion of the fleeing ex-president of the Confederacy was nebulous. In effect there was very little to be gained by his continued incarceration. Accordingly, Lubbock was released in November 1865. An order from the War Department dated November 23 declared:

> The President of the United States directs that F. R. Lubbock, a prisoner confined at Fort Delaware, be released on taking the oath of allegiance to the Government of the United States prescribed in the amnesty proclamation of President Johnson, and giving his parole to proceed to the place of his residence and remain there to abide the orders of the President of the United States. Transportation will be furnished him to his place of residence. You will please report the receipt and execution of this order and the place to which Colonel Lubbock proposes to go.[6]

Now only Burton Harrison remained. Prior to the end of the war, Harrison had become engaged to Miss Constance Cary. Miss Cary was residing in Baltimore and had not heard from her fiancée for several months; in fact, she had assumed that he was still at Old Capitol Prison in Washington. Following his release in late July, Major Douglas was able to deliver to Miss Cary several letters from Harrison informing her of his imprisonment at Fort Delaware. Constance was determined to see that her future husband was well treated and moved, with her mother, to Woodbury, New Jersey. She decided to go to Pea Patch and make an effort to enter the fort. In a diary entry she recorded the details of her experience:

From the village on the opposite shore of the Delaware River we sailed in a leaky fishing boat across a roughening, swelling tide. Arrived at the moated fortress on the bank, we sent in our cards by a soldier to the commandant. To our delight no question was made about receiving us and crossing a bridge to enter the gloomy corridors, we were soon in the presence of the redoubted chief. Had I divined the general's kind heart was already enlisted for the prisoner . . . then I should not have been so faint hearted. The general asked my mother if she could trust him to show me the interior of the fortress. He led, I followed to a door opening on the inner court where bidden to look toward the battlements, I saw my prisoner standing indeed between two bayonets in a casemate but alive and well, waving his hat like a school boy and uttering a great, irresponsible shout of joy.[7]

The Schoepfs developed an intimate friendship with Burton Harrison and Constance Cary. Throughout the period of his incarceration Harrison's only social intercourse was with General Schoepf. Efforts were made to secure Harrison's release, but as late as November 1865 his case remained in limbo. A letter to President Johnson from a Baltimore solicitor outlined the case for his release:

Among the number of those now in confinement for having participated in the late rebellion is Burton N. Harrison, of Mississippi, private secretary to Jefferson Davis. Mr. Harrison occupied the position of assistant professor in the University of Mississippi when that State seceded, and, as would have been the case with most young men, felt highly flattered at the, to him, honorable position which was offered him by Mr. Davis. Suffice it to say he accepted. Mr. Harrison is a graduate of Yale College, an Old Line Whig, and conservative in his politics, and was esteemed and honored by his classmates and all who knew him for his gentlemanly feeling and high sense of honor. I therefore entreat Your Excellency that that freedom from confinement which has already been granted to so many men of more influence in the political world than he may be granted to him. He is at present, I believe, in Fort Delaware. I address myself to Your Excellency from no desire for notoriety, but from friendship and affection for my friend and classmate, who appears to have been forgotten by his friends. I would add that he is the only son of a widowed mother, to whose support he has always contributed.[8]

While the Harrison case remained unresolved, General Schoepf was dealing with the deconstruction of the POW camp he had been instrumental in erecting. The prison barracks were of little use to the postwar government and thus it was decided to dismantle them and sell the lumber. The process took some time, but by winter the barracks were gone, with most of the usable lumber sold to private citizens in Delaware. Following some debate about the usability of the hospitals, they too were dismantled and sold for scrap. The hospitals were thought to be viable until an inspection revealed the presence of vermin. In September the last of the volunteer troops were discharged, replaced with two companies of the 4th United State Artillery. The Schoepfs had made a decision to return to civilian life and purchase a farm in Maryland. In November they had agreed on a property in Hyattsville, Maryland, and had begun making preparations for their move. The last of Fort Delaware reports were complete in December. The prison had received 32,305 prisoners during the war. Of those, 2,460 had died from various diseases, smallpox being the principal killer, with scurvy a close second. Seven prisoners had been shot; one in violation of Special Order 157, two attempting to escape, and the rest by accident. The prisoner fund retained a balance of $316,000. The immense amount of food and clothing issued to the POWs was categorized and accounted for. In February 1865 alone, the prisoners at Fort Delaware received 1,686 blankets, 1,086 coats, 1,776 pairs of pants, 1,340 shirts, 1,448 pairs of underwear, 1,656 pairs of socks, and 1,475 pairs of shoes—all from private donations.[9] The enormous undertaking on the part of the Federal government was drawing to a close.

For Schoepf but one problem remained: Burton Harrison. Harrison's case was in the hands of Judge Advocate Holt by December of 1865. Whether or not he was an active traitor or simply an innocuous functionary was a matter of great debate. Holt's conclusion leaned toward the former. Holt stated his case in a December 21 report to the secretary of war:

> In the case of Burton N. Harrison, rebel, referred to me for report by your order of the 20th instant, I have the honor to submit as follows:
>
> This person is well known to the history of the rebellion as having occupied the position of private secretary to Jefferson Davis, with the military rank of colonel. In this close and confidential capacity he continued, even after the collapse of the military power of the insurgents and up to the very last moment of the life of the so-called Southern Confederacy, having been captured with his fugitive chief at Irwinville, Ga., on the 10th of May last. It is thus perceived that his fortunes were inseparably associated with those of

his principal in treason, and that his case could not Indeed be justly considered apart from that of the other. But it is not alone from the fact of this intimate and continued association with Davis that his relations to the latter as a criminal and traitor and his joint responsibility with him in his crimes are to be ascertained.

Holt continued by citing a letter to President Davis from a Confederate officer, Lt. W. Alston, in which Alston alludes to the plot to assassinate the heads of the Federal government. Harrison had provided the following referral to the Confederate secretary of war:

Lieut. W. Alston, Montgomery Sulphur Springs, Va. [No date.] Is lieutenant in General Duke's command. Accompanied raid into Kentucky and was captured, but escaped into Canada, from whence he found his way back. Been in bad health. Now offers his services to rid the country of some of its deadliest enemies. Asks for papers to permit him to travel within the jurisdiction of this Government. Would like to have an interview and explain.

By his referral, Holt claimed, Harrison was fully aware of and in support of the plot. He continued:

If he had not been himself an assassin at heart he would have shrunk from furthering such a villainous undertaking, and would have exposed and denounced it, as well as its author. Instead of this he becomes, without a scruple, the instrument by which this fiendish project is made to receive the grave consideration accorded to an important State paper, and as a man of intelligence and education, and in view of the position which he occupied, he must be held personally responsible for the sanction thus awarded to its proposals.

Lastly, Holt acknowledged a recent appeal for Harrison's freedom made by powerful politician Frank Blair, a relative of Constance Cary. Holt concluded with his recommendation:

In view of the facts surrounding the case of Harrison it is feared that the Government would gravely compromise itself by complying with this recommendation, which indeed would be ludicrous were it not for the strange insensibility which it manifests to the revolting guilt with which this man's name is connected. . . . No exercise of Executive clemency, therefore, can be advised in this case, and as for the application to be paroled, which invariably accompanies such communications, it can no more be recommended that this should be granted than that a full pardon should be acceded. To ask that faith be reposed in a party resting under imputations not only of the deepest dishonor and the most intense disloyalty, but also of the gravest crime, is, it is submitted, as unconscionable as it would be unfortunate for the Government to favorably consider such a request.[10]

But in spite of Mr. Holt's objections, the case of Burton Harrison was finally reaching a resolution. Evidently Mr. Blair's political clout outweighed any other consideration on the part of the government. Burton Harrison was scheduled for release. Accordingly, on January 16, 1866, Burton N. Harrison became the last prisoner to be released from the confines of Fort Delaware. By request, he was transported to Richmond, Virginia, where he intended to continue to fight to free Jefferson Davis. Harrison had made his farewells to General and Mrs. Schoepf the day before. General Schoepf was mustered out of the Federal service on the fifteenth and he and his family made passage to Baltimore to begin a new life. The parting of Harrison and Schoepf must have been an emotional scene. They had become quite close in the last six months of 1865. So close, in fact, that Schoepf would name one of his sons after his esteemed friend. Burton Harrison Schoepf was born on February 11, 1877.

# EPILOGUE

*"Were you looking to be held together by lawyers?*
*Or by an agreement on a paper? Or by arms?*
*Nay, nor the world, nor any living thing, will so cohere."*
                                                    —Walt Whitman

As Burton Harrison made his way back home, he witnessed the devastation wrought upon the land and upon its peoples. And for his people the devastation was complete and uncompromising. The War of Northern Aggression was now a memory. The South had fought. She had given a fourth of her male population to feed the beast. Her major cities had become pyres to the "lost cause." Southern leadership, representatives of the political, economic, and intellectual power of the Confederacy, were exiled, imprisoned, or dead. The Yankees, if not God, had trampled out the vintage with a terrible swift sword, and now visited the region as the locusts of the Old Testament. For Burton Harrison, for those who bore the battle, for those who had sustained the warriors, for the widow and the orphan, the events of the last four years were now surreal, emotional, and unforgettable. To be sure the disenfranchised citizens of the South endured daily reminders of the power of the central government and would continue to be so reminded for many years to come. But the high drama born of the crucible of war was no longer part of daily life—no more the sight of the boys, confident, bright, in perfect stride passing to the front; no more the sight of the stainless banner; no more the raw unbridled power of victory; no more the vision of broken lads laid in rows; no more the events which promised hope—only memories.

And so it had become throughout the reunited nation. The events that had consumed the emotions of all Americans were no longer tangible, and as time passed all that occurred became collections of thoughts and experiences told and retold. The physical healing of the body would be complete in a comparatively short span, but the emotional memory would require generations to mend. Throughout the land the stories of the great and small were told to an

147

increasingly eager audience. In the decades following the war thousands of books, periodicals, and newspaper stories dealt with the experience of the people in the War, "of the Rebellion," "of Northern Aggression," "the late unpleasantness," and the dozens of other monikers hung upon the Civil War. For Victorian America this was the healing. But, as in all things, the stories changed with the retelling. The history of the Southern Confederacy, told in countless parlors in the postwar years, was set to print by none other than Jefferson Davis and served for at least three generations of historians as the foundation upon which the remembrance of the Confederacy rested. Davis's story portrayed a government of nobility representing a noble people in pursuit of righteousness. The Confederacy's story would ever after be known as the "Lost Cause," enshrined in the hearts of generations of Americans. In many ways the old adage, "The South shall rise again," had become prophecy. Through Davis's work the Southern Confederacy was reborn. For many it was, and continued to be, as real as the high-backed rocker that graced many a veranda.

Jefferson Davis set in motion a healing process that gave honor back to his people. The success of his memoirs in the late nineteenth century inspired others to write of their experiences. Many individuals who had been imprisoned at Fort Delaware authored monographs describing their experience as prisoners of war. As the Confederacy came to live in memory, so too did Fort Delaware's POW camp. As time separated the veterans from events, the fallible nature of memory colored and blurred their accounts. The stories of prison life and the injustice of the Lincoln administration were amplified and embellished. Of the 32,000 men who had lived on Pea Patch Island as prisoners of war, few, at the time, reported the horror of their condition. To be sure, the plight of the prisoner of war was soul robbing. The boredom and hopelessness of their incarceration, especially in 1864, made life intolerable. As time passed and memory faded, the stories of horror increased, presenting a distortion of the truth.

Reverend Handy, railing against his enforced confinement, offered an inconsistent picture of the brutal life imposed on the POWs. Handy's description of the starvation, disease, and the bestiality of the Federal administration at Pea Patch seems oddly incongruous with his accounts of days spent organizing worship services, baptisms, and revival meetings, attended by prisoner and guard alike. His story of the heartlessness of the Federals illustrated by visions of men hanging by their thumbs, enforced labor, and the denial of even the simplest communication with loved ones back home is contradicted by the fact that his own wife was allowed to come to Pea Patch, take room and board at Mrs. Patterson's Inn, and eventually visit with her husband.

Private Richard Shotwell's memoir, filled with invective and bile, paints a picture of unrestrained cruelty administered by an incompetent Dutchman and aided and abetted by the equally cruel Captain Ahl and Lieutenant Wolf. The uncaring attitude of those in charge was mitigated by the occasional, but inconsistent, kindness of Captain Mlotkowski. Even the bad food became part of a sinister plot to exterminate the prison population. Another prisoner, Charles Ravenbach, tells of the Federal guard named "Old Hike Out" who routinely marched the prisoners to the north end of Pea Patch and stripped them of their possessions, including their clothes, forcing Southern men to brave the harsh winter naked. It is, however, impossible to believe that Mr. Hike Out could accomplish such a feat without at least one other prisoner noticing that he too was naked and destitute at the behest of the Yankees.

The powerful emotions generated by the conflict, and the need to make a story more interesting may be responsible for the distortion of events as retold by the aged veterans. That is not to say that Pea Patch Island prisoners did not suffer the cruelty of war or the base nature of the guards. Certainly the experiences of Col. E. Pope Jones and Pvt. John Bibb offer evidence of remarkable disregard for the dignity of human life. Prisoners were physically punished, bucked and gagged, hung by their thumbs, or attached to a ball and chain. The food was, for the most part, wretched and sometimes difficult to obtain. The quarters were exactly what they were intended to be, temporary. In all events the relentless nature of enforced boredom took a heavy toll on the POWs. The medical arts of the time held out no answers for the effective treatment of the sick and, as a result, many of those sick died. Life on Pea Patch Island was not a pleasant one for the prisoners. But it was tolerable and survivable. The fact that the death rate among the POWs was equal to the death rate from disease among the civilian population indicates an organized effort to care for those incarcerated. The smallpox epidemic of 1863 presented a grave threat to the prisoner population and, by contrast, little danger to the Federals stationed on the island. The smallpox vaccine had been a staple of health care in the North for several decades and most of the Federals had been inoculated against the pox prior to their arrival for service on the island. After all the POWs received the vaccine, the epidemic was cut short. But society tends to focus on the dramatic rather than the mundane, and the drama sells books; so in the exaggerated tales circulating in the years following the war, the memory of Fort Delaware and Pea Patch Island became something quite different than the reality of events during the war.

The architect of the Confederate government and initial chronicler of the lost cause, Jefferson Davis, already had personal ties to Fort Delaware and Pea Patch Island. It had been Davis's initiative that secured the necessary funds for the completion of Fort Delaware. Davis's private secretary and many members of his entourage were held at Fort Delaware pending the government's decision on what to do with them. But Davis's own incarceration following the war offers a surprising Fort Delaware connection. Upon his capture,

Davis was taken to Fort Monroe, on the Virginia Peninsula, and imprisoned, pending trial. His keeper was a brilliant general and rising star of the new army. Maj. Gen. Nelson Appleton Miles, former colonel of the fighting 61st New York Volunteer Infantry, was barely twenty-six years old when he was assigned the task of holding Jefferson Davis. Miles's invective toward the former president of the Confederacy knew no bounds, and Jefferson Davis was held in close confinement for almost two years. Miles was reported to have inflicted petty tortures upon Davis, denying him even the right to exercise. Thus confined the effects began to take their toll. Davis's health began to deteriorate. All the while it seemed the Federals were unsure of the legal grounds on which they held Davis. After almost two years of incarceration, word of Davis's condition reached the press and people began to question the wisdom and justice of the government as they continued to hold Davis without benefit of trial. The writ of habeas corpus had been restored in 1865, yet Davis was still in confinement with little recourse to have his day in court. By 1867 the clamor for either a trial or release of Davis urged the Johnson Administration to examine the wisdom of Davis's continued imprisonment. When it was reported that Davis was near death the government was forced to do something about the "Davis Matter."

The first step in making things right involved the relief of General Miles. Despite his protests, Nelson Miles was relieved of duty and ordered home to Massachusetts. The next step involved the selection of a general officer whose humane nature was well documented. The man chosen, whose temperament was ideally suited to this sort of situation, was former commandant of Fort Delaware, Henry S. Burton. Burton had done well following his transfer from Pea Patch in 1863. Initially assigned to the defenses at Washington, Burton accepted a colonel's commission and assignment at the front. Burton's gallantry during the siege of Petersburg earned him a promotion to brevet brigadier general. When Burton assumed command at Fort Monroe, his first order of business was to see to the prisoner. Burton brought in physicians, and released Davis from close confinement. Burton also broke with the hard-liners in the government and allowed Davis to see visitors. By the end of July 1867 the Davis case had come to end. The former Confederate president had been released on bail to await a trial that never came. Gen. Henry Burton signed as the officer in charge and handed Davis over to the Federal judiciary and, within a few hours, freedom. The story had come full circle.

# APPENDICES

## MONTHLY DEATH RATES AT FORT DELAWARE, 1862–1865

| Month | Deaths | Percentage of Population |
|---|---|---|
| July 1862 | 20 | .58% |
| Aug. 1862 | 3 | .3% |
| Sept. 1862 | 7 | .3% |
| Oct. 1862 | 14 | .5% |
| Nov. 1862 | 0 | 0% |
| Dec. 1862 | 3 | 2.4% |
| Jan. 1863 | 0 | 0% |
| Feb. 1863 | 0 | 0% |
| March 1863 | 0 | 0% |
| April 1863 | 4 | .6% |
| May 1863 | 5 | .3% |
| June 1863 | 66 | 1.7% |
| July 1863 | 111 | .8% |
| Aug. 1863 | 169 | 1.8% |
| Sept. 1863 | 327 | 3% |
| Oct. 1863 | 377 | 5% |
| Nov. 1863 | 156 | 5% |
| Dec. 1863 | 82 | 2.8% |
| Jan. 1864 | 78 | 2.8% |
| Feb. 1864 | 42 | 1.5% |
| March 1864 | 62 | 1.06% |
| April 1864 | 74 | 1.1% |
| May 1864 | 62 | .75% |
| June 1864 | 67 | .71% |
| July 1864 | 110 | 1.1% |
| Aug. 1864 | 88 | .94% |
| Sept. 1864 | 48 | .53% |
| Oct. 1864 | 10 | .12% |
| Nov. 1864 | 19 | .24% |
| Dec. 1864 | 28 | .36% |
| Jan. 1865 | 55 | .69% |
| Feb. 1865 | 60 | .74% |
| March 1865 | 93 | 1% |
| April 1865 | 106 | 1% |
| May 1865 | 60 | .72% |
| June 1865 | 41 | .57% |
| July 1865 | 3 | 2.7% |

AVERAGE MONTHLY DEATH RATE: 1.2% • AVERAGE MONTHLY DEATHS: 66 • AVERAGE DAILY DEATH RATE: 2.2 •
JULY–DEC. 1863: 1,222 DIED • AVERAGE MONTHLY DEATH RATE: 3% • AVERAGE MONTHLY DEATHS: 203 • AVERAGE DAILY RATE: 6

## PRISONER COUNT BY MONTH

| Month | Present at 1st of month | Joined | Total | Temporarily Transferred | Delivery or Exchange |
|---|---|---|---|---|---|
| July 1862 | 1,260 | 2,174 | 3,434 | — | 3,059 |
| Aug. 1862 | 355 | 127 | 482 | 14 | — |
| Sept. 1862 | 68 | 2402 | 2,470 | — | — |
| Oct. 1862 | 2,532 | 50 | 2,582 | — | 2,298 |
| Nov. 1862 | 84 | 39 | 123 | — | — |
| Dec. 1862 | 106 | 17 | 123 | — | 103 |
| Jan. 1863 | 5 | 12 | 17 | — | — |
| Feb. 1863 | 17 | 13 | 30 | — | — |
| March 1863 | 36 | 2 | 38 | 7 | — |
| April 1863 | 30 | 565 | 595 | 602 | — |
| May 1863 | 46 | 1,209 | 1,255 | 1,198 | — |
| June 1863 | 51 | 3,686 | 3737 | — | — |
| July 1863 | 3,673 | 8,922 | 12,595 | 743 | 2,462 |
| Aug. 1863 | 8,982 | 154 | 9,136 | 90 | — |
| Sept. 1863 | 8,822 | 19 | 8,841 | 1,977 | — |
| Oct. 1863 | 6,490 | 8 | 6,498 | 3,125 | — |
| Nov. 1863 | 2,987 | 33 | 3,020 | 5 | 26 |
| Dec. 1863 | 2,822 | 37 | 2,859 | 5 | — |
| Jan.1864 | 2,765 | 2 | 2,767 | 24 | — |
| Feb. 1864 | 2655 | 7 | 2,662 | 2 | — |
| March 1864 | 2,600 | 3,218 | 5,818 | 29 | — |
| April 1864 | 5,712 | 536 | 6,248 | 1 | — |
| May 1864 | 6,149 | 2,060 | 8,209 | 3 | — |
| June 1864 | 8,126 | 1,194 | 9,320 | 66 | — |
| July 1864 | 9,174 | 98 | 9,272 | 55 | — |
| Aug. 1864 | 9,095 | 223 | 9,318 | 636 | — |
| Sept. 1864 | 8,585 | 401 | 8,986 | 2 | 953 |
| Oct. 1864 | 7,979 | 166 | 8,145 | 488 | — |
| Nov. 1864 | 7,630 | 41 | 7,671 | 17 | — |
| Dec. 1864 | 7,625 | 115 | 7,740 | 54 | — |
| Jan. 1865 | 7,622 | 236 | 7,858 | 36 | — |
| Feb. 1865 | 7,732 | 313 | 8,045 | 1 | 1,039 |
| March 1865 | 6,842 | 2,057 | 8,899 | 4 | 1,038 |
| April 1865 | 7,676 | 899 | 8,575 | — | 88 |
| May 1865 | 8,261 | 9 | 8,270 | 1 | — |
| June 1865 | 7,126 | — | 7,126 | — | — |
| July 1865 | 109 | 1 | 110 | — | — |

| Died | Escaped | Released | Total Loss | Sick | Political Prisoners |
|---|---|---|---|---|---|
| 20 | — | — | 3,079 | — | — |
| 13 | — | 314 | 341 | — | — |
| 7 | — | 104 | 111 | — | 59 |
| 14 | — | 176 | 2,488 | 23 | 45 |
| — | — | 1 | 1 | — | 24 |
| 3 | — | 2 | 108 | — | 1 |
| — | — | — | — | 2 | — |
| — | — | — | — | — | — |
| — | — | 1 | 8 | — | — |
| 4 | — | 1 | 607 | 57 | 27 |
| 5 | — | 2 | 1205 | — | 33 |
| 66 | 1 | 181 | 248 | 248 | 44 |
| 111 | — | 297 | 3,613 | 300 | 52 |
| 169 | 8 | 47 | 314 | 350 | 77 |
| 327 | 10 | 37 | 2,351 | 400 | 111 |
| 377 | 4 | 5 | 3,511 | 625 | 49 |
| 156 | 1 | 10 | 198 | 600 | 54 |
| 82 | 1 | 6 | 94 | 596 | 51 |
| 78 | — | 10 | 112 | 419 | 48 |
| 42 | 1 | 17 | 62 | 439 | 44 |
| 62 | 1 | 14 | 106 | 567 | 43 |
| 74 | — | 24 | 99 | 723 | 39 |
| 62 | — | 18 | 83 | 603 | 99 |
| 67 | — | 13 | 146 | 638 | 111 |
| 110 | 10 | 2 | 177 | 686 | 111 |
| 88 | 1 | 8 | 733 | 548 | 73 |
| 48 | — | 4 | 1,007 | 355 | 99 |
| 10 | 2 | 14 | 514 | 206 | 92 |
| 19 | 1 | 9 | 46 | 399 | 421 |
| 28 | — | 36 | 118 | 562 | 71 |
| 55 | — | 35 | 126 | 641 | 86 |
| 60 | — | 103 | 1,203 | 468 | 92 |
| 93 | — | 88 | 1,223 | 637 | 105 |
| 106 | — | 120 | 314 | 528 | 73 |
| 60 | 11 | 1,072 | 1,144 | 544 | 70 |
| 41 | — | 6,977 | 7,018 | 26 | 55 |
| 3 | — | 105 | 108 | — | 14 |

## SUTLER'S PRICE LIST

Brash . . . . . . . . . . . . . . . . . . . . . . . . . . . . . . . . . . . . 25¢ per yard

Cotton Spools . . . . . . . . . . . . . . . . . . . . . . . . . . . . . 25¢ each
Cards, playing . . . . . . . . . . . . . . . . . . . . . . . . . . . . 35¢ per pack (Steamboat)
Cards, playing . . . . . . . . . . . . . . . . . . . . . . . . . . . . 75¢ per pack (Linen backs)
Candles, relauruntine. . . . . . . . . . . . . . . . . . . . . . . 55¢ per pound

Drawers, cotton. . . . . . . . . . . . . . . . . . . . . . . . . . . . from $1.50 to $3.00 per pair according to quality
Drawers, woolen . . . . . . . . . . . . . . . . . . . . . . . . . . from $2.50 to $3.75 per pair according to quality
Drilling, cotton . . . . . . . . . . . . . . . . . . . . . . . . . . . 80¢ per yard

Emery Paper . . . . . . . . . . . . . . . . . . . . . . . . . . . . . . 05¢ for 2 sheets
Envelopes . . . . . . . . . . . . . . . . . . . . . . . . . . . . . . . . 10¢ for a pack of 25
Essences of Cinnamon and Peppermint . . . . . . . . . . . 10¢ for a 12 oz. bottle

Fruits, canned . . . . . . . . . . . . . . . . . . . . . . . . . . . . . 60¢ per pint can, $1.00 per quart
French Mustard . . . . . . . . . . . . . . . . . . . . . . . . . . . 30¢ per bottle
Fishing Lines . . . . . . . . . . . . . . . . . . . . . . . . . . . . . 10¢ each
Fishing Hooks . . . . . . . . . . . . . . . . . . . . . . . . . . . . 05¢ for a pack of 7

Gions, woolen . . . . . . . . . . . . . . . . . . . . . . . . . . . . 75¢ per pair
Gions, cotton. . . . . . . . . . . . . . . . . . . . . . . . . . . . . 30¢ per pair
Ginger snacks or cakes. . . . . . . . . . . . . . . . . . . . . . 25¢ per pound
Ground ginger. . . . . . . . . . . . . . . . . . . . . . . . . . . . 65¢ per pound
Ground Pepper . . . . . . . . . . . . . . . . . . . . . . . . . . . 65¢ per pound

Hanker chefs, cotton . . . . . . . . . . . . . . . . . . . . . . . from 30¢ to $1.00 each
"            ", silk . . . . . . . . . . . . . . . . . . . . . . . . . from 75¢ to $1.50 each
Herrings, dried . . . . . . . . . . . . . . . . . . . . . . . . . . . 01¢ apiece
Half Hose, Men's cotton . . . . . . . . . . . . . . . . . . . . 50¢ per pair
Half Hose, Men's woolen. . . . . . . . . . . . . . . . . . . . 75¢ per pair
Hair dyes. . . . . . . . . . . . . . . . . . . . . . . . . . . . . . . . $1.00 per bottle
Hammers. . . . . . . . . . . . . . . . . . . . . . . . . . . . . . . . $1.00 each
Hams. . . . . . . . . . . . . . . . . . . . . . . . . . . . . . . . . . . 30¢ per pound

Ink. . . . . . . . . . . . . . . . . . . . . . . . . . . . . . . . . . . . . 10¢ per 1 oz. bottle

Jellies. . . . . . . . . . . . . . . . . . . . . . . . . . . . . . . . . . . 40¢ per glass

Knives, pocket . . . . . . . . . . . . . . . . . . . . . . . . . . . 25¢ to $2.00 according to quality

Lemons . . . . . . . . . . . . . . . . . . . . . . . . . . . . . . . . . 25 percent addition to the market price
Lemon syrup . . . . . . . . . . . . . . . . . . . . . . . . . . . . 75¢ per bottle
Lemon cakes . . . . . . . . . . . . . . . . . . . . . . . . . . . . 25¢ per pound
Letter paper, (congress) . . . . . . . . . . . . . . . . . . . . 02¢ per sheet
Letter paper, (notes). . . . . . . . . . . . . . . . . . . . . . . 01¢ per sheet
Looking glasses, pocket . . . . . . . . . . . . . . . . . . . . 15¢ for 2, 20¢ for 3
Lead Pencil . . . . . . . . . . . . . . . . . . . . . . . . . . . . . . 15¢ for 2
Licorice . . . . . . . . . . . . . . . . . . . . . . . . . . . . . . . . . 05¢ per oz.

Milk, fresh. . . . . . . . . . . . . . . . . . . . . . . . . . . . . . . 08¢ per quart
Milk, condensed . . . . . . . . . . . . . . . . . . . . . . . . . . 60¢ per can
Molasses, common . . . . . . . . . . . . . . . . . . . . . . . . $1.00 per gallon
Money wallet. . . . . . . . . . . . . . . . . . . . . . . . . . . . . 50¢ to $2.00 each
Matches. . . . . . . . . . . . . . . . . . . . . . . . . . . . . . . . . 03¢ per box
Melons . . . . . . . . . . . . . . . . . . . . . . . . . . . . . . . . . 15¢ each
Muslin, unbleached . . . . . . . . . . . . . . . . . . . . . . . 80¢ per yard
Mitts, woolen . . . . . . . . . . . . . . . . . . . . . . . . . . . . 75¢ per pair
Meats, canned . . . . . . . . . . . . . . . . . . . . . . . . . . . 70¢ per pint can, $1.25 per quart can

## SUTLER'S PRICE LIST *(continued)*

Needles . . . . . . . . . . . . . . . . . . . . . . . . . . . . . . . . . . . . . . 15¢ per paper of 25

Over shirts, woolen . . . . . . . . . . . . . . . . . . . . . . . . . . . from $2.00 to $4.00 each according to quality
Oranges . . . . . . . . . . . . . . . . . . . . . . . . . . . . . . . . . . . . 25% added onto the market price
Oysters, canned . . . . . . . . . . . . . . . . . . . . . . . . . . . . . . 35¢ for a 1 lb. can, 60¢ for a 2 lb. can
Oil, sweet, pint bottles . . . . . . . . . . . . . . . . . . . . . . . . . $1.00 each, 1 oz. bottles, 10¢ each
Oil, armor . . . . . . . . . . . . . . . . . . . . . . . . . . . . . . . . . . . 10¢ per bottle
Oilcloth satchels . . . . . . . . . . . . . . . . . . . . . . . . . . . . . . $2.00 each

Pen holders . . . . . . . . . . . . . . . . . . . . . . . . . . . . . . . . . . 05¢ for 2
Pens, steel . . . . . . . . . . . . . . . . . . . . . . . . . . . . . . . . . . . 3 for 05¢
Pins . . . . . . . . . . . . . . . . . . . . . . . . . . . . . . . . . . . . . . . . 15¢ per paper
Pipes, briar wood . . . . . . . . . . . . . . . . . . . . . . . . . . . . . 35¢ each
Pipes, gutta percha . . . . . . . . . . . . . . . . . . . . . . . . . . . . 80¢ each
Pepper sauce . . . . . . . . . . . . . . . . . . . . . . . . . . . . . . . . . 30¢ per bottle
Potatoes, per bushel . . . . . . . . . . . . . . . . . . . . . . . . . . . 25% added onto the market price
Peaches, per basket . . . . . . . . . . . . . . . . . . . . . . . . . . . . "                                    "
Peaches, dried . . . . . . . . . . . . . . . . . . . . . . . . . . . . . . . 25¢ per pound
Perfume . . . . . . . . . . . . . . . . . . . . . . . . . . . . . . . . . . . . 30¢ to 75¢ per bottle
Postage stamps . . . . . . . . . . . . . . . . . . . . . . . . . . . . . . at Government value

Raisins . . . . . . . . . . . . . . . . . . . . . . . . . . . . . . . . . . . . . [No price given]
Razors . . . . . . . . . . . . . . . . . . . . . . . . . . . . . . . . . . . . . from 75¢ to $2.00 each
Razor straps . . . . . . . . . . . . . . . . . . . . . . . . . . . . . . . . from 25¢ to $1.00 each

Shirts, cotton . . . . . . . . . . . . . . . . . . . . . . . . . . . . . . . from $2.00 to $5.00 according to quality
Syrup . . . . . . . . . . . . . . . . . . . . . . . . . . . . . . . . . . . . . $1.40 per gallon
Soap, fine . . . . . . . . . . . . . . . . . . . . . . . . . . . . . . . . . . 10¢ per cake
Soap, shaving . . . . . . . . . . . . . . . . . . . . . . . . . . . . . . . 10¢ per cake
Soap, laundry . . . . . . . . . . . . . . . . . . . . . . . . . . . . . . . 20¢ per pound
Suspenders . . . . . . . . . . . . . . . . . . . . . . . . . . . . . . . . . from 50¢ to $1.00 per pair
Scissors, small size . . . . . . . . . . . . . . . . . . . . . . . . . . . . 25¢, large $1.00
Shoestrings (cotton, 3/4 yd) . . . . . . . . . . . . . . . . . . . . . . 05¢ for 2
Sauce, cranberry . . . . . . . . . . . . . . . . . . . . . . . . . . . . . . 60¢ per can or bottle
Sauce, Worcester shire . . . . . . . . . . . . . . . . . . . . . . . . . $1.00 per pint bottle, $1.75 per quart
Sardines . . . . . . . . . . . . . . . . . . . . . . . . . . . . . . . . . . . 1/4 box – 60¢, 1/2 box – $1.00
Soused, pigs feet . . . . . . . . . . . . . . . . . . . . . . . . . . . . . 15¢ each
Soused, sheeps tongue . . . . . . . . . . . . . . . . . . . . . . . . . 15¢ each

Tacks (6 oz and 8 oz) . . . . . . . . . . . . . . . . . . . . . . . . . . 15¢ per paper
Towels . . . . . . . . . . . . . . . . . . . . . . . . . . . . . . . . . . . . . 35¢ per yard
Tin cup (pints) . . . . . . . . . . . . . . . . . . . . . . . . . . . . . . 20¢ each, 30¢ for quarts
Thread, black linen . . . . . . . . . . . . . . . . . . . . . . . . . . . . 10¢ per skein
Tobacco-black 12's . . . . . . . . . . . . . . . . . . . . . . . . . . . . 10¢ per plug (10 plugs to a pound)
"         "-Natural Leaf . . . . . . . . . . . . . . . . . . . . . . . . . . . 60¢ (3)
"         "-Navy . . . . . . . . . . . . . . . . . . . . . . . . . . . . . . . . . $1.25 per pound
"         "-Solace . . . . . . . . . . . . . . . . . . . . . . . . . . . . . . . 25¢ for 2 papers
"         "-Sunny Side . . . . . . . . . . . . . . . . . . . . . . . . . . . "                                    "
"         "-Killikinid . . . . . . . . . . . . . . . . . . . . . . . . . . . . $1.25 per pound
"         "-Lynchburg . . . . . . . . . . . . . . . . . . . . . . . . . . . . $1.50 per pound
"         "-Idol . . . . . . . . . . . . . . . . . . . . . . . . . . . . . . . . 20¢ per paper of 4 oz.
"         "-common cut and dry . . . . . . . . . . . . . . . . . . . . 75¢ per pound
Tripoli . . . . . . . . . . . . . . . . . . . . . . . . . . . . . . . . . . . . . 05¢ per paper

## "ROSTER OF FIRST FIFTY CONFEDERATES SENT TO CHARLESTON, S.C.

| Name | Rank | Regiment or County and State |
| --- | --- | --- |
| Johnson, Edward | Major-general | C. S. Army |
| Gardner, Franklin | Major-general | Commanding Port Hudson |
| Archer, J.J. | Brigadier-general | C. S. Army |
| Steuart, George H. | Brigadier-general | C. S. Army |
| Thompson, M. Jeff | Brigadier-general | C. S. Army |
| Carter, R. Welby | Colonel | 1st Va. Cavalry |
| Cobb, N. | Colonel | 44th Va. Infantry |
| Duke, Basil W. | Colonel | 2nd Ky. Cavalry |
| Ferguson, M. J. | Colonel | 16th Va. Cavalry |
| Hanks, J. M. | Colonel | Buford's Brigade |
| Morgan, Richard C. | Colonel | Morgan's Cavalry |
| Pell, James A. | Colonel | Forrest's Cavalry |
| Peebles, W.H. | Colonel | 44th Ga. Infantry |
| Vandeventer, A.S. | Colonel | 50th Va. Infantry |
| Ward, William W. | Colonel | Ward's Tenn. Cavalry |
| Barbour, William M. | Colonel | 37th N.C. Infantry |
| Brown, J. N. | Colonel | 14th S.C. Infantry |
| Jaquess, J. A. | Colonel | Gardner's staff |
| Caudill, B. E. | Colonel | 11th Ky. Infantry. |
| Forney, W. H. | Colonel | 10th Ala. Infantry |
| Brewer, James F. | Lieutenant-colonel | McDonald's Battalion |
| Daugherty, F. H. | Lieutenant-colonel | 8th Tenn. Cavalry |
| Davant, P. E. | Lieutenant-colonel | 38th Ga. Infantry |
| Fitzgerald, J. P. | Lieutenant-colonel | 23d Va. Infantry |
| Haynes, C. L. | Lieutenant-colonel | 27th Va. Infantry |
| Patton, O. A. | Lieutenant-colonel | Patton's Ky. Rangers |
| Parsley, W. M. | Lieutenant-colonel | 3rd N.C. Infantry |
| Swingley, A. L. | Lieutenant-colonel | Forrest's Brigade |
| Tucker, Joseph T. | Lieutenant-colonel | Chenault's Cavalry |
| Martz, D. H. L. | Lieutenant-colonel | 10th Va. Infantry |
| Dupree, A. | Lieutenant-colonel | Gardner's staff |
| Jackson,Thomas C. | Lieutenant-colonel | Anderson's Brigade |
| Smith, M. J. | Lieutenant-colonel | C. S. Army |
| Anderson, D. W. | Major | 44th Va. Infantry |
| Caldwell, J. W. | Major | 1st Ky. Cavalry |
| Carson, J. T. | Major | 12th Ga. Infantry |
| Ennett, W. T. | Major | 3d N.C. Infantry |
| Groce, J. E. | Major | Gen. Wharton's staff |
| Higley Horace A. | Major | Gen. Bragg's staff |
| Henry, E. M. | Major | Hunter's Cavalry |
| Nash, E. A. | Major | 4th Ga. Infantry |
| Perkins, L. J. | Major | 50th Va. Infantry |
| Smith. George H. | Major | Gen. Wheeler's staff |
| Sanders, E. J. | Major | Sanders' battalion |
| Steele, T. | Major | 7th Ky. Cavalry |
| Webber, Thomas B. | Major | 2nd Ky. Cavalry |
| Wilson, J. M. | Major | 7th La. Infantry |
| Manning, W. H. | Major | 6th La. Infantry |
| Upshaw, T. E. | Major | 13th Va. Cavalry |
| Warley, F. F. | Major | 2nd S.C. artillery |

## IN JUNE 1864 TO STAND UNDER FIRE OF OWN GUNS."

| Where Captured | When Captured |
| --- | --- |
| Wilderness, Va. | May 12,1864 |
| Port Hudson | July 9,1863 |
| Gettysburg, Pa. | July 3,1863 |
| Wilderness, Va. | May 12,1864 |
| Randolph Co., Ky. | Aug. 22,1863 |
| Loudoun Co., Va. | Dec. 17,1863 |
| Wilderness, Va. | May 12,1864 |
| New Lisbon, Ohio | July 26, 1863 |
| Wayne Co., Tenn. | Feb. 16, 1864 |
| Anderson, Ky. | July 20,1863 |
| Buffington, Ohio | July 19, 1863 |
| Paris, Ky. | Jan. 6,1864 |
| Wilderness, Va. | May 12,1864 |
| Wilderness, Va. | May 12, 1864 |
| Buffington Island, Ohio | July 19, 1863 |
| Spotsylvania, Va. | May 12, 1864 |
| North Anna River | May 23, 1864 |
| Port Hudson | July 9, 1863 |
| Wise Co., Va. | July 7, 1863 |
| Gettysburg, Pa. | July 2, 1863 |
| Hampshire Co., Va. | Jan. 5, 1864 |
| Livingston, Tenn. | Feb. 8, 1864 |
| Wilderness, Va. | May 12, 1864 |
| Wilderness, Va. | May 12, 1864 |
| Wilderness, Va. | May 12, 1864 |
| Morgan Co., Ky. | Oct. 15, 1863 |
| Wilderness, Va. | May 12, 1864 |
| Bolivar, Tenn. | Jan. 20, 1864 |
| Cheshire, Ohio | July 20, 1863 |
| Wilderness, Va. | May 12, 1864 |
| Port Hudson | July 9, 1863 |
| Gettysburg, Pa. | July 3, 1863 |
| Port Hudson | July 9, 1863 |
| Wilderness, Va. | May 12, 1864 |
| Shelbyville, Tenn. | Oct. 7, 1863 |
| Wilderness, Va. | May 12, 1864 |
| Wilderness, Va. | May 12, 1864 |
| Natchez, Miss. | Dec. 14, 1863 |
| New Lisbon, Ohio | July 26, 1863 |
| Stone's River, Tenn. | Oct. 7, 1863 |
| Wilderness, Va. | May 12, 1864 |
| Wilderness, Va. | May 12, 1864 |
| Knoxville, Tenn. | Dec. 5, 1863 |
| Aberdeen, Miss. | Feb. 19, 1864 |
| New Lisbon, Ohio | July 20, 1863 |
| New Lisbon, Ohio | July 26, 1863 |
| Wilderness, Va. | May 12, 1864 |
| Wilderness, Va. | May 12, 1864 |
| Spotsylvania, Va. | May 14, 1864 |
| Charleston Harbor | Sept. 4, 1863 |

# NOTES

## INTRODUCTION

1. This figure does not include the deaths of Federals, both active soldiers and convicts. Fort Delaware housed prisoners of war, prisoners of state, and Federal soldier convicts. The number cited here includes only Confederate prisoners of war.

## CHAPTER 1: PRELUDE

1. Alexander B. Cooper, Esq., papers, Historical Society of Delaware, Wilmington, Del.
2. *Coastal Defense Study Group Journal* (Nov. 1995): 118 (cited hereafter as *CDSG*).
3. Ibid., 35.
4. Ibid.
5. The following is the act, in part, of the Delaware State Legislature ceding the island to the Federal government: "Be it enacted, etc., That all the right, title and claim which this state has to the jurisdiction and soil of the island in Delaware, commonly called the pea patch, and the same is hereby, ceded to the United States of America, for the purpose of erecting forts, batteries, and fortifications, for the protection of the river Delaware and the adjacent country."
6. Martello Towers were commonly used as seacoast defensive structures in the late seventeenth and early eighteenth centuries. The Martello Tower derived its name from the remarkable performance in 1794 of a fortification under attack by the British in the Bay of Martello, on Corsica. The tower was a forty-foot-high conical edifice, capable of

mounting six guns. In the Martello episode, as described by Henry W. Halleck, *Elements of Military Art and Science* (Washington, D.C.: Government Printing Office, 1846), 164–65, the English ships *Fortitude* (seventy-four guns) and *Juno* (thirty-two guns) were repulsed and damaged considerably by fire from the tower, which mounted only one barbette gun. The *Fortitude* lost seven men and was set ablaze. The thirty men stationed inside the tower remained unhurt; only three men served the gun during the fight.

7. *CDSG*, 36.

8. Ibid.

9. Ibid., 37.

10. Ibid. The Newbold plans were referring to the area known locally as Reybold's Landing. It is marked by present-day Fort Dupont.

11. In the U.S. Army of the nineteenth century, a ranking system had been devised that compensated for the slow and cumbersome system in use to advance career officers in rank. By law, the army could assign only a limited number of officers for each grade of service. Once those slots were filled, the rank was unavailable until the present officers died or resigned. Thus it was practically impossible to advance in grade during peacetime. The Brevet promotion was created as a temporary fix, activated during wartime as the army increased its size. The individual holding the Brevet rank could be addressed at that rank but was paid according to his Regular rank. Lieutenant Colonel Totten had been awarded a brevet promotion for gallant and meritorious service at the battle of Plattsburg on 11 September 1814, but he was not promoted to Regular lieutenant colonelcy until 1828.

12. The battle of Fort McHenry had demonstrated the invulnerability of star-shaped masonry forts.

13. Under the presidency of Col. Samuel B. Archer, inspector general, the board consisted of: Maj. Alexander C. W. Fanning, 2nd U.S. Artillery; Maj. James H. Hook, 4th U.S. Artillery; Maj. James Kearney, Topographical Engineers; Maj. Thomas Stockton, 3rd U.S. Artillery; Capt. William Wade, 4th U.S. Artillery; and Capt. Felix Ansart, 3rd U.S. Artillery. Capt. Francis Smith Belton, 3rd U.S. Artillery, served as supernumerary. Appearing as counsel for Babcock were the Honorable Louis McLane and George Reed Jr., Esq.

14. "The Old Star Fort Delaware," *Fort Delaware Society Notes* (Jan. 1961): 2. The fire had far-reaching ramifications for the government. The following statement from Lorenzo Thomas in 1862 regarding the liability of the government for such losses reflects the precedent set in 1832 when the soldiers sued the United States for the loss of their personal property.

> I will cite as a sufficient instance the act of July 14, 1832, page 512, U.S. Statutes at Large, Private Laws for 1789 to 1815. This act authorizes the Second Auditor of the Treasury and requires him to ascertain and pay the amount of property lost by each officer and soldier in the conflagration of Fort Delaware, which occurred February 8, 1831.

Thomas used this decision and subsequent statute to argue for just compensation for soldiers' loss of personal property during the Civil War; see *Official Records of the War of the Rebellion*, ser. II, vol. 117, 37 (cited hereafter as *O.R.*).

15. U.S. Army Corps of Engineers, *The District: A History of the Philadelphia District, 1866–1971* (Washington, D.C.: U.S. Government Printing Office, 1976), 46–60 (cited hereafter as *The District*).
16. Ibid.
17. Manuscript, drawer 49, sheet 1, RG 77, National Archives Branch Depository, Philadelphia.
18. *The District*, 46.
19. Fort Delaware Papers, Historical Society of Delaware, Wilmington, Del.
20. Sergeant's ruling had far-reaching effects. He established the border between New Jersey and Delaware as the high-tide mark of the eastern shore of the Delaware River. When the tide recedes, the exposed mud is technically Delaware. Sergeant also established the right of the Federal government to select and appropriate property deemed essential to the national defense, provided just compensation is awarded.
21. Surgeon Spencer, "Description of Military Posts," RG 393, National Archives.
22. James St. Clair Morton, "Memoir of Major John Sanders, Corps of Engineers, U.S. Army," (Pittsburgh, 1861), 59.
23. The island fortification called Alcatraz, as well as Corregidor in the Philippine Islands, owes much to the work of Totten and Sanders.
24. George Brinton McClellan to Elizabeth McClellan, 7 July 1851, George Brinton McClellan Papers, Library of Congress.
25. *The District*, 55.
26. Ibid., 56.

## CHAPTER 2: 1861

1. Fort Delaware's Engineer's Report, RG 77, National Archives Branch Depository, Philadelphia.
2. *O.R.*, ser. I, vol. 5, 61.

3. W. Emerson Wilson Papers, Fort Delaware Society Archives, Delaware City, Del.

4. Ibid.

5. *The District*, 60.

6. Richard Thomas to John Mattapony, 26 April 1861, *O.R.*, ser. II, vol. 105, 401.

7. *O.R.*, ser. II, vol. 115, 399.

8. Ibid., 391–94.

9. Ezra J. Warner, *Generals in Blue* (Baton Rouge: Louisiana State University Press, 1964), 126.

10. *O.R.*, ser. II, vol. 114, 587.

11. Ibid., 592.

12. Ibid., 58.

13. Julia Jefferson Papers, Historical Society of Delaware, Wilmington, Del. The note, dated 8 Nov. 1861, reads: "Sir, the box of clothing for the prisoners of war was received yesterday and the contents distributed. They commission me to communicate their heartfelt gratitude to the donors for the gift so timely and acceptable."

14. *O.R.*, ser. II, vol. 115, 95.

## CHAPTER 3: 1862

1. Fort Delaware Post Council Records, RG 393, National Archives.

2. Gibson is referring to the collecting tanks located on the parapet. These tanks collected rainwater and were connected to the filtration system leading to the cisterns. The water for drinking was to be drawn before it drained into the cisterns.

3. Fort Delaware Post Council Records.

4. "Letters of George M. Green," *Fort Delaware Society Notes* (Jan. 1957): 1.

5. Ibid.

6. Fort Delaware Post Council Records. The following Special Order No. 28, dated 11 April 1862, indicates how lax the system had become: "Upon the recommendation of the Surgeon, Lieut. Charles Martin, Corps of Marine Artillery, P.V., has leave to be absent forty-eight hours. If at the expiration of that time his health should not permit his return, he will report by letter to these headquarters, specifying his address. By command of A. A. Gibson, Capt. 2nd Artillery."

7. "Letters of George M. Green," 1.

8. *O.R.*, ser. I, vol. 115, 269.

9. Ibid., vol. 122, 934.

10. "Letters of George M. Green," 1.

11. *O.R.* ser. I, vol. 9, 19.

12. United States of America, *Revised United States Army Regulations of 1861* (Washington, D.C.: Government Printing Office, 1863), 159.
13. Ibid.
14. *O.R.*, ser. II, vol. 116, 470.
15. "Letters of George M. Green," 1.
16. *O.R.*, ser. II, vol. 116, 445.
17. Ibid., 449.
18. "Letters of George M. Green," 1.
19. Ibid.
20. *O.R.*, ser. II, vol. 117, 23.
21. Gibson's reprimand to his garrison reads in part:

> The Commanding Officer is subjected to the mortification of announcing that a Federal Prisoner has escaped from the Guard and deserted from the Service. This confirms the apprehension which he has entertained, that the troops at this Post are not fully sensible of the exaction and vigilance indispensable to the proper discipline of service on guard. . . . The looseness which has been frequently observed, especially of the non-commissioned officers is a scandal to the military profession, for which the officers are truly responsible. . . . Great allowance has been made for inexperience, but the Commanding Officer has been disappointed in the failure of the troops to cultivate the pride of doing things in a military way— "up to the hub." The effort to become soldiers will be futile if the ambition is wanting to excel.

See Fort Delaware Post Council Records.
22. *O.R.*, ser. II, vol. 117, 121.
23. *Civil War Quarterly* 10 (1998): 37.
24. Fort Delaware Papers, Historical Society of Delaware, Wilmington, Del.
25. Ibid.
26. *O.R.*, ser. II, vol. 117, 225–27.
27. Ibid.
28. Ibid., 267–68.
29. Ibid., 834.
30. Robert Atkinson Diary, 21 Aug. 1862.

31. Ibid.

32. W. Emerson Wilson ed., *A Fort Delaware Journal: The Diary of a Yankee Private, A. J. Hamilton, 1862–1865* (Wilmington, Del.: Fort Delaware Society, 1981), 8.

33. Fort Delaware Post Council Records.

34. Atkinson is mistakenly referring to Capt. Stanislaus Mlotkowski.

35. Atkinson Diary, 22 Aug. 1862.

36. Ibid.

37. *O.R.*, ser. II, vol. 117, 662.

38. Passenger lines were required to keep complete passenger records to be turned over to U.S. authorities when disembarking. An extensive search of these records indicates that Kossuth, with an entourage, came to the U.S. via an Austrian navy vessel, unnamed. Evidently a naval vessel was not required to keep the same passenger records, so the authors cannot name the members of his group for certain. A further search of 1851 records revealed that Albin Schoepf did not officially arrive in the U.S. in 1851, but family records indicate that Schoepf was indeed in the U.S. in the year 1851. Conjecture allows for Schoepf's arrival in New York with Kossuth, but this cannot be proved conclusively.

39. William Kesley Boynton, "Albin F. Schoepf: A Family Biography," vol. 35, no. 4608, Holt Papers, Library of Congress.

40. *O.R.*, ser. I, vol. 4, 312.

41. Ibid., ser. I, vol. 22, 7.

**CHAPTER 4: 1863**

1. Russell Duncan, ed., *Blue-Eyed Child of Fortune* (Athens: University of Georgia Press, 1992), 104, 210.

2. Alexander Hamilton Diary, 10 Sept. 1862, Historical Society of Delaware, Wilmington, Del.

3. Henry Clay Dickinson, *The Diary of Henry Dickinson* (Denver: William Haffner, 1913). 13.

4. *O.R.*, ser. I, vol. 22, 492.

5. Ibid., 459–61.

6. Ibid., 543–48.

7. *O.R.*, ser. II, vol. 118, 217–21.

8. *O.R.*, ser. II, vol. 119, 427.

9. *O.R.* ser. II, vol. 118, 488.

10. Ibid.

11. *O.R.* ser. II, vol. 119, 23.

12. Fort Delaware Post Council Records.

13. "The Maple Leaf," *Fort Delaware Society Notes* (Feb. 1994): 18–20.

14. *O.R.*, ser. II, vol. 118, 764.

15. *O.R.*, ser. II, vol. 115, 402.

16. Ibid., 408.

17. *O.R.*, ser. II, vol. 115, 410.

18. Tom Jenkins Journal, 11 July 1863, Fort Delaware Society Archives, Delaware City, Del.

19. *O.R.*, ser. II, vol. 119, 156.

20. Joseph E. Purvis Diary, 28 July 1863, Fort Delaware Society Archives, Delaware City, Del.

21. Jenkins Journal, 3 Aug. 1863.

22. *Richmond Dispatch*, 28 Aug. 1863, Fort Delaware Society Archives, Delaware City, Del.

23. *Fort Delaware Society Notes* (Feb. 1994):

24. Purvis Diary, 28 July 1863.

25. Jenkins Journal, 17 July 1863.

26. Purvis Diary, 13 July 1863.

27. Ibid.

28. Jenkins Journal, 12 July 1863.

29. Ibid.

30. James McCowan Diary, 3 Aug. 1864, Fort Delaware Society Archives, Delaware City, Del.

31. Purvis Diary, 17 July 1863.

32. Ibid.

33. *O.R.*, ser. II, vol. 119, 441–66.

## CHAPTER 5: 1864

1. Article in a Steubenville, Ohio newspaper by "G.F.," 22 Aug. 1864, Fort Delaware Society Archives, Delaware City, Del.

2. P. Jamison Joselyn, "Our Soldiers at Fort Delaware," *Fort Delaware Society Notes* (Feb. 1994): 4.

3. Robert E. Denney, ed., *Civil War Prisons and Escapes* (New York: Sterling Publishing, 1993), 212–13.

4. Hamilton Diary, 10 Sept. 1862.

5. James I. Robertson, Jr. and the editors of Time-Life, *Tenting Tonight: The Soldier's Life* (Alexandria, Va.: Time-Life, 1985), 119.

6. *O.R.*, ser. II, vol. 120, 1256.

7. Lewis H. George manuscript, Fort Delaware Society Archives, Delaware City, Del.

8. *O.R.*, ser. II, vol. 120, 453–55.

9. Ibid.

10. Ibid.

11. Ibid.

12. I. Handy, *United States Bonds; or, Duress by Federal Authorities* (Baltimore: Turnville Bros., 1874), 514.

13. Wilson, *A Fort Delaware Journal,* 58.

14. Ibid.

15. Ibid.

16. *O.R.*, ser. II, vol. 7, 763.

17. *O.R.*, ser II, vol. 120, 156.

## CHAPTER 6: 1865

1. "New Diary Discovered," *Fort Delaware Society Notes* (Dec. 1957): 2–3.

2. *The Life of Belle Boyd in Camp and Prison,* Fort Delaware Society Archives, Delaware City, Del., 421.

3. *Fort Delaware Prison Times*, April 1865, Fort Delaware Society Archives, Delaware City, Del.

4. "New Diary Discovered," 2–3.

5. Hamilton Diary, 15 April 1865.

6. *O.R.*, ser. II, vol. 121, 817.

7. Cary Harrison, *Recollections Grave and Gray* (New York: Charles Scribner and Sons, 1911), 242.

8. *O.R.*, ser. II, vol. 121, 775.

9. Ibid.

10. *O.R.*, ser. II, vol. 21, 839.

# BIBLIOGRAPHY

**BOOKS**

Baker, John Calhoun. *Directors and Their Functions.* Boston: Harvard University Press, 1945.

Casey, Silas. *Infantry Tactics for the Instruction, Exercise, and Maneuvers of the Soldier: A Company, Line of Skirmishers, Battalion, Brigade, or Corps D'armée.* Dayton, Ohio: Morningside Bookshop, 1985.

Confederate States of America. *Regulations for the Army of the Confederate States, 1863.* Richmond: J.W. Randolph, 1863.

Davis, Burke. *The Long Surrender.* New York: Random House, 1985.

Denney, Robert E., ed. *Civil War Prisons and Escapes.* New York: Sterling Publishing, 1993.

Dickinson, Henry Clay. *The Diary of Henry Dickinson.* Denver: William Haffner, 1913.

Drucker, Peter F. *Concept of the Corporation.* New Brunswick, N.J.: Transaction Publishers, 1993.

Duncan, Russell. *Blue-Eyed Child of Fortune.* Athens: University of Georgia Press, 1992.

Folsom, Burton W., Jr. *The Myth of the Robber Barons.* Herndon, Va.: Young America's Foundation, 1996.

Foote, Shelby. *The Civil War, a Narrative: Fredericksburg to Meridian.* New York: Random House, 1963.

Halleck, Henry W. *Elements of Military Art and Science.* Washington, D.C.: Government Printing Office, 1846.

Handy, I. *United States Bonds; or, Duress by Federal Authorities.* Baltimore: Turnville Bros., 1874.

Harrison, Cary. *Recollections Grave and Gray*. New York: Charles Scribner and Sons, 1911.

Hassler, Warren W., Jr. *General George B. McClellan*. Baton Rouge: Louisiana State University Press, 1957.

Hidy, Ralph W., and Muriel E. Hidy. *Pioneering in Big Business, 1882–1911*. New York: Harper and Brothers, 1955.

Jackson, Donald Dale, and the editors of Time-Life. *Twenty Million Yankees: The Northern Home Front*. Alexandria, Va.: Time-Life, 1985.

Joslyn, Mauriel. *The Biographical Roster of the Immortal 600*. Shippensburg, Pa.: White Mane, 1992.

———. *Immortal Captives: The Story of 600 Confederate Officers and the United States Prisoner of War Policy*. Shippensburg, Pa.: White Mane, 1996.

Kautz, August V. *The Company Clerk: Showing How and When to Make Out All the Returns, Reports, Rolls, and Other Papers, and What to Do with Them*. Philadelphia: J. B. Lippincott, 1865.

Le Grand, Louis. *The Military Handbook*. New York: Beadle, 1862.

Livermore, Thomas L. *Numbers and Losses in the Civil War in America, 1861–65*. Dayton, Ohio: Morningside Bookshop, 1986.

McClellan, George. *Manual of Bayonet Exercise: Prepared for the Use of the Army of the United States*. Philadelphia: J. B. Lippincott, 1852.

Mescher, Virginia. *Price Comparisons, Price Increases, and Salaries of Jobs in the South during the Civil War*. Burke, Va.: Nature's Finest, 1994.

Munroe, John A. *History of Delaware*. Newark: University of Delaware Press, 1979.

Nevins, Allan. *John D. Rockefeller: The Heroic Age of American Enterprise*. New York: Charles Scribner's Sons, 1940.

———. *The War for the Union*. New York: Charles Scribner's Sons, 1971.

Phisterer, Frederick. *Statistical Record of the Armies of the United States*. 1883. Reprint, Wilmington, N.C.: Broadfoot, 1989.

Plum, William R. *The Military Telegraph*. New York: Arno Press, 1974.

Porter, Glenn. *The Rise of Big Business, 1860–1920*. 2nd ed. Wheeling, Ill.: Harlan Davidson, 1992.

Robertson, James I., Jr., and the editors of Time-Life. *Tenting Tonight: The Soldier's Life*. Alexandria, Va.: Time-Life, 1984.

Sears, Stephen W. *George B. McClellan: The Young Napoleon*. New York: Ticknor and Fields, 1988.

Shannon, Fred A. *The Organization and Administration of the Union Army, 1861–1865*. 2 vols. Gloucester, Mass.: Peter Smith, 1965.

Taylor, Frank. *Philadelphia in the Civil War, 1861–1865*. 1913. Reprint, Glenside, Pa.: J. M. Santarelli, 1991.

U.S. Army Crops of Engineers. *The District: A History of the Philadelphia District, 1866–1971*. Washington, D.C.: U.S. Government Printing Office, 1976.

United States of America. *Official Army Register of the Volunteer Force of the United States Army*. Washington, D.C.: Adjutant General's Office, 1865.

United States of America. *Revised United States Army Regulations of 1861*. Washington, D.C.: Government Printing Office, 1863.

Ward, James A. *That Man Haupt: A Biography of Herman Haupt*. Baton Rouge: Louisiana State University Press, 1973.

Warner, Ezra J. *Generals in Gray*. Baton Rouge: Louisiana State University Press, 1959.

———. *Generals in Blue*. Baton Rouge: Louisiana State University Press, 1964.

Weigley, Russell F. *Quartermaster General of the Union Army: A Biography of M.C. Meigs*. New York: Columbia University Press, 1959.

Wilson, W. Emerson, ed. *A Fort Delaware Journal: The Diary of a Yankee Private, A. J. Hamilton, 1862–1865*. Wilmington, Del.: Fort Delaware Society, 1981.


ARTICLES

*Civil War Quarterly* 10 (1998): 37.

*Coastal Defense Study Group Journal* (Nov. 1995): 1–118.

Joselyn, P. Jamison. "Our Soldiers at Fort Delaware." *Fort Delaware Society Notes* (Feb. 1994): 4.

"Letters of George M. Green." *Fort Delaware Society Notes* (Jan. 1957): 1.

"New Diary Discovered." *Fort Delaware Society Notes* (Dec. 1957): 2–3.

"The Maple Leaf." *Fort Delaware Society Notes* (Feb. 1994): 18–20.

"The Old Star Fort Delaware." *Fort Delaware Society Notes* (Jan. 1961): 2.


NEWSPAPERS

*Fort Delaware Prison Times*

*Richmond Dispatch*


MANUSCRIPT SOURCES

Atkinson, Robert. Diary. Fort Delaware Society Archives, Delaware City, Del.

Boyd, Belle. "The Life of Belle Boyd in Camp and Prison." Fort Delaware Society Archives, Delaware City, Del., 1865.

Boynton, William Kesley. "Albin F. Schoepf: A Family Biography." Vol. 35, no. 4608, Holt Papers. Library of Congress.

Cooper, Alexander B., Esq. Papers. Historical Society of Delaware. Wilmington, Del.

Fort Delaware's Engineer's Report. RG 77. National Archives Branch Depository, Philadelphia.

Fort Delaware Papers. Historical Society of Delaware, Wilmington, Del.

Fort Delaware Post Council Records. RG 393. National Archives.

George, Lewis H. Manuscript. Fort Delaware Society Archives, Delaware City, Del.

Green, George M. Letters. Fort Delaware Society Notes, Delaware City, Del.

Hamilton, Alexander J. Diary. Historical Society of Delaware, Wilmington, Del.

Jefferson, Julia. Papers. Historical Society of Delaware, Wilmington, Del.

Jenkins, Tom. Journal. Fort Delaware Society Archives, Delaware City, Del.

Manuscript. Drawer 49, sheet 1. RG 77. National Archives Depository Branch, Philadelphia.

McClellan, George B. Letters. George Brinton McClellan Papers. Library of Congress.

McCowan, James. Diary. Fort Delaware Society Archives, Delaware City, Del.

Morton, James St. Clair. "Memoir of Major John Sanders, Corps of Engineers, U.S. Army." Pittsburgh, 1861.

Purvis, Joseph E. Diary. Fort Delaware Society Archives, Delaware City, Del.

Spencer, Surgeon. RG 393. "Description of Military Posts." National Archives.

Wilson, W. Emerson. Papers. Fort Delaware Society Archives, Delaware City, Del.

# INDEX